Disaster Writing

NEW WORLD STUDIES

J. Michael Dash, *Editor*

Frank Moya Pons and
Sandra Pouchet Paquet,
Associate Editors

Disaster Writing

THE CULTURAL POLITICS OF CATASTROPHE IN LATIN AMERICA

Mark D. Anderson

University of Virginia Press

Charlottesville and London

University of Virginia Press
Printed in the United States of America on acid-free paper
First published 2011

9 8 7 6 5 4 3 2 1

Library of Congress Cataloging-in-Publication Data
Anderson, Mark D., 1974–
    Disaster writing : the cultural politics of catastrophe in Latin America
/ Mark D. Anderson.
        p.   cm. — (New world studies)
    Includes bibliographical references and index.
    ISBN 978-0-8139-3196-8 (cloth : acid-free paper)
    ISBN 978-0-8139-3197-5 (pbk. : acid-free paper)
    ISBN 978-0-8139-3203-3 (e-book)
    1. Latin American literature—History and criticism.   2. Disasters in
literature.   3. Catastrophes (Geology) in literature.   4. Literature and
society—Latin America.   5. National characteristics in literature.   I. Title.
PQ7081.A566   2011
860.9'3556—dc22

                                                        2011015738

THE
AMERICAN
LITERATURES
INITIATIVE

A book in the American Literatures Initiative (ALI), a collaborative
publishing project of NYU Press, Fordham University Press, Rutgers
University Press, Temple University Press, and the University of Virginia
Press. The Initiative is supported by The Andrew W. Mellon Foundation.
For more information, please visit www.americanliteratures.org.

For Norma and Natalia,
who preserve me from the posthuman

Contents

Acknowledgments

I AM SURE THAT WHEN Bill Megenney decided to include Graciliano Ramos's *Vidas secas* and Rachel de Queiroz's *O quinze* in a master's course on Brazilian literature for Spanish speakers at the University of California, Riverside, he had few ulterior motives beyond finding texts relatively easy to read in Portuguese and his own love for the Nordeste. Neither he nor I could then imagine that, ten years later, the fascination with disaster narratives that those two texts elicited in me would give birth to this monstrous project spanning nations and literally thousands of texts relating to drought, flooding, hurricanes, earthquakes, landslides, sinkholes, and volcanic eruptions. Thanks, Bill.

I am deeply grateful to the many friends and colleagues who have supported me during the torturous intellectual wanderings through texts and continents that led me, against even my own expectations, to conceive and bring to fruition this book. I appreciate particularly the time and acuity that Ignacio López-Calvo, Susan Quinlan, Betina Kaplan, and the editors and anonymous readers at the University of Virginia Press and the American Literatures Initiative dedicated to my manuscript, as well as all the others whose conversation influenced my thinking on the topic in a more indirect but no less influential way. I also wish to thank those authors and researchers whose work I cite, for their explorations of disaster opened an entirely unsuspected world of inquiry to my eyes. I am deeply indebted to the Kluge Center at the Library of Congress and its staff for their support, especially Carolyn Brown and Mary Lou Reker, but also to the other Kluge fellows and all the people who brought the ridiculous number of books I ordered to my cubicle. I appreciate deeply the research funding and other support provided for this project by the administration and my colleagues at the University of North Texas and the University of Georgia.

I would also like to thank professor Raymond Leslie Williams, whose excellent advice continues to guide me unerringly through the world of academia long after I diverged from the path we laid out together all those years ago.

Finally, I owe a great deal to the many people who recounted their own experiences of disaster to me, for without them, I could easily have lost sight of the humanity of disaster behind the towering skyline of verbal constructs and political edifices that envelop it.

Introduction

Approaching Disaster

Man uses his old disasters as a mirror
—Roque Dalton, "Arte poética"

NOTHING SHAKES ONE'S WORLDVIEW more than the experience of a natural disaster. Disaster by definition is conceived of as a rupture or inversion of the normal order of things; natural disaster denotes that moment of disjuncture when nature topples what we see as the natural order of human dominance. The natural environment that sustains human populations appears to rebel against us, wreaking havoc on our lives and throwing into question our very identities, as disaster reconfigures suddenly and brutally the lifelong relationships that we have fostered with other people and the places we inhabit. Replenishing rains that nourish lives and livelihoods suddenly transform into raging torrents of destruction that erase the signs of human dominance from the landscape. Hurricanes converge sea and sky, those media so central in a modern economy reliant on transportation and communications, into monstrous vortices that devour everything in their path, leaving behind apocalyptic swathes of death and destruction. The metaphorical solidity of the earth, ubiquitous in the construction of identity and worldview, is uprooted abruptly by earthquake, sweeping the ground from beneath our feet and reducing to rubble our literal and conceptual edifices. In natural disaster, the elements appear to rise up against human civilization, rending violently ideology, institutions, and identity.

Anthropological and sociological researchers have demonstrated that disaster events do not simply owe their existence to the presence of catastrophic natural forces, but rather represent the intersection of natural hazards such as earthquakes, hurricanes, and volcanic eruptions with human populations in varying states of economic, social, and cultural vulnerability.[1] In this sense, "natural" disasters embody yet another facet of human interaction with the environment and as such must be mediated through culture. Recent catastrophes such as the 2004 tsunami in Indonesia, the 2005 Hurricane Katrina in the United States, the 2008 Sichuan earthquake in China, and the 2010 earthquakes in Haiti and Chile have reminded us not only that natural disasters embody the destructive potential to lay waste to entire cities or even regions and jeopardize countless lives but also that they give rise to powerful political and cultural discourses.

I invoke culture in its anthropological dimension as the collective procedures and system of mediation of social and natural environments, as well as in its more specific connotations as the discursive articulation and artistic product of that process. On the one hand, individuals and nations require potent cultural discourses to mediate the psychological trauma that natural disasters inflict by forcing a jarring realization of the frailty of the collective human project to dominate nature. On the other hand, natural disasters make inescapable the axiom that culture is never apolitical; rather, politics represents the process by which cultural trends are formalized and institutionalized as political power.[2] Political power is at a premium during the recovery process, and this power is also channeled or refuted through cultural mediation. As culture is never monolithic but rather a flexible system of interrelations between multiple actors, cultural responses to disaster are as varied as those affected by it. Not all cultural responses are equal, however, and disasters result in fierce competition over which interpretations hold sway over the collective imagination and, more to the point, the political establishment. This process of negotiation dictates how a society responds to disaster as a whole, usually via political mediation, and it leads to cultural change as the experience of disaster is integrated into a society's worldview through normalizing mechanisms.[3]

The chapters that follow elucidate the way in which the cultural and, more specifically, literary mediation of natural disasters informs political policy in Latin America. I am particularly interested in the political implications of the process of defining disasters and how textualization is used to negotiate political power. I begin by addressing some general theoretical concerns dealing with the conceptual relationship between nature and disaster, how disaster is defined through narrative, and why disaster narratives have powerful political implications. As it is impossible to understand cultural trends without historical context, I provide a brief historical overview of disaster narratives and their representations of the relations between culture, politics, and disaster in distinct historical periods in Latin America. I emphasize particularly the shift from perceiving danger as subject to human rather than divine agency that occurred with the rise of modernity. Finally, I provide a brief summary of the ensuing chapters and address some practical concerns that influence the organization of my book.

From Normal Nature to Natural Disaster

The term *natural disaster* describes not a human object subject to non-human agency but rather a series of interactions between people and their environment that occur beyond the bounds of certain socially defined limits. In its broadest sense, *disaster* simply connotes disordering, a breaking of limits or structural norms in which nonhuman nature may or may not be implicated. Indeed, from the prevalent perspective of modern risk assessment, which is a technology designed to restore human agency over the unknown, *disaster* merely indicates the surpassing of thresholds of acceptable or foreseeable social and economic losses. What constitutes those thresholds varies widely, however, leading to a situation in which the definition of *disaster* depends almost solely on the individual or collective "eye of the beholder." Until experience strikes, at least, disasters are open signifiers, to be molded to the parameters of those who use the term. This abstractness makes disaster highly useful in political discourse, as political actors easily put definitions of disaster to work in the task of forging or deauthorizing political platforms and ideologies.

Robert Kastenbaum points out that disasters have traditionally been endowed with meaning: conceived as messages from God(s) or nature, they must be read and interpreted (69). The communicative act is one-sided, though, leaning heavily on interpretation, since it is not at all clear who is the sender. Even if one believes that nonhuman nature possesses its own subjectivity, as do pantheists, animists, and some deep ecologists, it is undeniable that natural phenomena have no inherent meaning discernable by humans outside that which we assign them, a fact that is evidenced by the enormous divergence in the views that different cultures hold of them. One could certainly argue (and many have) that nature plays a constitutive role in the construction of human subjectivity through processes of identification: that is to say, that humans define themselves through nature, and therefore it is nature, as humanity's primordial other, that stimulated the human invention of culture in the first place in order to mediate the relationship and create meaning from it. Indeed, prominent anthropologists such as Claude Lévi-Strauss have long held that the nature-human binomial is constitutive in the construction of culture.[4] Others trace this dualism to the origins of Western culture rather than human culture in general. J. Baird Callicot in particular sees it as the product of the convergence of classical thought and mythology with Judeo-Christian theology, while Charles Taliaferro locates its consolidation in the rise of modern science, which discarded Hobbesian materialism for Descartian dualism.[5] Likewise, John M. Meyer points out throughout his book *Political Nature* that many of the earliest thinkers in the Western tradition founded their theories of politics, or social organization, on the dialectic between nature and human culture, among them Aristotle and Hobbes.

On the other hand, even though conceptual division by species exists to a degree in all cultures, it is much less prominent in many non-Western cultures, in which humans often share kinship with plants, animals, and even geographic features (Whitt et al. 4–8). In fact, many cultures do not recognize the broad abstract category of "nature," as Marilyn Strathern's reevaluation of the Hager culture makes clear. As she writes, "There is no culture, in the sense of the cumulative works of man, and no nature to be tamed and made productive" (219). Nonetheless, even in cases such as this, there are always species or substances that are excluded from the kinship relationship, which still creates an "othering," if along somewhat different lines.

In any case, the genealogy of the term reveals that nature has neither collective agency as subject nor fixed meaning as object outside of the dualistic relationship with human culture—"nature" is always defined in opposition, whether to the human, the rational, or some other criterion. Beyond this chicken-and-egg conundrum, however, the relationship between humans and nature cannot remain entirely in the negative or oppositional: the daily human experience of the natural environment has certainly led to identification with some aspects of nature, a kind of conceptual domestication that has resulted in a third, mediating space between what we consider human and nonhuman, what might be referred to as "normal nature." Indeed, Strathern notes that even in dualistic models, the conceptual relationship between nature and culture is never static but rather involves tension. As she writes, "There is more than the notion of nature and culture as the halves of a whole (dichotomy)" (180). Normal nature clearly acquires meaning beyond the negative through human interaction; but again, this meaning is relative, dependent on individual subjectivities and social mediation.

This concept of nature being normalized through human interaction is perhaps best represented in the practice of landscaping. As Stephen Daniels has pointed out in his study of the political symbolism of landscaping in later-Georgian England, "Planting accentuated the impression of power in the land. Avenues, ridings, belts, clumps, and screens were arranged to emphasize the apparent as well as the actual extent and unity of an estate. Formal styles of parkland planting, with long vistas radiating from the country house, expressed a military sense of command" (45). Landscaping creates a third space in which nonhuman nature is incorporated into the sphere of human social control, normalizing it as society's stage rather than its other. It seems clear, moreover, that actual human alteration of the environment is unnecessary to achieve this culturing of nonhuman nature: any environment becomes landscape if it is conceived of as a space for human enterprise, rather than as its antagonist.

Disaster, as the negative of normalcy, is also the negative of normal nature. That is to say that disaster represents the inversion of the normalized relationship between humans and their environments, both "natural" and human made. Disaster unmakes landscapes, estranging nature from the human. Susanna Hoffman underscores this disjunction when she points out that what I have called "normal nature" is often endowed with maternal properties, becoming a nurturing, benefic Mother Nature, while disasters are frequently viewed as unnatural and described with a lexicon of monstrosity and aberration (126). The attempt to reconcile this rupture and to restore human agency has led some people to attribute disasters to human abuses: nature is a battered mother, mistreated and exploited by her human children, and disaster is seen as both retribution and an opportunity for new beginnings (Hoffman 121–26). In this maternal framework, the recovery from disaster is represented as a cyclical rebirth (Hoffman 133). Alternately, Western culture has a long history of viewing nature as fallen and evil, a threat rather than an ally, one that must be overcome through divine or technological intervention (Oliver-Smith, "Theorizing" 30–31). This stance can surely be attributed to fears of impending disaster.

Although both these inscriptions of nature appear premodern in origin, they have highly utilitarian uses in modern economics and the politics and policies that support them. As Mike Davis points out, for much of the past century "market-driven urbanization has transgressed environmental common sense," leading to a situation in which "the social construction of 'natural' disaster is largely hidden from view by a way of thinking that simultaneously imposes false expectations on the environment and then explains the inevitable disappointments as proof of a malign and hostile nature" (9). Although Davis focuses on Southern

California, this statement goes a long way toward explaining the high toll in human lives and material possessions incurred by "megadisasters" worldwide in recent years. Indeed, many researchers have pointed out that natural hazards such as hurricanes, earthquakes, and volcanic eruptions are the norm rather than the exception. What is exceptional is the degree of urbanization in the past century and the accompanying increase in human vulnerability to natural hazards.[6]

As the variety of perspectives analyzed by these authors makes clear, disaster is a conceptual negative that has no inherent meaning beyond opposition to socially defined normality. Notions of disaster are inevitably tied up with definitions of what constitutes loss, that is, absence. The loss may be material or psychological, the absence of freedoms, of normality, even of "progress" and "development": for many people, "underdevelopment" entails a permanent state of disaster. As the case may be, the very breadth of the category *disaster* indicates its abstract and negative qualities.

Individual and collective experiences of specific disasters, however, cannot be left in abstract terms. As common as they may be, natural disasters lie far enough outside the human experience of "normal nature" that they must be endowed with their own meaning when they are encountered, which can only happen through inscription within the existing cultural system. Through personal experience, disasters cease to embody abstract opposites of normal life and become extraordinarily concrete events with very real effects at every level of individual and social life. The definition of disaster as the absence of normalcy does not suffice to describe catastrophic experience; localized interpretations must be wrought in order to explain and justify what has happened. Furthermore, these interpretations must be collectivized and incorporated into a historical framework.[7] Although these collective interpretations are constructed locally at the disaster site, they are not entirely autonomous. They must be negotiated through dialogue with existing local traditions as well as broader national and globalized frameworks of knowledge. It is through this process of dialogue and negotiation that disaster narratives emerge to explain individual and collective experiences of the catastrophe.

Theorists from Gramsci to Foucault have demonstrated that discourse never exists outside ideology, a consideration that Kastenbaum takes into account when he declares that "explaining disaster asserts knowledge and power" (69). Even when disasters are not mediated by formal literary or cultural production, the process of narrating the disaster mobilizes existing social and political power relations at the same time that it renegotiates them. Simply choosing disaster as the narrative thread that ties together the different elements that come into play in any narrative constitutes a political posture: disaster narratives serve to legitimize and to delegitimize political discourse, always in competition with rival versions.[8] The process of negotiating interpretation leads to prevailing and subordinated disaster narratives whose positions reflect the political heft and poise of their authors. In the end, the triumphant version of events, often formulated through consensus with various competing accounts, achieves canonical status as the basis for political action, and frequently, but not always, it persists as memory in the popular imagination. In this way, each disaster engenders its own language, whose terms are often as symbolic as directly allusive. Furthermore, each disaster narrative embodies the process of the negotiation of meaning: its language bears the marks of competing, often contradictory interpretations like scars. It is through close examination of these linguistic wounds that one can arrive at an understanding of the politics of interpretation.

Given the deadly effects of natural disasters, however, one may well ask whether reducing disaster to a symbolic order is a valid approach to conceptualizing very real human suffering, or is it simply a semantic game for intellectuals sequestered from the reality of catastrophe? There is surely no shortage of opinions on the subject, and many of them lean toward a "stick to the facts" kind of approach. I certainly have no dispute with irrefutable facts, but I do question the way in which the facts become self-evident, as well as their meaning and coherence. I argue that disaster narratives not only organize the facts into a coherent, meaningful explanation of catastrophic experience but that they also factualize their version of events through the careful use of documentary and testimonial modes of discourse. As the case may be, my study of the relationships between disaster narratives and the politics of disaster reveals the very concrete social and political power of literary representations of natural disasters in Latin America.

Latin American Disaster Writing in Historical Perspective

Of necessity, natural disasters have formed an inextricable part of culture in Latin America since long before the region was conceptualized as such. To be certain, Latin America is a landscape largely inscribed by disaster: it is a geography molded by violent geological cataclysms inlaid with the cultural interpretations of its human inhabitants. One is never far from disaster in either space or time in Latin America. Much of this is purely geographical, of course. For the entirety of its western limits, Latin America bounds the infamous Pacific ring of fire, with its plethora of earth-shaking geological phenomena. In its northern reaches lie the Caribbean's hurricane-generating tropical waters, which also constitute an active seismic zone, as the 2010 Haiti earthquake reminded us. The Atlantic coast seems relatively tame by comparison, if one discounts the perennial cycle of drought and flooding that characterizes much of the region's climate. On the other hand, much of Latin America has also been molded by human transformations of the landscape, whether comparatively benign feats of indigenous engineering or more disastrous alterations of the environment such as desertification due to deforestation, erosion, and the importation of nonnative species such as European cows and sheep.[9]

The looming shadow of disaster does not tell the whole story of its relationship with culture in Latin America, however. Disaster is not the same as hazard, as researchers in a variety of fields have made abundantly clear.[10] Potentially catastrophic geological phenomena such as earthquakes and volcanic eruptions only become disasters when they affect humans negatively and on a large scale. Latin America comprises some of the oldest continuously inhabited spaces in the world, many of which exist in highly geologically active areas such as coastal Peru, the Andean highlands, the Caribbean, northern Central America, and Mexico. Situations arose in which successive cultures were forced to coexist with recurring disaster over long periods of time. In order to survive, they had to devise strategies for mediating and mitigating the effects of disaster on their daily lives.

In many cases, disaster dynamized culture. As Greg Bankoff has shown, natural hazards are agents of cultural formation as much as physical events (3). Cultures form through the process of adaption to distinct environments; "cultures of disaster" form when frequently occurring natural hazards are integrated into the schema of daily life (Bankoff 3–4). The repeated experience of disaster in Latin America led to commonsense solutions such as dispersed settlement patterns as well as technological innovation such as terracing and the use of interlocking polyfaceted blocks in construction by Andean civilizations, impressive feats of aquatic engineering in Lake Texcoco, and irrigation and wetlands agriculture throughout Latin America.[11] It also fostered innovation in collective cooperation, the organization of labor, and the elaboration of complex worldviews and conceptual mechanisms for mediating humans' relationship with their environment—especially religious ritual but also poetry, song, and myth. In rare cases, some cultures benefited directly from natural phenomena that we now regard as disastrous, as in the case of the indigenous harnessing of the flood cycle in the Amazon (Miller 16–17). On the other hand, disasters such as drought, volcanic eruption, and hurricanes have long been thought to have contributed to the waning of civilizations, from Cuicuilco and the classic Mayan city-states in Mesoamerica to the Moche and the Wari in what is now Peru.[12]

Pre-Columbian indigenous civilizations throughout Latin America incorporated the experience of disaster into their worldview and cultural practices, constructing mythological and theological frameworks for mediating these events. In Mesoamerica in particular, disasters were viewed as manifestations of divine power and presence. The Aztecs and their predecessors had a pantheon of deities dedicated to disaster, ranging from Atlacoya, the goddess of drought, to Atlacamani, goddess of storms and hurricanes; Chantico, goddess of fire and volcanoes; and Tepeyollotl, "heart of the mountains," who was associated with earthquakes. Tellingly, Mesoamerican creation myths postulated four geneses (or suns) preceding the present time, each of which had ended violently in cataclysm. Similarly, the K'iché Mayas included several deities associated with disaster in their *Popol Vuh*: among them, Hurakan, the "heart of the sky," whose potent name persists in our conceptualization of the phenomenon today; the creation deity Tojil, who was associated with lightning, thunder, and heavy rain; Ah Kin, who controlled disease and drought; and Cabrakan, the Mayan equivalent of Tepeyollotl. Looking southward, the inhabitants of the Andean cordillera believed that creation deity Pachamama's colossal footsteps provoked earthquakes as she wandered throughout her domain. Deities such as Catequil, Kon, Illapa, and Pariacaca were associated with storms, especially thunder and lightning, and Pachacamac, the supreme creator deity, was reputed to have sent a flood to kill humans who had disrespected him, although one senses the influence of Catholic syncretism in this myth. Furthermore, indigenous groups throughout the Andes worshiped at *guacas*, local geographic features whose resident deities were often associated with seismic activity, and the Mapuche in southern Chile and Argentina revered spirit beings known as Pillán, to whom volcanic eruptions were frequently attributed.[13]

Using colonial chronicles and indigenous sources, María Eugenia Petit-Breuilh Sepúlveda has delineated a series of parallels between cultural practices and beliefs relating to disasters throughout Mesoamerica, the Andes, and southern Chile. In particular, she notes commonalities in the sanctification of the geography, in which prominent features such as mountains and volcanoes became the abode of gods, but she also describes how the landscape itself was inspirited with supernatural beings and the souls of ancestors who continued to act in human history. In fact, humans and geological phenomena were linked through a conceptual chain in which there was no clear division between human and nonhuman nature: they had all arisen from a single genealogy.[14] Human originary myths were often linked to emergence from the earth, particularly from caves and volcanic craters, which were symbolic of the birth canal (Petit-Breuilh 27). In some societies, humans were even viewed as direct descendants of volcanoes, as was the case with the indigenous residents of the flanks of the Chimborazo volcano in Ecuador or the Mapuches in Chile (Petit-Breuilh 24, 26). Likewise, indigenous mythology is rife with legends of humans turned to stones and volcanoes, whose spirits made the earth rumble when displeased or to warn of impending danger.[15] Disasters revealed the humanity of nature: far from the alien, unfeeling force that nature represents for modernity, the indigenous environment displayed emotions such as love and jealousy and reacted to stimuli in much the same way as humans. This familiarity with the landscape did not ensure freedom from disaster, however: in this framework, disasters were most often conceived as punishment for a society's failure to keep its tutelary gods or ancestors happy.

Pre-Columbian religious interpretations of disasters, despite their spiritual bent, were often used for political purposes. Indeed, there was rarely a clear separation between religion and politics in indigenous societies. As Petit-Breuilh points out, many indigenous societies charged a particular caste or group with conserving traditions and religious rites as well as elaborating politically coherent narratives for new situations, including disaster (27). These were the people who would reconcile disaster with preexisting narratives, often in a way that would reinforce or underscore their own political power or standing. For instance, many disasters were attributed to the wrath of gods who had to be appeased through ritual cleansing and/or sacrifice. Deciding what or who was responsible for the "contamination" could be a highly politicized selection process, one that was used on more than one occasion to eliminate rivals. Likewise, in societies that practiced human sacrifice, the choosing of the sacrificial victim(s) often implied a political decision, whether sacrifice was a burden reserved for slaves and prisoners of war or an honor bestowed on the most pure or highest nobility.

On the other hand, disasters underpinned foundational narratives that justified the dominion of some groups over others. For instance, the Inca creation narrative included a massive flood in which all humanity was destroyed due to its failure to keep a taboo. The only survivors were the ancestors of the Incas; as the most direct descendants of these founding fathers, their dominion over the other tribes was justified (Petit-Breuilh 31). Many groups throughout Mesoamerica had similar myths of regeneration following catastrophe that legitimized them as the true descendants of divinity and, as such, the possessors of the divine right to rule. Such myths served a political function when the Spanish arrived as well, providing fodder for opponents of indigenous enslavement, such as Bartolomé de las Casas. Indigenous stories of massive floods held great significance for Catholic missionaries, who were preoccupied with verifying that the indigenous people were descendants of Noah and therefore true humans with a soul (Petit-Breuilh 32–33).

Disaster narratives had important political ramifications in indigenous societies, but most political debate that occurred would have taken place in oral rather than written spaces, which are what concern me in this book. As in other cultures of the time period, writing had a primarily hegemonic function in those indigenous cultures that used it. The theocratic state maintained a monopoly on interpretation and worldview that was not subject to public debate. The textualization of disaster narratives in codices, stelae, and murals served primarily to reinforce oral myths and state-sanctioned explanations with the authority of sacred iconography. In this setting, indigenous disaster writing did not usually offer a forum for renegotiating power relationships.

The Spaniards and Portuguese brought their own religious views of disaster with them upon arriving on American shores. Although drought was common and earthquakes occurred infrequently (the most notorious was the 1755 earthquake that severely damaged Lisbon), the Iberian Peninsula had a history relatively free of natural disasters, and they did not play a major role in the Iberian worldview.[16] Nevertheless, when seafaring Spaniards first encountered the fearsome Caribbean hurricanes, they appealed for protection to Catholic saints traditionally associated with protection at sea, such as San Cristóbal (St. Christopher) and the Virgen del Carmen, also known as the "Star of the Sea." Indeed, Columbus himself described how he pled for divine aid as he rode out a hurricane that sank three or more ships in the harbor of the Isabella settlement in June 1495, during his second voyage.[17] During the colonial time period, Spaniards frequently referred to religious signs sent by God to warn of impending disaster, such as the image of the Virgin crying and sweating before the devastating 1687 earthquake in Lima (Aldana 172). In fact, two incarnations of Christ became associated with seismic events in Peru: "Nuestro Señor de los Terremotos" (Our Lord of the Earthquakes), whose procession takes place in Cuzco on the anniversary of the 1586 earthquake that decimated the region, and the "Cristo Morado" (The Purple Christ), "Nuestro Señor de los Milagros" (Our Lord of Miracles), whose image survived a massive tsunami that devastated the predominantly black-freedman neighborhood of Callao in Lima in 1746.[18]

On the other hand, Spanish colonizers at a loss to explain convincingly the magnitude of disasters that they experienced in the New World incorporated elements of indigenous worldviews into their conceptualization of the phenomena. According to some accounts at least, Hurakan was not worshiped only by Mayas: he was also a Taíno deity that the Spaniards inducted into their reading of the disaster as the embodiment of evil.[19] Once again, syncretism seems to be at work, as Native American cultures rarely shared the Judeo-Christian dualistic conceptualization of the universe as segregated between good and evil. The Spaniards, in keeping with their colonial project, postulated hurricanes as manifestations of diabolic power that attempted to thwart their divine mission to convert the New World to Christianity, rather than the more common Judeo-Christian view of disaster as trial or punishment sent by God.

Writing was generally more accessible to the Iberian population of the time period than to their indigenous counterparts, and it was often used in Spanish and Portuguese society as a space for the debate of moral and political issues. It seems somewhat incongruous, therefore, that the textualization of disaster for political purposes was not prominent in colonial chronicles and correspondence. Despite the many disasters that the Iberian colonizers experienced in the New World, some of which were highly catastrophic, the written references to them are surprisingly sparse. Disasters rarely receive more than a passing mention even in instances in which entire cities were destroyed, as was the case when a volcanic lahar leveled the colonial capital of Guatemala in 1541. I believe that this is due to two main considerations. The many chronicles and histories not directly commissioned by the empire were written primarily to persuade it to respond to individual and collective legal petitions; therefore, their narratives tend to focus on human agency (their authors' heroic deeds) rather than what they would have viewed as divine acts.[20] On the other hand, an overemphasis on disaster could undermine Iberian claims of divine authorization for the colonial enterprise. Particularly in light of accusations of Spanish abuses such as those leveled by Bartolomé de las Casas, the divine-retribution paradigm of disasters to which the Spaniards subscribed would suggest that they were deserving of punishment rather than reward. Perhaps for these reasons, disasters are mostly mentioned in these texts as curiosities, distanced historically and geographically from the narrating voice. There are, of course, exceptions, particularly in cases in which it benefited writers to engage tropes of victimization to attract aid.[21]

Africans thrust onto New World shores by the slave trade and their descendants appealed to deities of syncretic religions such as Santería/Lukumí and Candomblé for protection during disasters. In Cuba, for instance, Orishas such as Changó, Ainá, and Exú are associated with fire, thunder, and lightning; Oyá with wind and lightning; Aganjú with volcanoes; and Yemanyá and Oranyán with movements of the sea and the earth, respectively. Among the more engaging deities linked specifically to disaster are Ayarakotó, who warns humanity when a tsunami is about to strike, her roaring voice preceding the tidal wave, and Oshumaré, who restores environmental balance following a storm, returning excess water to the sky (M. Ramos 26, 28). Very few firsthand textual accounts of Africans' and their descendants' experiences in the colonial New World exist, but many disaster narratives were handed down through oral history, some of which were directly confrontational to the hegemonic interpretations of the Spanish and Portuguese empires.

Despite a degree of transculturation in the interpretation of natural disasters during the colonial period, the perspectives cannot be simply lumped together. It is true that most disaster narratives during this time period are religious in nature, but there was by no means consensus regarding which religion was involved or what the meaning of the divine message was. To the chagrin of the Spaniards, indigenous peoples frequently conceived of postconquest disasters as the vengeance of their gods for Spanish abuses. Alternately, if the disasters mainly affected the indigenous people, they were often viewed as punishment for abandoning traditional beliefs for Catholicism (Petit-Breuilh 51).[22] One might surmise that for the people of African descent, as in the case of the indigenous people, disaster could represent divine vengeance on oppressors. However, black people in colonial Latin America were not typically identified with the land to the same degree as indigenous people—they were seen as "uprooted," as it were, and as such had less of a spiritual connection to the local landscape and its convulsions.[23] Furthermore, in places like colonial Peru, black people often lived in the areas most vulnerable to disaster; as such, they were the most affected by these events. They may have viewed disasters as an opportunity to escape their oppression, however: with the social organization in shambles following disaster, surely many slaves fled, and colonial powers frequently documented their fear of uprisings during disasters such as the 1746 earthquake in Peru (Aldana 178).

Nonetheless, until the principles of the Enlightenment began to take hold in the late eighteenth century, the dominant interpretations of the disasters themselves were rarely disputed publicly due to the authoritarian position of the church and the state in the production of disaster narratives. As Claudio Lomnitz has pointed out, there was little space for civic debate (in writing or elsewhere) in Mexico during the colonial period; the same could be said of most of the Iberian colonies (146–53). The notable exception was in the sphere of local politics, but participation was carefully limited by factors such as race and gender (Lomnitz 147–48). Even though newspapers were introduced in Latin America in the 1720s, they did not become a forum for public debate until the late eighteenth century, and even then discussions were limited to scientific and technical questions (Lomnitz 147–48). Newspapers did not acquire their primacy in the constitution of the public sphere until after independence in the nineteenth century; any reports on disasters published in them up until that point only reinforced the disaster narratives sanctioned by the colonial powers. In this scenario, there was very limited room for subalterns of any kind to influence policy through writing or otherwise.

Without a doubt, the primary genres for the production of disaster narratives in the colonial time period were designed to reinforce existing hierarchies of power: official reports and correspondence, church records, chronicles, and, later, newspapers. Of course, private correspondence, diaries, and travel accounts provide a more intimate look at interpretation, but as the only people who had the means to write tended to be inscribed in positions of power, they typically diverge little from official accounts in their interpretations of events. The most contestatory forms of colonial disaster narratives, oral accounts whispered from the shadows of power, have by now largely disappeared or remain only in trace form in popular cultural practices. In any case, formal and informal censorship forced these oral accounts to be framed primarily as folk stories whose content was only obliquely confrontational to power.

This is not to say that there was no room for negotiation. Susana Aldana Rivera notes that in any context in which paternalist politics hold sway, disaster creates a sudden confrontation between the state and its citizens (189–90). As she argues so convincingly, disasters in colonial Latin America were frequently used by different social sectors to renegotiate power relationships. In particular, she cites the example of indigenous people in northern Peru who learned to use real or perceived drought as a mechanism for reducing the tribute levied on them, as well as the manipulation of the facts by the elite in official accounts for personal gain (188, 191). As the case may be, subalterns had little recourse but to work from within the frameworks set up by those in positions of power. As Lomnitz underscores, popular political agency was generally limited to appealing to the mediation of political or religious representatives assigned them by the empire (150, 275). With these representatives mediating, often in writing, details might be disputed, but the master narrative was never in question. The religious hegemony of the Catholic Church was never seriously threatened, and in the political realm there were only very limited elections to be lost due to bungled disaster responses; only the local officials of municipal *cabildos* were subject to vote. Of course, rioting and revolution were always a possibility, one that was taken very seriously by the colonial authorities.

With this brief and highly reductive overview of the early history of the cultural politics of disaster narratives in Latin America, I do not mean to imply, as have some observers, that Latin American cultures are somehow traumatized by a state of permanent or unending catastrophe. Instead, I am interested in the historical development of mechanisms for the cultural mediation of crisis and disaster and, more specifically, in the way in which written representations of disasters have been used to construct local concepts of risk, vulnerability, loss, and recovery for political purposes. As fascinating as pre-Columbian and colonial disaster narratives may be, they tend to engender religious interpretations of disaster that minimize (perhaps purposefully) the political aspects and implications of disaster management. Religious interpretations of disaster waned with modernity, however, or at least they lost their hegemonic position, becoming subject to dispute and refutation.

As Niklas Luhmann has argued, the Enlightenment focus on human agency led to a fundamental transformation in the way in which the Western world conceived of danger and security, displacing them from the realm of divine intervention to human domains of discourse and probabilities.[24] Threats began to be conceived in calculable terms of risk, rather than indefinite, divine danger. In political terms, this implied a shift of power from the church to the state: whereas the church had formerly been charged with assuaging the threat of disaster, the government became responsible for calculating and managing the risks it posed. Likewise, Enlightenment notions of political representation and consensus government meant that divisiveness in politics became much more acceptable than in religion, particularly with the demise of the concept of divine authority. For this reason, modern discourse on disaster encompasses a much wider variety of interpretations, whose political validity depends on a process of negotiation that, if not nonexistent during the colonial period in Latin America, was minimal due to the autocratic government and the hegemony of the Catholic Church. As Claudio Lomnitz has argued, "With independence, a nationally articulated sphere emerged for the first time, with the commercial press and Congress as its two main forums. This transition meant that arbitration from the political center was no longer the only, or even necessarily the principal, way of arguing for the rights of a collective actor" (150). Although the political forms that emerged in Latin America with independence were imperfect and constantly changing, they nevertheless provided a space for the public negotiation of policy and power relations. And, as Lomnitz argues, these negotiations were often carried out through writing.

Luhmann associates the rise of the concept of risk with a displacement in language in which theological discourse was replaced by the specialized language of statistics and probabilities. Louis Anthony Cox notes, however, that "risks cannot be directly observed or measured. Therefore they must be inferred from models, knowledge, assumptions, and data" (4). In this sense, statistics in risk assessment function symbolically, as abstract, representative values rather than entirely known quantities. I argue, moreover, that statistics are not the only kind of symbol used in risk analysis; literary tropes often assume similar functions. Furthermore, even when statistics are used, they must be explained to policymakers using more expository modes of discourse. As Anthony Oliver-Smith points out, "The perception of risk, vulnerability, and even impact is clearly mediated through linguistic and cultural grids" ("Theorizing" 38). Indeed, a common criticism of statistical risk analysis is the way in which it dehumanizes human identities through symbolic abstraction, converting people into numbers and human behavior into formulas.

For policymakers as well as the general public, statistics are meaningless until they are reinscribed within a story, which however removed from the original context, nevertheless forms a discursive whole, the textual embodiment of disaster. In other words, for raw data to be put into practice and policy, it must be shaped into a narrative. The numbers and formulas become the supporting evidence of a collective local, regional, or national disaster narrative of which the mortality statistics and sum of material damage form the conclusion. Risk assessment, therefore, is carried out through a variety of techniques that include qualitative as well as quantitative aspects. Furthermore, these narratives of risk often contain a manifest ideological bent in that they intend to influence policymaking with the goal of maximizing economic profit and political currency while minimizing losses of either. As Mary Douglas points out, in today's usage, *risk* is no longer a neutral term denoting the probabilities of both positive and negative outcomes. It has become conflated with danger, leading to a situation in which "the evaluation is a political, aesthetic, and moral matter" (31). In this sense, risk analysis has undeniable ethical implications despite its claimed objectivity in statistics.

Risk as a concept became prevalent during the nineteenth-century neocolonial enterprise as part of what Bankoff has called the colonial "rendering the world unsafe" that led to the classification of the tropics as "danger zones" that could only be neutralized by replicating the conditions of Western, developed nations (6–8). Today's prevalence of statistical analysis in risk assessment, however, only reached culmination with the academic ultraspecialization and computerization in the period since World War II, and even then only in the most technified societies. This does not mean that risk analysis has not been carried out even in situations in which statistics were imprecise or unavailable, or when probabilities could not be formulated adequately, whether due to lack of information or excess of variables. As scholars such as Elaine Freedgood have shown, literary discourse has often assumed the guise of risk assessment, and it has been employed to those ends by political actors.[25]

Following independence, many Latin American nations looked to the United States and Europe for models of development, including mechanisms for mediating crisis. Nevertheless, limited resources and internal politics frequently slowed the implementation of the technocratic infrastructure associated with modern government, with its network of governmental agencies and academic institutions for mediating contingencies such as disaster. In lieu of technical specialization, literature became a key space in which notions of risk and vulnerability were formulated and debated. In Latin America, literary works often served to theorize disaster, creating an interpretative system for dealing with catastrophe in which society, politics, and cultural practice converged. Literary analysis permitted Latin American societies to take a step back from disaster and to assume a more critical stance toward highly traumatic experience. At the same time, literature constitutes a powerful method of persuasion: the rhetoric of disaster and crisis was particularly effective in promoting ideological points of view, particularly given the atmosphere of irrefutability that disaster narratives generate.

Latin American disaster narratives owe their potency in part to the starring role of nature in the national foundation narratives that appeared following independence. Throughout the nineteenth century, *criollo* writers—that is, authors of predominantly European heritage such as Brazilian José de Alencar, Colombian Jorge Isaacs, Cubans José María Heredia and José Martí, Peruvian José Santos Chocano, and Venezuelan Andrés Bello, to name only a few—were obliged to turn to local landscapes as the sign of national distinctiveness. As members of the white cultural elite educated in European knowledge and aesthetics, they were unable to appeal convincingly to racial or cultural idiosyncrasies to reject the colonial order and found a new national aesthetics; emplacement became the solution for breaking with their Iberian heritage. Paradise was a key locus in the national imaginary created by these writers, who were deeply influenced by the Romantic sublimation of national landscapes.[26] The utopian landscape would sustain the nation economically, through natural abundance, as well as culturally, through the symbolic appropriation of nature as the rich repository of national values. Clearly, there was little place for disaster in national narratives rooted in paradise. Furthermore, for much of the nineteenth century, the ravages caused by natural disasters were secondary to those caused by political disasters. As in the colonial period, disaster narratives existed largely on the margins of literature and politics, with a few exceptions.

A more critical view of the relations between humans and nature in Latin America arose only in the late nineteenth century, when greater political stability and the modernization that accompanied the first wave of liberal globalization led to drastic transformations of the national landscape. During this time period, the growth in the lettered middle class led to a much larger audience for literature, while the continued hegemony of what Uruguayan cultural critic Ángel Rama called the *ciudad letrada* (lettered city) assured the political ascendancy of writing.[27] For these reasons, literature became an important tool for assessing and mediating the changes that were occurring in the national landscape, including its social, political, and environmental components. Confronted with internal displacement toward urban areas as well as massive waves of European immigration, on the one hand, and English and US capitalization of the economic landscape, on the other, Latin American authors turned to the rural interiors of their nations as the setting for new foundational narratives that attempted to resolve the complex tensions between modernization and local traditions.[28] Alternatively labeled regionalist, *criollista*, or telluric fiction, these "novels of the land" evoked tropes developed by José Martí in his 1891 essay "Nuestra América," with its concept of the patriarchal "natural man," who despite his European or *mestizo* racial makeup becomes autochthonous by rooting himself in the land and rejecting foreign values. In order to combat the notion that modernization could only by achieved by importing European values or even Europeans themselves, regionalist works such as Argentinean Ricardo Güiraldes's *Don Segundo Sombra* (1926), Brazilian José de Américo Almeida's *A bagaceira* (*Trash*; 1928), and Venezuelan Rómulo Gallegos's *Doña Bárbara* (1929) put to work the modern discourse of the collective labor of the human domination of nature to legitimize local elites' claims to a land won by sacrifice and toil. At the same time, these works comprised a kind of risk assessment in themselves, judging the dangers posed to projects of national integration by marginalized environments and their human inhabitants.

Despite the continued feminization of the land (captured famously in Gallegos's title, *Doña Bárbara*, in which the female title character is inextricably tied to the barbarous landscape of the Venezuelan *llanos*), regionalist depictions of nature broke with the romantic trope of feminine passivity; the rebellious land had to be conquered with a combination of masculine virility and modern technology. In fact, the romantic tropes of paradise cede in many of these works to a hostile nature that threatens to devour modern man (and the protagonists are always men), as is the case in works such as Brazilian Alberto Rangel's *Inferno verde* (*Green Hell*; 1908) and Colombian José Eustasio Rivera's *La vorágine* (*The Vortex*; 1924). Despite appearances, nonetheless, even in *La vorágine* nature does not triumph over man: rather than the malice or rebellion of nature, the protagonists owe their downfall to human exploitation in the rubber industry and the political failure to impose the rule of law uniformly throughout the nation. In reality, these works reinforced human agency over nature, revealing how human enterprise had reached into even the most inaccessible, marginal environments and calling for the rectification of incomplete or imperfect development in those areas. Read as a corpus, the gist of Latin American regionalist writing was that in-vogue European theories of environmental determinism, which suggested that underdevelopment was the product of environmental maladaptation and/or genetic inferiority, could be overcome with modern education and private initiative. As Jennifer L. French has shown, these are not works that reject liberal capitalism outright; rather, they propose liberal modernization from the inside.

While disaster writing cannot be pigeonholed to a particular period or style of literary production, it is clear that it arises in dialogue with the dominant modes of nature writing, a term that I use in its broadest sense. By definition, disaster writing must address the disjunction that occurs when a catastrophe precipitates a drastic reevaluation of our relationships with nature. In this sense, disaster writing from the 1920s onward would seemingly contradict the positive views of human-nature relations presented in regionalist fiction, for example, in which humans dominate nature and make it more productive through literal and symbolic cultivation. In reality, however, disaster narratives often complement these projects, representing a continuation of regionalism's focus on the risks that underdevelopment and marginalized environments entailed for the nation. They deploy a variety of strategies to normalize or restore the conceptual relationships that have been disarticulated during disaster. A key mechanism is the focus on politics: by representing disasters as political rather than natural or divine events, human agency over nature is restored, even if in a nuanced way. Through narrative, humans are able to harness disaster, converting destruction and mortality into matters of human error (vulnerability) and channeling it to political ends in contesting autocratic political orders or engaging in nation building. The chapters that follow focus specifically on how disaster narratives undertake this transference from natural to human agency through inscription within a political framework.

The Modern Grammar of Disaster

With the emergence of risk assessment as the primary tool for judging danger and potential threats in the twentieth century, a grammar of disaster arose for mediating catastrophic events that included key concepts such as risk, vulnerability, trauma, and normalization. In reality, vulnerability is the concept that underpins the entire system of assessment; it defines risk and the potential for trauma, as well as inscribing the boundaries between normality (as security) and the normalization of insecurity—that is to say, which perennial threats are unacceptable socially according to local parameters as well as the modern discourse of human rights. And in any case of risk assessment, defining vulnerability is a highly politicized process, one that is most often undertaken retrospectively, after the fact of disaster. This belated relationship with disaster means that concepts of vulnerability are entangled with the assignment of blame, which cannot fail to have political consequences.

The political implications of assessing vulnerability are not always immediately evident, however, due to the perception that disasters constitute abnormal situations. In the context of socially constructed normality, disaster is viewed as a liminal state, an anomaly that interrupts history. As Susanna Hoffman has argued, the specter of disaster is particularly disturbing because it disorders not only space but also time (124). Conceptually, disaster disrupts the historical progression leading to modernity, and when disaster is recurring, it creates the impression of entrapping humanity in cyclical time (Hoffman 132). In this sense, disasters, like nature itself, are often conceived of as existing beyond history and, therefore, politics.[29]

Nevertheless, researchers such as Kenneth Hewitt have revealed the fallacy of this perspective: rather than representing the collapse of historically constituted social and political order, disasters reveal the normal order of subordination and inequality ("Idea" 24–27). In this framework, disasters, rather than isolated events, represent the culmination of historical processes that have resulted in certain populations living in a state of heightened vulnerability, which explains how a single disaster affects people from distinct social groups in very different ways (Oliver-Smith, "Theorizing" 23–27). As Greg Bankoff has made clear, "For those who can expect to experience repeated disasters in both their personal lives and in the histories of their communities, the concept of hazard as a distinct phenomenon is often not a very meaningful one. There is no very clear separation between it, environmental degradation, poverty, marginalization, disempowerment, and disentitlement" (179). In this scenario, the disaster is not at all an abnormal event; it is the convergence of multiple factors that have placed a certain population in a vulnerable state over a significant period of time.

Although the anthropologists, sociologists, and geographers I have cited highlight the historical construction of situations of vulnerability, which are inextricable from political and economic power relations, they pay little shrift to the political implications of definitions of vulnerability. The neutral language in which they couch their theories constructs a universalist perspective of vulnerability that, while a useful conceptual tool, becomes much stickier when applied locally. In local contexts, defining vulnerability often constitutes a highly charged political act. The works I study all play off definitions of the grammar of disaster for political purposes, redefining concepts of risk, vulnerability, trauma, and normalization in order to promote and, in many cases, institutionalize highly politicized interpretations of particular disaster events.

This book examines the political ramifications of narratives dealing with two types of disasters: sudden-onset, single events, which often strike with little or no warning, and long-term, recurring disasters. Each kind of disaster gives rise to distinct forms of cultural production and political interpretations. Disaster narratives that arise following a single, powerful event such as an earthquake or hurricane tend toward the extemporaneous. They most often mirror existing forms and draw on latent political narratives to endow the event with social meaning. The suddenness of the catastrophic event frequently makes it useful as an image of political rupture, providing space for criticisms of the existing order. On the other hand, adept regimes are sometimes able to incorporate the disaster into their own foundational narratives, thus turning it to legitimizing purposes. Production typically tapers off as the disaster recedes into the past and new sources of legitimization must be sought to actualize the pertinent political narratives. Sometimes anniversary memorials are able to replenish the political currency of past disasters, however, particularly when political events endow the disaster with renewed relevance, and one sees a resurgence of disaster writing ten or twenty years after the catastrophic event.

Disasters that recur over time, such as cycles of drought or volcanic activity, however, often lead to the formation of a tradition of disaster narratives that engenders its own aesthetics, allowing it to transcend its moment. The repetition of tropes and plot lines over decades or generations creates a powerful, self-sustaining disaster narrative that canonizes the disaster culturally while institutionalizing the political interpretations associated with it. In this way, disaster narratives associated with long-term, recurring disasters often give rise to powerful foundational narratives of their own that sustain particular political orders. Nonetheless, dissident groups may use single disaster events within a chronology of recurring disaster to subvert or redirect these foundational narratives, opening them to contestation.

Sudden disaster events often thrust into the spotlight the normal degree of subordination and inequality that exist within a society, but they also open that order to revision through political negotiation. This process of renegotiation does not always lead to a reduction in disparities, however; many times they are deepened. Perhaps nowhere is this clearer than in the way in which Dominican dictator Rafael Leonidas Trujillo used his response to and interpretation of Cyclone San Zenón, which leveled Santo Domingo scarcely two weeks after he seized power in a military coup in 1930, to found a new social and political order. Tellingly, his regime used representations of the hurricane both to legitimize his rupture with the prior political order and to anchor a new foundational narrative of Dominican history as an enduring disaster to which he was the sole remedy. In contrast to the typical view of disasters as interrupting or existing outside of history, Trujillo inscribed Cyclone San Zenón as a key marker in a national history characterized by vulnerability to a series of political, economic, and natural catastrophes.

Chapter 1 of this book, entitled "Disaster and the 'New Patria': Cyclone San Zenón and Trujillo's Rewriting of the Dominican Republic," examines the way in which Trujillo's regime used literary works written by supporters as well as the literal rewriting of the national landscape to legitimize his interpretation of Dominican history, while limiting competing interpretations of both the hurricane and his policies through autocratic repression and censorship. Playing off what Hoffman calls the "creative destruction" paradigm of disasters, in which the disaster response represents the possibility of rebirth and renewal on a blank site, Trujillo's regime used the rebuilding process following the hurricane not only to consolidate his political power but also to extend political change to ideological transformation in the creation of a "Nueva Patria" (New Homeland).[30] Trujillo's manipulation of the meaning of the 1930 hurricane to consolidate and justify his regime reveals transparently the powerful political utility of cultural representations of disaster.

If the interpretation of single disaster events such as Cyclone San Zenón may be engaged in the service of powerful political narratives legitimizing and even institutionalizing political orders, it comes as no surprise that cultural representations of recurring disasters such as drought in northeastern Brazil can have even more substantial political utility. Notably, the earliest representations of drought in northeastern Brazil, such as those depicting the 1877–1879 "Great Drought," treated it in a way not so different from Trujillo's inlaying of the 1930 hurricane within a Dominican history of disaster. The trope of state vulnerability to a variety of disasters, political as well as natural, weighs heavily in these early representations of drought. Indeed, during the postindependence period of the "Old Republic" (1889–1930) up through the consolidation of Getúlio Vargas's Estado Novo, Brazilian intellectuals frequently viewed the state as a fragile entity, vulnerable to foreign intervention or invasion, racial uprisings, the restoration of the monarchy, and internal secessions. These fears came to a head during the 1897

Canudos War, in which a group of several thousand religious zealots who had settled on a plot of land in the interior of the northern state of Bahia came to be seen as a threat to the nation. Their initial triumphs over federal troops confirmed this view, and the government ended up sending a massive military expedition to eradicate the rebels, the story of which is retold in Euclides da Cunha's masterpiece *Os sertões* (*Rebellion in the Backlands*; 1902). Tellingly, Cunha's text postulates the Northeast's drought-stricken environment as the prime factor in creating a rebellious race that he denominates the *sertanejo*, which is unable to adapt to modern democracy and therefore threatens the continued existence of the Brazilian state.

Nowhere is the direct role of literature in dictating governmental policies toward disaster more clear than in the long history of drought in northeastern Brazil. This disaster constitutes a unique case in catastrophes of national significance: through literary mediation, the *seca*, or drought, in the Northeast has come to embody what Antonio Callado has called a "traditional Brazilian calamity" (5). Tellingly, many of the literary works that deal with it have been canonized as Brazilian classics. Chapter 2, entitled "Drought and the Literary Construction of Risk in Northeastern Brazil," analyzes the long tradition of drought narratives inaugurated with José de Alencar's *O sertanejo* (1875) and continuing in the works of writers such as José do Patrocínio, Rodolfo Teófilo, Euclides da Cunha, José Américo de Almeida, Rachel de Queiroz, and Graciliano Ramos, to name only a few of the most well-known authors associated with drought. I argue that the centrality of literary mediation of the disaster depended not on the social prestige or value of literature but rather on its concrete political uses in creating formulas for assessing the risks that drought and the Northeast in general posed to national political and economical projects. Due to the scarcity of data on the northeastern *sertões*, which were frequently referred to as *"terra incógnita"* (unknown lands), literary tropes substituted for the statistics and scientific measurements that are typically used in risk assessment. Beginning with the 1930s, however, literature slowly ceded its role in risk assessment to academic specialists in economics and the social sciences, which appeared in Brazil as distinct disciplines in the decades that followed.

Trujillo's autocratic manipulation of disaster imagery to consolidate and justify his power was relatively transparent: even when works were signed by different authors and written in different styles, the thematic unity and repetition of propaganda is always discernable. Similarly, the Brazilian discourse on drought was most often elaborated by intellectuals from outside the affected region, leading to remarkable consistency in interpretations of the disaster and the politics surrounding it. Things become considerably more complex, however, when literary tropes and themes cannot be traced to a single source, and competing representations of disaster vie for discursive legitimacy. Such is the case in chapter 3, which focuses on the forceful jousting for control over volcanic imagery in Central American literature and politics. "Volcanic Identities: Explosive Nationalism and the Disastered Subject in Central American Literature" scrutinizes the role that imagery arising from a long history of volcanic activity has played in the ongoing process of the construction and negotiation of ethnic and national identities in Central America. I am particularly interested in the way that volcanic imagery was used to mediate interactions between individual and collective identities in the works of canonical and less known authors such as Rubén Darío, Luis de Lión, Claribel Alegría, Manlío Argueta, Roque Dalton, and José Coronel Urtecho. Volcanoes figured frequently as benign beacons of nationalism in official iconography throughout Central American history, but revolutionary social movements often turned volcanic imagery against autocratic symbolic orders. They emphasized the metaphorical potential of eruption, especially that of the indigenous inhabitants of the volcanoes' flanks. At the same time, many Central American works associate imagery of volcanic eruptions and other disasters with the psychological trauma inflicted on the individual living under repressive regimes, resulting in representations of what I call the "disastered" subject. The competition for control over volcanic iconography in Central American literature and culture brings to light the impressive political potency of disaster discourse, as well as the competition over its legitimizing symbolism as the authentic, autochthonous expression of the land.

Chapter 4, entitled "Fault Lines: Mexico's 1985 Earthquake and the Politics of Narration," studies in greater detail the relationships between politics, disaster narratives, and social identity, focusing on the struggle for control over the interpretation of a single, powerful event: the 1985 earthquake in Mexico City. Unlike Trujillo's rescription of the Dominican Republic following Cyclone San Zenón, in which the regime's rendition of the disaster became one of its most powerful defenses and legitimizing mechanisms, the official version of the earthquake, constructed by Mexico's ruling Partido Revolucionario Institucional (PRI), failed in its bid for discursive control of the disaster, being forced to cede legitimacy first to informal, popular accounts of the event and soon after to a coordinated literary attack that effectively abolished the last vestiges of governmental claims to popular, revolutionary embodiment and encompassment.

I argue that the key point of dispute in the wrangling over interpretation of the disaster was the definition of vulnerability and the assignment of risk. Ben Wisner comments in his study of vulnerability that in situations in which the state exercises repression against its own citizens, the state itself may come to be considered a hazard (134). Even when repression is absent, citizens may assume this viewpoint when the state fails to respond adequately to their needs during situations of disaster, particularly when they recognize that the modern state distributes risk in a highly unequal fashion (Wisner 134). This view of the state as hazard was widely promoted by the cultural representations of the Mexico City earthquake. These works construct a series of political identities based on the response to the disaster, pitting the common people against the state. They take an openly antagonistic position toward the PRI, disputing not only the government's version of events but also the discursive foundations of the PRI's legitimacy as the embodiment of popular revolutionary change in Mexico. They depict the earthquake's effects as the collapse of the governmental edifice, extending discursively the populace's vulnerability to disaster, which they blamed on the PRI, to the political system itself. The antagonism was due largely to the government's refusal to cede any authority to disaster victims, who self-organized in rescue brigades, at the same time that it reacted inefficiently to the disaster. This technocratic attitude made it impossible to negotiate a consensus view of the disaster that would have allowed the government to reengage its citizens and reauthorize itself as their agent.

Why the Comparative Approach?

I believe that comparative analysis is particularly fruitful when dealing with cultural representations of natural disasters for a variety of reasons. On the one hand, comparison opens apparently self-contained discourse to reevaluation. This is particularly important when one deals with traumatic events such as disasters, in which it becomes very difficult to extricate oneself emotionally from the narratives of suffering and loss. On the other hand, disaster studies as a field has largely focused on developing theory and related practices that are applicable across the board, to any disaster in any context. These theories are often presented in scientific modes of discourse that appear depoliticized: the goal is saving lives, not amassing political currency. I use a comparative approach to enter into dialogue with the universalist assumptions of disaster theory on its own comparative terrain, in order to interrogate the political implications of theorizing natural disasters, whether as particular events or as a category.

Each disaster that I study resulted in the construction of one or more, often competing local theoretical frameworks for explaining and mitigating the disaster in question. Due to the convergence of the historical institution that Ángel Rama called the *ciudad letrada* and the humanist tradition of indistinct academic divisions, literature has long functioned in Latin America as an interdisciplinary space for drafting cultural, social, and political theory. It comes as no surprise, therefore, that much of the theorizing of these local disasters took place in literary texts. The literary divide between fiction and fact, or abstraction and practicality, however, meant that the legitimacy of these local theoretical formulations of disaster depended on their relationship to political and economic power: they had to prove their relevancy. And they often negotiated this power through dialogue with the Western academic tradition, in which theory is conceived of as centralized and universal in scope. For these reasons, my study is also interdisciplinary: I show how local writers dialogue with key Western theoretical concepts such as development, risk, trauma, and vulnerability that originated in a variety of disciplines from economics to sociology but that have recently converged in disaster studies.

Having established the utility of a comparative approach to studying disasters in Latin America, the question remains as to why I chose these disasters in particular (the 1930 hurricane in the Dominican Republic, drought in northeastern Brazil, volcanic imagery in Central America, and the 1985 earthquake in Mexico City) to the exclusion of innumerable others, many of which were more recent or devastating materially. First, as I consider the role that disasters played in politics primarily at the national scale, I wanted to avoid endorsing or naturalizing the view of any one nation as a "disastered state," particularly given the political ends to which such views of national histories were put to use in Mexico and the Dominican Republic.[31] Comparing traumatic ideologies of Dominican and Mexican history with Brazilian representations of the Northeast in a similar mode, for instance, has been very revealing, considering that the latter place one region and its residents in direct opposition to the national ideology of Brazil as tropical and racial paradise. Brazilian discourse on drought reveals in greater relief the mechanisms of inclusion and exclusion in national concepts of citizenship that come into play in the representation of disaster, a situation that illuminates the murkier consequences of the symbolic use of disaster imagery in Dominican and Mexican national histories.

At the same time, the disasters that I have selected are closer to the nation than others have been. They are disasters that became iconic and/or "paradigmatic"—that is to say, they acquired national symbolism and precipitated or consolidated cultural and political shifts through literary mediation. One might say that I chose disasters that became politically central through literary canonization, or vice versa. My selections have therefore been dictated to some degree by the quality and the quantity of the cultural works that represent particular disasters. Contrary to appearances, these are not arbitrary criteria. The volume of literature written about a particular disaster and the involvement of canonical literary figures are prime indicators of its cultural and political relevancy for the nation. Likewise, more developed and sophisticated cultural production on a disaster allows for a deeper reading of the forces at work. It is for this reason that I do not study the recent (2010) disasters in Haiti and Chile. As horrifyingly mesmerizing as they may be, a modicum of historical distance is necessary to judge the implications of literary and artistic production for political change.

Finally, my readers may wonder why I do not dedicate any chapter to so-called man-made disasters such as environmental degradation or genocide (although both these topics do actually surface throughout the book). I would point out that the distinction between natural and man-made disasters mirrors what environmental theorists have derided as modernity's false dualism between humans and nonhuman nature. From a practical point of view, recent geographical and sociological research suggests that even "natural" disasters are most often man-made in the sense that their catastrophic effects on human populations depend on social and economic problems of vulnerability and the unequal distribution of risk.[32] From a more theoretical vantage point, I have argued that nature is delimited as the negative to the human in a classic case of othering discourse, in which the object is defined only in opposition to the subject. Similarly, disaster is defined as the negative to normalcy, and normalcy is socially defined, not natural. In this sense, both *disaster* and *nature* are socially constructed human concepts. The pages that follow concentrate precisely on the framing of disasters as natural versus political events, and how concepts of *the natural* and *disaster* are constructed or dismantled in literature and other cultural media for political purposes.

1 Disaster and the "New Patria"

Cyclone San Zenón and Trujillo's Rewriting of the Dominican Republic

In this home, Trujillo is boss.
—Trujillo-era slogan

THE HURRICANE THAT STRUCK the Dominican Republic on September 2 and 3, 1930, caused unprecedented damage to the nation's capital, disrupting severely the nation's infrastructure as well as its self-image. Santo Domingo's iconic Río Ozama overflowed with the hurricane's intense rains, washing out key bridges and port facilities and flooding the neighborhoods along its banks, while winds of up to 150 miles per hour wreaked havoc on tin-roofed, wooden buildings that had been constructed during the period of rapid urbanization from the end of the nineteenth century through the US occupation (1916–1924). Thousands were killed, and a much greater number were left without food or shelter. Despite the massive scale of the destruction and having consolidated his power mere weeks earlier, Dominican dictator Rafael Leonidas Trujillo responded in a highly efficient manner to the disaster, putting to use his military training in organizing the relief efforts. In the years that followed, Trujillo and his collaborators used his response to Cyclone San Zenón as a key trope in the narrative legitimizing his rule, which lasted from 1930 until his assassination in 1961.

Trujillo's renaming of Santo Domingo following the hurricane's leveling of the city in 1930 was not simply another of the megalomaniac acts that characterized his regime. Beyond his penchant for the unsubtle performance of power, Trujillo's rewriting of Santo Domingo's urban landscape as Ciudad Trujillo signified a radical rescription of Dominican history and, in the eyes of the regime, its future. Indeed, the incredible devastation wreaked by the hurricane scarcely two weeks after a military coup culminated in Trujillo's likely fraudulent election as president allowed him not only to consolidate his power by declaring a state of emergency and martial law but also to remake the capital in his image. His rewriting impulse did not stop at the city limits, however, but radiated forth to encompass the entire nation: Trujillo became the most common toponym in the Dominican Republic, appearing from the capital to the Haitian border in private homes and public parks, on street signs, bridges, public works projects, hillsides, and mountaintops. Two provinces were even rechristened in the family name.[1] This rescription was not limited simply to changing the place names to reflect his regime; it also implied the physical reconstruction of Santo Domingo and much of the countryside to his specifications, as well as the ideological transformation of Dominican society.

The Dominican Genealogy of Disaster

The Trujillan penchant for what might be termed "branding," given the marriage of national politics and personal economics for which the regime was famous, adds credence to exiled Dominican politician Juan Bosch's claim that the dictator had turned the Dominican Republic into his private corporation.[2] Indeed, the dividing line between public and private property became quite blurred during his administration; he frequently "borrowed" from the national treasury, pawning his personal property to the nation for exorbitant prices in order to free up capital for the expansion of his economic empire, only to buy it back a few years later (Turits 242–43). In this context, the proliferation of the Trujillo surname throughout the country could be construed as simple political branding, an act of staking his claim completely in keeping with his possessive, patriarchal image. While this scenario cannot be dismissed, upon closer examination the effects of Trujillo's substitution of the names of bridges, parks, streets, and even mountaintops with the family surname has much more profound implications, for the names they supplanted were not without prior history.

In the eyes of the regime, the old names begged replacement because they denoted an outmoded and ultimately failed past of colonial servitude and threatened sovereignty. The past had been a disaster, and it could only be rectified through the complete physical transformation of the landscape and the consequent modification of the defeatist psychology of its inhabitants. Trujillo's rescription of these places was not necessarily intended to erase history completely, however; the Trujillan iconography was meant to serve a supplemental role to the past, acknowledging it but also marking a clear rupture with it. The past was past, and this was modernity.

A key move in Trujillo's rewriting of the Dominican Republic was to replace the existing *ciudad letrada*, which was composed primarily of members of the postindependence oligarchy, with a new group of intellectuals and bureaucrats who swore absolute loyalty to his regime. Indeed, Trujillo's strategy of rewriting history through transforming place was not an entirely novel idea: the old order had made use of place names and historical markers to maintain its social and political hegemony, tracing its legitimacy back to the colonial period and particularly to the Colón (Columbus) family.[3] In order to carry out the remaking of places with historical meanings contrary to Trujillo's political designs, it would be necessary to replace the custodians of the oligarchy's national history with his own. This new intellectual class was charged with the task of creating the discursive underpinnings of his power by assembling a body of cultural texts that would simultaneously justify and obscure the repressive acts carried out by his government. Tellingly, not only do many of these texts refer to the 1930 Cyclone San Zenón, but they actually use it as a key argument in their vindication of the dictator's tactics. The hurricane became the cornerstone of what might be termed Trujillo's politics of disaster: that is, the discursive construction of a catastrophic national history characterized by perpetual vulnerability to attacks from outside sources, both human and natural.

This tragic view of Dominican history reappears in works written by Trujillo supporters throughout the "Era of Trujillo," some of them even published under his name. The majority of these texts, almost in their entirety aimed at offsetting criticisms of human rights abuses from abroad while trumpeting the regime's modernizing achievements, open by positing Dominican history as a series of failed development projects, whose truncation is due to vulnerability to nefarious external and, occasionally, internal forces. For this reason, Colombian author José Antonio Osorio Lizarazo, who found refuge in the Dominican Republic as a political exile and became one of Trujillo's most prolific and ardent defenders, initiates his overview of Dominican History in his eloquent if biased *La isla iluminada* (*The Illumined Island*; 1947) with the declaration that "a series of misfortunes, wars, massacres, prosperities, assaults of Nature, determine its history, convulsed and agitated like that of no other nation in the Americas" (42).[4] Likewise, Dominican writer Túlio Céstero Burgos reproduces this vision of the national past in his somewhat less polished *Filosofía de un régimen . . .* (A Regime's Philosophy . . .; 1951), claiming that "the sinister past of our nationality, which flourishes today, lies there, in ruins, like a stigma" (22).[5] Indeed, he refers variously to "a sordid past, littered with rubbish" (29) and "our shameful past" (45) characterized by "fratricidal storms" (58). Henry Gazón Bona propagates a similar view of the nation's architectural history, alluding to the period since independence as an "abysm" of "artistic apathy," whose primary characteristic was the profanation of venerable colonial art and architecture by "indifferent barbarians during a time of heretic rulers" (1). Trujillan ideology painted the Dominican Republic's history preceding his rise to power as a failure in every sense: a failure to modernize, a failure to become truly independent or to create a viable national culture, a failure to thwart the "barbaric" influence of black Haiti, and a failure to throw off the yoke of Yankee imperialism.

According to the official line, this catastrophic history took its toll on the Dominican psychology as well, creating a pessimistic being with no sense of historical agency. Trujillo himself, or his ghostwriter at any rate, emphasizes this point in *The Basic Policies of a Regime* (1960): "Always the people were faced by uncertainty, discord, the ruin of their hopes, the crushing of their vital instincts. All this frustration was causing to be forged a special psychology, a typical but unique sensitivity, a way of being unlike that of any of the other peoples of America" (29). Trujillo argues that although this traumatized historical subject was adept at surviving the vicissitudes that it was forced to confront, its defeatist mentality was altogether unfit for the modern paradigm of progress. The Dominican subject's wounded psyche was a reactive, not a proactive, force and, as such, could only weather life's storms but not rebuild in the wake of their destruction.

Naturally, only Trujillo's regime could put an end to the Dominican Republic's tragic destiny by effectively neutralizing the threats that had created it and thus transforming the national psychology into a positive, proactive historical force. The Dominican Republic's catastrophic history had to be rewritten, its failed culture of disaster replaced with a new outlook based on select modern Western values and the removal of what the regime perceived as the impediments to this transformation. Consequently, Osorio offers only four options for the future of the Caribbean nation: yet another invasion by Haiti and a subsequent regression to African barbarism, exploitive occupation by the United States, interminable civil wars, or Trujillo (23). Clearly, only one of them guarantees its survival as an autonomous state. The Dominican Republican being a democracy, the people were free to choose.

Tellingly, the "special psychology" created by the Dominican Republic's unique geography and history was also used to justify Trujillo's singular brand of democracy. Regarding this point, Osorio presents an interesting argument in favor of "historical, geographical, and ethnic relativity" based almost entirely on nineteenth-century racialist theories of environmental determinism (11). While his vocabulary may anticipate current theories of anthropological relativism, his thrust has little to do with cultural plurality: on the contrary, a few pages onward he makes clear that "the concept of democracy is contingent on multiple eventualities" (13). At root is an attack on the universal application of Western notions of democracy and human rights; he promotes "a local concept of democracy," in which more important than the right to vote and individual guarantees are "prosperity and collective well-being, the fullness of spiritual freedom, the authentic happiness of the people" (13).[6] He describes a utilitarian democracy that depends on individual material well-being rather than political representation. In any case, for Osorio representation has already been achieved: further on, he describes "a perfect copenetration of the people, who command, with their commander" (20–21).[7] Trujillo is invested with the power of the people not by vote but through embodiment: he is the *pueblo*.

Chronicling the Future

Robert Kastenbaum asserts correctly that "no matter how a disaster may be explained, the catastrophe can serve as a powerful explanation of other events" (69). This was certainly the case with the Trujillo regime; beyond chance or the will of God, there could be no concrete explanation of why the 1930 hurricane struck Santo Domingo, but the catastrophe was propitious for the regime's construction of this worldview in which the nation's physical and moral integrity was perceived as perpetually vulnerable to multiple threats. This politics of fear led to the perception of everyday life as a perpetual state of emergency, providing the ideal justification for Trujillo's authoritarianism and repressive tactics. Indeed, governments the world over have a history of responding to perceived emergency through totalitarianism, although relatively few have reached Trujillo's extremes.

The regime saw its response to the hurricane as the first step in constructing a "magnificent new nation" that would leave behind its catastrophic past (Trujillo 16). This project required "eliminating the factors of political disorder, financial oppression, juridical imprecision, and economic serfdom, replacing the public's pessimism and feelings of incapacity by self-confidence and creative willpower to carry out a fundamental transformation" (Trujillo 18). Alongside this chillingly nonchalant proposal for the elimination of political opponents, the oligarchy, and anyone else who stood in his way, the psychological transformation of the Dominican people became a key factor in his plan to remake the nation. Trujillo saw this refashioning of the national subject as the only possible route to modernity, and whoever refused to assume this transformational, ultimately antihistorical identity was labeled a traitor and forcibly (and sometimes permanently) removed from the nation. In this way, Trujillo hoped to fabricate a homogeneous, national "culture of disaster" capable of dealing with any internal or external threat in a preemptive and, from his point of view, constructive manner. And in his mind, there was no separation between the new national psychology and the physical modernization of the national landscape; the transformation of the directionless peasants, who still formed the majority of the population, into modern workers would be both a catalyst for and a product of development.

While the destruction wreaked by the hurricane did not give birth to this project of the construction of the "Nueva Patria," or "New Homeland," it both hastened and facilitated its execution. On this point, Trujillo states,

> I had scarcely begun to undertake this staggering program when—sixteen days after my inauguration—a tremendous cataclysm destroyed the nation's capital.
>
> The San Zenón Hurricane, as it came to be known, left thousands of victims, a wrecked city, and a grisly panorama of death and desolation. The tragedy had the effect of precipitating my plans. It created sadly propitious circumstances for their implementation. I could exercise my capacity for organization and leadership, which had been developed during my military career. I was able with this demonstration to restore some degree of confidence, which was the foundation of the moral reconstruction I proposed. (31)

The natural disaster thus exercised a triple function in the regime's politics: first, as a proving ground in which Trujillo could demonstrate the effectiveness of his leadership abilities; second, as an experimental laboratory for the totalitarian policies that he would later implement in response to future contingencies or perceived disasters; and third, as a platform for the construction of this new national psychology that would replace the defeatism that, according to his analysis of the nation's history, had characterized the Dominican collective consciousness since colonial times. Indeed, enforced solidarity under his leadership became the cornerstone of this new national "can-do" psychology:

> The efficiency with which I met the terrible consequences of the storm and the readiness with which I took charge of the situation—without having had

time to organize the government that was to attempt to lead a country already struggling against growing and implacable menaces and which was so financially subjugated that it lacked even minimum autonomy— enabled me to restore confidence, stimulate effort, overcome pessimism (further exacerbated by the catastrophe) and rehabilitate our noble hopes and ambitions, prove the power of unity and cooperation, and awaken some of the qualities dormant in the national character. In other words, there was a demonstration of what a people is capable of doing by acting with faith, decision and method under competent, vigorous leadership. (Trujillo 31)

In this way, Trujillo's response to the devastation caused by hurricane San Zenón gave rise to a consistent politics of disaster that would characterize his approach to future perceived threats. This would represent the concretization of what Valentina Peguero terms the "militarization" of Dominican culture, implementing a kind of obligatory collectivism and social solidarity under Trujillo's command. This collectivism *à la force* was central not only to the social organization of his power but also to his discourse of democracy through embodiment.

A key step in Trujillo's strategy to consolidate power using the hurricane was to transform the catastrophe from an experience of individual loss into a national disaster mediated by the state. His regime used a variety of mechanisms to collectivize the disaster, including involving the public directly in the relief effort, creating centers where people met to receive food and medicine, and coordinating the popular perception of the disaster through the use of media. Indeed, newspapers played a fundamental role in this process. As Ramón Lugo Lovatón points out, even in the midst of the general devastation and the interruption of most public services, Santo Domingo's newspapers continued printing, falling silent for only two days immediately following the cataclysm (67). Benedict Anderson's seminal study has made clear the fundamental role that newspapers have played historically in the creation of the national civic imaginary and collective feelings of sharing a historical moment.[8] Trujillo, like so many politicians before and after him, took advantage of this cultural tradition in order to construct a public disaster culture capable of coping with the hurricane as well as future threats such as communism, Haitian immigration, US intervention, and any other challenge to his hegemony.

In fact, Lugo's chronicles themselves played an important role in collectivizing the catastrophe. Now united in a single book under the title

Escombros: Huracán del 1930 (Rubble: The Hurricane of 1930; 1955), these thirty chronicles originally appeared in the *Listín Diario* alongside the "extraordinary emergency measures undertaken by the young commander President Trujillo" that were awaited impatiently each morning by the reading public (Lugo 10).[9] Lugo's chronicles thus functioned as a sort of cultural component of the emergency measures that Trujillo put into place, creating a view of the disaster as a shared, collective experience that went beyond feelings of personal loss. Written in a unique mixture of journalistic styles and literary registers, Lugo's rather uneven prose fuses Romantic descriptions and patheticism, occasional *Modernista* turns of phrase, and avant-garde imagery and aesthetics. He intersperses relatively objective reporting with moments of poetic ecstasy, in which the hurricane is represented variously as a simple natural phenomenon, an apocalyptic beast, and an *artiste* of destruction that paints the disaster with vivid colors and violent brush strokes (45).

A singular text in terms of disaster narratives, *Escombros* purports to give a firsthand view of events: its author claims to have written the chronicles in the midst of the hurricane, hunched over his typewriter as the winds demolished the city around him (10). The chronicles trace the full course of the disaster from the proverbial calm before the storm through the successful reconstruction and "progress" achieved by Trujillo by 1955, when the bound volume was published in celebration of Trujillo's "silver" anniversary. They narrate the terrifying experience of the hurricane itself, including harrowing tales of survival, the government's initial response, the recovery initiatives, and the process of psychological healing.

Despite Lugo's precise descriptions of the hurricane's effects and the use of statistics to root his texts in objectivism, the author frequently falls into a trance of poetic delirium, transporting the reader beyond the sordid enumeration of victims and decimation. Indeed, Lugo's chronicles greatly exceed the bounds of documentation: in the chronicle entitled "Vorágine: Sangre y Zinc" (Vortex: Blood and Zinc), for example, the hurricane's ravages are recounted not by the principal narrative voice but by Santo Domingo's oldest colonial monuments. The Torre del Homenaje narrates the collapse of the Río Ozama bridge; El Castillo de San Gerónimo keeps the reader up-to-date on what is occurring in the area around the Avenida Independencia; El Alcázar de Diego Colón chronicles the destruction in the Santa Bárbara neighborhood. The personification of Santo Domingo's colonial architecture, with its national, collective symbolism, as witness of the hurricane's destruction initiates the amplification of the disaster beyond the bounds of individual loss; it provides a panoramic view of the catastrophe through impartial eyes. As the author writes, "One must really have a soul of stone, like that of our Torre de Homenaje, to be a mute and impassible witness of such a great tragedy" (40). This objectivism would ostensibly lead the individual to break out of the carapace of his own subjectivity and experience the disaster collectively.

The collectivization of the disaster acquires even greater centrality in the chronicle dedicated to the day after, entitled simply "Santo Domingo, September 4, Dawn." After summarizing the panorama of destruction that meets the eye upon emerging from one's place of refuge, the author focuses on the individual experience of material loss: "Our bedroom runs toward us. The mind reconstructs it just as it was, and one by one we think of all its details. We remember a painting that someone gave to us. The portrait of a friend with a glowing dedication. Our bed, fluffed for the last time the night before" (52).[10] In spite of the personal significance of the items lost, the experience of loss itself becomes a unifying factor: "Throughout the city of Santo Domingo, fifty thousand Jeremiahs lament the ruins of their homes" (52).[11] The individual materialism gives way to a more humane outlook as the observer is confronted with the collective tragedy. The shared psychological trauma becomes the point of departure for a new social solidarity.

This unification reaches beyond all social and racial boundaries. The hurricane has had a leveling effect, destroying, at least momentarily, class and racial distinctions that had formerly seemed as eternal as the city's colonial monuments: "The poor, the rich, the white, and the man of color, all suffer this terrible dawn, the saddest of all" (52). Confronted with loss and death, social differences are temporarily set aside. Santo Domingo the stratified city of colonial heritage becomes Santo Domingo the horizontal social community, homeless in its own land, unified through pain and loss: "Santo Domingo lies in ruins. Santo Domingo is all rubble. Santo Domingo is all wailing" (52).[12] In case any shadow of a doubt remains, Lugo clarifies for the unperceptive reader: "Here, in these pages, the protagonist of the story, the main character, is all the people of Santo Domingo. We must speak of all. We must speak of the banker, the writer, the professional, the bureaucrat, the worker in general. We must speak of the poor and the rich, of the healthy and the sick. We must enter into the home of the weak as well as the powerful. What we really have here is the Dominican home, the home of us all, in ruins" (54).[13] The demolition of the city's architectural distinctions thus acquires metaphorical properties in the social realm; the edifices of the wealthy no longer hold their sway over the shacks of the destitute. They are all rubble. In this postapocalyptic climate, humanity has been reduced to its lowest common denominator: suffering. The collective nature of the disaster has provoked an unexpected "dawn of equality" (55) that ostensibly does away with the colonial hierarchies that had thrust the majority of Dominicans to the lower rungs of society.

At the same time, Lugo's use of the home as a metaphor for the nation is clearly not accidental (or original), and it prefigures the paternalistic demagoguery employed by Trujillo, in which he postulates himself as the father of the Dominican household. The family home has been destroyed, and the children must look to Father to rebuild it or at least to coordinate its reconstruction. Appealing to biblical imagery with Lacanian overtones, in one scene Lugo describes Trujillo strolling through the ruins of the city accompanied by a scribe with a notebook, literally speaking into being the future of the city and the nation (126). The authoritative word of the father and the originary word of God as creator converge into one, reiterating the imagery of Trujillo as God's representative on earth and perhaps even suggesting the elimination of "representative" from the equation.

In any case, the hurricane has created a provisional democracy of need that sets the stage for Trujillo's rhetoric of social solidarity under his command. The rich as well as the poor hover around the "street corners of hunger," as Lugo entitles one chronicle, clamoring desperately for a handout. Indeed, he describes how the "entire population has a common stomach with no bread and a common throat with terrible thirst" (89). This commonality, however, in spite of its enormous vitality and force, has not yet taken form or direction. It could become either a positive or a negative agent. While he speaks of the "dawn of mutual assistance and hope" (54), he also warns that the starving masses have become a "human hurricane" with a destructive potential to rival that of the natural disaster itself (91). The nation has reached a crucial juncture in its history, a social crisis that can lead equally to a transition toward the new nation envisioned by Trujillo or a collapse into primitivism, which Lugo associates with Africa.

In fact, it initially seems that things are taking the latter direction, with squatters building flimsy sheds from rubble on destroyed lots, "without ventilation, without bathrooms, without yards, without anything" (105). The proud colonial capital has begun a dangerous regression that reaches back, beyond even the underdeveloped countryside over which it presides, to the impenetrable jungles of black Africa. In the absence of electricity, the city becomes full of bonfires, which "illuminate frightfully the South, next to the Antillean Sea. This makes one believe that he lives no longer in Santo Domingo, that he has leaped in a single bound to Southern Africa, to the Congo, for example, and he suffers there a long, cruel exile. The Dominican people of the Capital suffer a terrible deportation without leaving their city. Ripley's 'Believe It or Not'" (114–15).[14] The entire city runs the formerly inconceivable risk of being deported from modernity, of being exiled to an earlier point in the positivist paradigm of human progress, with its racist, colonial characterization of Africa as the embodiment of undeveloped barbarity. And in light of the anti-Haitian sentiment common at the moment, which is echoed in other parts of Lugo's book, the association of the nation's capital with Africa is particularly poignant. The Dominican Republic confronts its deepest fear: that it will become black Haiti. Clearly, something had to be done.

Beyond the material regression of Santo Domingo to the barbaric past, the disaster also threatens to precipitate a catastrophe in social psychology. Feelings of individual and collective impotence emerge following the confrontation with the wrath of nature and the traumatic realization of the fragility of the modern project to dominate it completely. Lugo details these psychological effects of disaster, emphasizing the loss of agency: "The individual becomes immersed in the idea that life is truly bitter. He comes to think that nothing is worth worrying about anymore and that he should stop caring to a degree that borders on the shameful" (78).[15] This resignation is not limited to individual affairs, however; the fatalism leads to a state of collective depression and stagnation in which rebuilding and the return to normality appear inconceivable. Order itself is threatened as the catastrophe comes to be perceived as the normal state of affairs: "The disaster makes become normal, before our very eyes, what we thought yesterday to be extremely abnormal" (79).[16] Class distinctions have been leveled; even the oligarchy has been reduced to begging on street corners and taking refuge in shacks and shantytowns. The social order, with its role in enforcing traditional norms and mores, lies buried beneath the rubble of its monuments and institutions. The hurricane has passed, but the Dominican society and economy have fallen into shambles.

As is perennial in Trujillan discourse, there is but a single remedy for this panorama of individual fatalism and collective despair: Trujillo's new social psychology. Lugo makes this transition rather subtly at first, using playful metaphors of modern industrialization: "We need an artificial factory of encouragement. We need machinery to make willpower. We need a mechanism to produce joy. We need special gears whose only purpose is to produce optimism" (83).[17] Indeed, the chronicler has already shown how feelings of collective loss have led to social solidarity; now the only element missing is decisive leadership to channel the relief effort. Trujillo's new state will provide this, transforming the disastered national psychology into a model of modern optimism and industrial willpower. As he writes in the following passage: "Únicamente Trujillo" (83). Only Trujillo.

It has already become clear that the Boss's relief effort was not limited only to succoring needy citizens and restoring order. In fact, Lugo fuses together the massive effort to restore communications and remove the wreckage from the city's streets with the remaking of the Dominican psychology: "The removers of obstacles and rubble, those who practice the action of removal, cleaning, clearing, have advanced a great deal, within a terrible sluggishness, their work in our old Ciudad Primada [First City]. They are scouring hardened hearts and moldy souls as well; they clean in both homes and public byways, wherever material or spiritual ruins contribute to keeping the will and the sky gray" (165).[18] At first glance, Lugo's metaphor of "cleaning" appears relatively innocuous: it entails only the removal of the obstacles that are restraining the optimism that Trujillo will inspire in his followers. However, in the context of the events that followed, it takes on more sinister overtones. In the years to come, Trujillo's regime "cleaned house," forcibly removing undesirable individuals and ideologies from the nation, with no regard for distinctions between private and public spaces. Trujillan iconography intruded into the private sphere through the obligatory branding of homes as Trujillist. It was when that iconography was rejected that the repressive apparatuses of the state entered into action, at best punishing the infringers with humiliation, imprisonment, and torture and at worst disappearing them forever. And several authors claim that this "house-cleaning" had already begun when the hurricane struck: rumors cited by Jesús de Galíndez, among others, state that not only victims of the hurricanes were incinerated in the mass cremations at the Plaza Colombina—several political opponents apparently vanished in the flames as well (20).

In fact, the political reality contradicts the semblance of national unity promoted by the regime following the disaster. Together with social and class divisions, the catastrophe seemed to have set aside political rivalries. However, closer scrutiny of the cultural production associated with the hurricane reveals another story. In spite of Lugo's claim to represent impartially the disaster, his volume is filled with political rhetoric supporting the Trujillo regime, as is befitting the uncle of Lina Lovatón, Trujillo's most prized mistress. It is certainly no coincidence that the book appeared in 1955, the "Year of the Benefactor of the Nation." Indeed, Lugo's introduction echoes Trujillo's assessment of the Dominican psychology, while simultaneously underscoring the political implications of the hurricane by comparing it to a political uprising: "The cyclonic hecatomb constituted a coup d'état of nature; it was for the Republic like an abrupt awakening from a deep sleep of centuries. We were truly deep asleep with the hereditary sloth produced by the violent crossing of antagonistic races" (13).[19] He represents the natural disaster almost as if it were a planned phase of Trujillo's political project; it complements and completes the military uprising initiated months earlier, demolishing outmoded institutions in preparation for the reconstruction of the nation. Paradoxically, the hurricane has become an agent of modernity.

Lugo's introduction (written after the fact, in the year of publication of the anthology, 1955) sets the stage for reading the tome within the code of the official discourse, which he further reinforces by returning to the topos of Dominican history as a disaster. The hurricane's destruction deals the final blow to the Dominican Republic's aborted trajectory toward modernization; Santo Domingo is reduced to representing the "ruins of modernity" (111). "Santo Domingo has failed miserably" (113), and in keeping with the modern tradition of urban symbolism, the capital becomes metonymically a symbol of the nation's legacy of failed modernity. The story does not end there, however. Lugo posits his texts not only as chronicles of the disaster but also as foundational narratives of the rebirth of the nation, with the hurricane playing a necessarily destructive role in leveling the nation's obstacles to modernity. As he concludes his introduction, "But all tragedies are at once graves and cradles, endings and beginnings, final resting places and paths to the future. A propitious moment presented itself for the appearance of a man, and he did, in fact, appear, with the destiny of one who carries, in his mind and soul, extraordinary powers" (13).[20] In this way, he posits the hurricane's ravages as a point of departure for the reconstruction of the nation under Trujillo's guidance.

Although the introduction was written expressly for the celebration of Trujillo's twenty-fifth anniversary in power and thus obligatorily spouts the praises of the dictator, Lugo's chronicles prefigured this prophetic tone twenty-five years earlier. Indeed, a chronicle with the purposeful title "Today, Yesterday, Tomorrow" predicts, "We will not be the ones who receive tomorrow the results of this great catastrophe. Our children and grandchildren will be the ones who gather its fruits. Twenty, thirty, fifty years from now, the tree of today's hurricane will bloom in the souls of our new generations with white flowers, flowers with a new perfume as a symbol of new life" (124).[21] The hurricane's destruction has sown the seeds of change that will give rise to positive fruits in the future, allowing the nation to blossom into modernity. The capital will rise again, more glorious than ever before: "Santo Domingo will bloom as a modern city, in size and progress, over what we water today with tears and hopelessness" (125).[22]

Disaster Tourism/Voyeurism

There remains an aspect of Lugo's work that deserves an aside. About midway through his chronicles, a strange bifurcation of audience occurs. While the early chronicles appear to address almost exclusively the residents of Santo Domingo affected directly by the disaster, these later texts take a sudden interest in an outside reader. They seemingly transform the disaster yet again from a collective tragedy into a gruesome spectacle for a kind of disaster tourist or voyeur whom the narrative voice addresses directly: "Come, stranger. Take my hand and I will guide you to just one of the street corners of the city so that you can contemplate the victims. Come, follow me. Step carefully so that you don't hurt yourself with a nail or cut yourself on a piece of tin. Look at the damage. Examine everything carefully because you won't contemplate a similar tragedy for a long time" (65).[23] The invitation that Lugo proffers to this outside reader, to this stranger or foreigner, does not constitute a simple appeal for international aid. Its vividness and involvedness penetrate much beyond that point. Nor is it solely a Debordian spectacle of reality. At the very least, the verb *examine* carries legal connotations, and in the context of the criticisms of the Trujillo regime's human rights abuses, it implies the gathering of evidence for the purpose of making a judgment.

Throughout the chapters that follow, Lugo's narrative voice becomes the guide of a sort of disaster tour that draws in people unaffected by the catastrophe. He uses the denomination *"extranjero"* in its widest sense, meaning not only a foreigner in relation to the Dominican Republic but anyone who did not experience the disaster in person. In a way analogous to his move to collectivize the disaster beyond the bounds of individual loss in his earlier chronicles, here he attempts to bridge the gap between subject and object, between experience and observation. From the point of view of trauma theory, Lugo's interest in engaging the outside observer may be seen as an allegorical strategy for resolving the schism between the experiencing and the observing selves that develops when the mind is unable to assimilate fully the traumatic event.[24] Taken at its more concrete face value, Lugo draws the foreign reader in, converting the disaster from local into ostensibly universal experience through tropes of human suffering. The suggestion that the observer may actually sustain physical wounds (cuts from a nail or a piece of tin roofing) implies an immediacy that nullifies observational distance or abstraction. The threat of physical harm as well as the psychological trauma that contemplating one's own mortality in the faces of those to be cremated, for instance, precludes that possibility. The promised tour is a ploy; Lugo does not allow the reader to remain a voyeur entertained at the expense of others. Thus forced to experience the catastrophe oneself, even if to a minimal or artificial degree, the reader is in a much more receptive position with respect to the ideological bent of Lugo's book. With one's own physical integrity and peace of mind suddenly at risk, Trujillo's authoritarian leadership and disaster-relief policies seem more acceptable. Lugo has effectively dismantled critical distance, drawing the reader into the sphere of Trujillo's control. After all, incorporating opponents into his regime was Trujillo's preferred strategy for minimizing resistance to his rule. By the end of *Escombros*, the reader has been persuaded, if not to collaborate with the regime, at least to reevaluate his or her position.

The Rewriting of the Nation

Lugo and Trujillo's other literary collaborators were responsible for creating a new foundational narrative of the nation to support Trujillo's ideology on the symbolic plane, but the rewriting impulse did not end at the page's edge. Acutely aware of the power and poetics of naming, Trujillo's regime rewrote the Dominican landscape both figuratively and literally: the relentless renaming impulse accompanied a profound and forceful shift in the concept of Dominican citizenship in which the dictator inscribed himself as the ideal national subject and the future of the nation. The visual omnipresence of the dictator's name and likeness not only promoted a populist cult of personality; it also made concrete the inescapability of this new postulation of *dominicanidad*, or Dominicanness. The new consciousness extended to every corner of Dominican life, breaking even the traditional boundaries between the public and private spheres and drawing formerly neglected rural spaces into its concept of civic and political participation in national life.

José Antonio Osorio Lizarazo provides extensive enumeration of this discursive transformation of the Dominican landscape in *La isla iluminada*. He notes that the Dominican Republic has been rewritten in a literal sense, through the superposition of Trujillan iconography over the cultural landscape: "You see phrases in which the people express their feelings everywhere, in their yards, on the walls of buildings, even inside private homes. Truckers rechristen their vehicles with laudatory names. The president's photograph decorates homes, and everything is named with words that are associated with him" (26).[25] Notably, Osorio shifts the agency for the physical rewriting of the national landscape to the Dominican people rather than the regime itself, portraying it as an homage rendered to their leader. This was a transparent strategy that Trujillo's regime employed repeatedly throughout his thirty years in power. In fact, Osorio claims that the motion to rename Santo Domingo as Ciudad Trujillo in honor of the self-styled *Benefactor de la Patria*'s reconstruction of the city following the hurricane was put on the table by the president of the Senate while Trujillo was on vacation and that the dictator expressed his inconformity with this proposal in an open letter to the Dominican people that Osorio includes in a footnote in the book.

Jesús de Galíndez, the Basque exile who is believed to have been abducted and murdered by the regime for writing an unflattering doctoral thesis on the "Era of Trujillo," confirms this version of the events, although he is somewhat more skeptical about Trujillo's nonparticipation (31–32). In any case, following a referendum, in which official sources counted six hundred thousand votes in favor of the name change, and lengthy, if vacuous, discussion in the congressional chambers, on January 11, 1936, the rechristening ceremony was held in the cultural heart of the nation, the Parque Colón. The name change was further commemorated one year later with the construction of a massive obelisk at the end of the newly finished Malecón, or Avenida George Washington.[26] Hurricane-devastated, colonial Santo Domingo was thus discursively reborn from its ashes, or rubble, as the case may be, as the modern Ciudad Trujillo.

Luis Alemar, in his chapter on the name change, transcribes the speeches of each region's senator as well as Vice President Jacinto B. Peynado's panegyric at the dedication of the obelisk. Alemar's effusive treatment of Trujillo's renaming impulse verges on sarcasm, which proves an interesting strategy for resistance in a dictatorship that practiced iron-handed censorship. While he flatters the dictator shamelessly in several parts of the work, the evocation and praises of the oligarchy's names (many of whom were anti-Trujillan) in relation with the proud colonial heritage and architectural history of Santo Domingo contrast with the cursory treatment that the Trujillan names receive. The latter typically appear at the end of a long pedigree, including brief biographies of illustrious figures, following a curt, introductory "now": "this historic and ancient city of Santo Domingo, now Ciudad Trujillo" (34), or "Avenue José Trujillo Valdez, before called Duarte, in remembrance of the glorious founder of the Republic" (195). In this way, Alemar reveals the upper classes' scarcely concealed scorn for the upstart dictator's humble background, an attitude that resulted in humiliating reprisals by the dictator as well as the eventual participation of several members of the oligarchy in the successful plot to assassinate him in 1961.

In any case, the name changes were not simply cosmetic: the physical transformation of place nearly always accompanied the regime's discursive redefinition of local toponyms. Santo Domingo itself was only rechristened once Trujillo's process of reconstruction, which implied a fundamental transformation of the urban landscape of the hurricane-ravaged capital, was completed. Osorio describes this transformation in more than glowing terms: "Propelled by [Trujillo's] dynamic will, the city rose from its own ruins, much more beautiful, reconstructed in cement, with a young and audacious architecture. It is today, in its appearance, its comfort, its seductions, its services, and its hygiene, one of the most modern cities of the Antilles" (26–27).[27] The new city was intended to embody the epitome of Western civilization—it would be a monument to modernity; the old, ramshackle wooden architecture replaced by the concrete face of the twentieth century. At the same time, the reconstruction in concrete reminded one of Santo Domingo's colonial heritage; the solidity of Ciudad Trujillo reflected what Osorio called the Spanish "criteria of eternity" that had permitted the colonial stone buildings to survive the hurricane's devastation (42). Trujillo's city would construct a bridge between the solid colonial past and the modern present, bypassing almost entirely what his regime viewed as the disastrous history since independence.

Indeed, the actual renaming or marking of place was seen as the culmination of the process of modernization and development that Trujillo carried out following Western models. Osorio makes this clear in another passage, describing a kind of laudatory rural graffiti: "On a public fountain, a rough hand, with almost indecipherable writing, has stamped: 'Let us bless Trujillo, who gives us our water.' The police have erased this hyperbolic inscription. But we are talking about a region that was sterile and barren and is now fertile and prodigiously cultivated due to a colossal hydraulic engineering project that Trujillo personally ordered and oversaw" (26).[28] The *Benefactor de la Patria*'s public works projects did not function only as mechanisms for modernizing the countryside and increasing agricultural production; they also played an important role in garnering popular rural support for his regime. As historian Richard Lee Turits points out, public works that benefited agriculture, together with an aggressive program of land distribution to peasants, formed the basis of the considerable support that he was able to amass in the rural sector.[29] There was a trade-off: the peasants received arable land and increased access to the national market, but in return they were required to sacrifice their traditional, somewhat wild freedom and the unrestricted use of communal lands and to support Trujillo's regime by attending political rallies and incorporating his political discourse into their everyday lives.[30] The latter included hanging portraits of the dictator in their homes, inscribing laudatory messages on their property, such as the one cited earlier, using a new calendar based on the "Era of Trujillo," and even displaying a sign that was particularly contentious for many people in the patriarchal society: "In this home, Trujillo is boss" (Turits 229). Likewise, this political clientelism implied an iron censorship: one could never display, publicly or privately, any animosity or even neutrality toward the regime.

Trujillo's rewriting impulse was not associated only with public works, however. It also evoked the dark side of modernity, with its obsession with security and the discourse of risk. Osorio also mentions that

> close to the border with Haiti, you can see on a hill the phrase that has drawn biting criticism: "God and Trujillo." The police also destroyed it over and over again, prohibited it with sanctions, kept watch over the place. But on the border, life was tremendously unsafe, the towns were assaulted periodically by Haitians, who took by force women, crops, and cattle. Trujillo organized the security of the border and, with a wise mixture of diplomacy and energy, transformed that dangerous place into a series of centers of progress where life is easy and safe. And the sign keeps reappearing. (26)[31]

Once again, this superposition of Trujillan iconography over the Dominican landscape is attributed to the Dominicans themselves, who wish to honor their leader. However, in this case the visual impact of the public works that Trujillo has constructed reaches beyond simply providing evidence of progress. Osorio posits Trujillo's reinscription of the border landscape within the Western paradigm of development as a strategy to put an end to the cultural and supposed racial porosity of the border. Indeed, the giant letters proclaiming "God and Trujillo" dominate the cultural landscape from their prominent position on the hillside, warding off the looming disaster of Haitian occupation by making clear that this is the land of Catholics, not worshipers of Haitian *Vaudou*, and that Trujillo is in control. Even the illiterate could doubtlessly recognize the import of this unequivocal branding of the border with Trujillo's private-property sign, and no Haitian could fail to remember those fateful days in 1937 in which Trujillo authorized the massacre of thousands of Haitian workers and squatters in this same area.

This inscription plays with the discourse of risk control, border vulnerability, and development, postulating that a developed border is a safe border; in reality, however, the border is "secure" because of institutional violence, not Trujillo's public works programs. The modernization is primarily performative: it reiterates visually the discursive divide that Trujillo's regime constructed between the modern, civilized Dominican subject and the barbaric, black Haitian object.[32] In this way, the Trujillo regime's transformation of the visual and physical landscape of the border complements and reinforces his alteration of its historical porosity through state violence.

A Geography of Surveillance

As the refashioning of the border revealed, not all of Trujillo's public works programs were dedicated solely to reconstructing the capital or modernizing rural life, and few if any were free of ideological and political functionality. Each piece of the regime's reconstruction plan formed part of a carefully orchestrated web of propaganda, intimidation, and political pandering. As Raphael Fischler points out, planning itself embodies a communicative exercise in power and a powerful means of persuasion and establishing legitimacy.[33] Trujillo's regime shared this view; in *La arquitectura dominicana en la Era de Trujillo* (Dominican Architecture in the Era of Trujillo; 1949), one of its most prolific architects, Henry Gazón Bona, compared architecture to literature in its communicative properties (82). Theorists such as Henri LeFebvre have shown that this relationship is much more complex: while architecture does indeed function within a communicative code, it also configures and reproduces social or lived space through what LeFebvre calls "spatial practice" (26–36). This does not, however, contradict Gazón Bona's point of view but rather complements it. Trujillo's goal was to transform not only Santo Domingo's architecture and urban codes but also Dominican social space. Indeed, Trujillo's regime clearly intuited what LeFebvre later put into words: that "a revolution that does not produce a new space has not realized its full potential; indeed it has failed in that it has not changed life itself, but has merely changed ideological superstructures, institutions, or political apparatuses" (54). In any case, Trujillo was not the first in the Dominican Republic to use architecture and urban planning as instruments of social control; the Spanish colonizers, steeped in the Roman tradition, had been masters of conveying imperial power through urban landscapes.

In fact, Santo Domingo's first urban building codes were established by Spanish governor and "Capitán General" Felipe Ribero y Lemoyne during the brief reannexation of the nation by Spain (1861–1865), revealing neocolonial overtones. Not coincidentally, these codes were taken nearly verbatim from the rules that were in effect in Cuba, where they played a role in quelling the nascent independence movement. According to these rules, new building projects had to be approved by a licensed architect. Not surprisingly, all the architects were from Spain and licensed by the colonial authorities, thus allowing the imperial power to maintain absolute control over all new construction, as well as to compile an archive of plans and maps in case military intervention became necessary.[34] Likewise, the codes specified the dimensions of streets and required the construction of sidewalks for foot traffic as well as streetlamps for nighttime illumination (Fondeur).

As progressive as such measures may appear, they cannot be separated from the Spanish neocolonial project. As urban sociologists such as Richard Sennett point out, the rise of modern urban planning, with its straight, wide streets that provide easy, rapid access to the heart of cities, was closely associated with the need to mobilize troops to quell urban uprisings (89). According to Sennett, contemporary city planning emerged from Napoleon III's project to rebuild Paris during the 1860s. The specialist in charge of the project, Baron Haussmann, wished to limit urban unrest and its potential material effects by replacing dilapidated housing, grouping social classes into distinct zones, and cutting through the mess of twisted, medieval streets that could be barricaded by rebellious workers with long, wide, and straight avenues that would facilitate traffic and commerce, allow for rapid troop mobilization, and form a barrier between socially segregated neighborhoods (Sennett 87–

90). The building codes put in place by the Spanish for Santo Domingo mirrored these practical goals, prohibiting, for instance, the adobe construction techniques used by the poor, effectively displacing them to more easily controlled worker tenements owned by the often foreign bourgeoisie or exiling them beyond the city limits.

The Spanish building codes remained in effect following the War of Restoration and Isabel II's annulment of the annexation in 1865, and urban planning continued to play an important role in social control in the subsequent years. Indeed, urban planning and modernization of the nation's infrastructure were important projects under Ulises "Lilís" Heureaux, the late nineteenth-century dictator whom many people view as a precursor of Trujillo, and in 1900 General Casimiro Nemesio de Moya mapped the capital with security issues in mind (Brea García, "Vicisitudes"). However, these earlier efforts could not compare with Trujillo's manipulation of the urban landscape as a social control mechanism. His refashioning of the capital was carried out by a team of official architects that included figures such as Guillermo González Sánchez (commonly considered the "father" of modern architecture in the Dominican Republic), Henry Gazón Bona, José Antonio Caro Álvarez, nationalized Italian Guido D'Alessandro Lombardi, and urban engineer José Ramón "Moncito" Báez López-Penha. Working in teams or individually, these men were responsible for planning and rebuilding Santo Domingo following the destruction caused by Cyclone San Zenón in 1930, as well as for other modernization projects throughout the nation. Together they constructed the urban face of the regime, Ciudad Trujillo.

Trujillo's urban planning incorporated multiple functions: it was designed not only to provide modern facilities and services to Ciudad Trujillo's inhabitants but also to expedite the Dominican Republic's entrance into global commerce by creating a standardized business environment compatible with foreign interests, as well as to take on a role in security. As Arturo Escobar has noted, the professionalization of development was requisite for integration into the global economy.[35] Indeed, regarding the relationship between globalized capitalism and architectural uniformity, LeFebvre has written that "repetitious spaces are the outcome of repetitive gestures (those of the workers) associated with instruments which are both duplicable and designed to duplicate: machines, bulldozers, concrete-mixers, cranes, pneumatic drills, and so on" (75). In a broader take, Beaverstock, Taylor, and Smith use the terms "global capacity" and "global competence" to underpin their reworking of Peter Hall's concept of "world cities," urban conglomerations that play central roles in the processes of globalization by concentrating multinational commercial and legal services in regional hubs (446). While Ciudad Trujillo predates the present moment of hyperglobalization to which these latter authors refer, Trujillo clearly intended to situate the Dominican capital on the map of world trade by increasing its capacities and competence for dealing with global commerce through creating a compatible business environment.

At the same time, Trujillo's modern urban planning sought to minimize disorder and opposition, to impress friends, and to intimidate foes. His rewriting of toponyms and architectural transformation of the landscape throughout the Dominican Republic served as cultural reminders of the penetration of his regime into every corner of national life. In this sense, the detested declaration "God in the Heavens, Trujillo on Earth" was not entirely an exaggeration; in the Dominican Republic, only God could trump the sensation of omnipotence that the dictator's regime fostered. And "the Boss" consciously exploited this connection to create an atmosphere of total surveillance: his statues and busts dominated the communal public spaces, their blank eyes a constant admonition that Trujillo was watching from above. Frequently endowed with phallic symbolism, these self-aggrandizing monuments reinforced visually the myth of omnipotence and the vertical hierarchy of the patriarchal order, with Trujillo as its maximum embodiment. At the same time, their central placement worked within Trujillo's planning of public spaces to augment his control and to limit points of gathering of possible opposition.

The erection of statues and busts of the leader was the culmination of a beautification process in which the nation's urban parks and central plazas were transformed from open spaces of public gathering into labyrinthine tropical gardens. The revamped public spaces were fragmented with geometrical patterns traced by paths lined with abundant greenery and cool arboreal canopies that invited one to sink docilely into the benches in their shade. And, naturally, all paths led to Trujillo, or to his statue in any event. Intentionally more restful than the traditional, open earthen, cobblestone, or concrete plazas, these eye-pleasing green parks exercised a double security function, soothing the public soul, thereby making it less likely to rebel, and limiting severely the space available for large-scale public gatherings and protests should instances of public disorder arise. The only centric urban open spaces that remained were those designated by Trujillo for the obligatory demonstrations of public support for his agenda, and these spaces were selected carefully for their proximity to his mechanisms of control and surveillance (i.e., police stations and military bases). In any case, together with the signs proclaiming his authority throughout virtually all public and private spaces, Trujillo's monuments completed the tangible illusion of omnipresence and omniscience. His presence in word and image was a visual reminder of the political reality of unrelenting control.

Creating a (Disastrous) Culture of Catastrophe

Anthropologist Jon Anderson has noted that "in acute crises where disaster-culture patterns are absent or lack development, interpretations tend to be extemporaneous, unstable, and individualized, and definitions of the situation remain private" (299). Lugo documented this state of national unreadiness in his chronicles in *Escombros*, revealing that there were no collective cultural patterns in the Dominican Republic for dealing effectively with a disaster of the magnitude of Cyclone San Zenón. The initial reaction was each for his or her own. Of course, this was not by any means the first time that a hurricane had struck the Dominican Republic; Columbus observed one in Hispaniola as early as 1495, and another reportedly destroyed Santo Domingo in 1504, shortly after its founding, forcing it to be relocated to the higher bank of the Ozama River.[36] A series of hurricanes also struck the area throughout the sixteenth and seventeenth centuries, demolishing churches and other buildings and ruining repeatedly the cacao crop.[37] In fact, statistics show that a tropical system brushes by or makes landfall on the Dominican Republic every 4.69 years on average.[38] Through a stroke of luck or natural patterns, however, no storm had damaged the capital severely since independence, although several had struck it, including an estimated Category 3 hurricane in 1883[39]—this in spite of the fact that several powerful tropical systems had pummeled other parts of the nation, such as an 1893 hurricane that devastated the northern coast, leaving hundreds dead.[40] This long vacation from the effects of disaster in the capital left the citizenry without a solid cultural background for dealing with catastrophe. Similarly, the nation's recent history of political conflict, dictatorships, and US intervention did not foment the development of institutionalized disaster-response strategies at either the local or national levels. Without collective cultural or institutional strategies for coping with disaster, it could only be conceptualized in a private manner, and to return to Anderson's words, responses were "extemporaneous, unstable, and individualized" (299).

This lack of a collective culture for dealing with catastrophe left the population feeling entirely vulnerable when Cyclone San Zenón struck in 1930, which may be why Trujillo's authoritarian actions and rhetoric proved so effective. As Lugo's chronicles reveal, Trujillo used the state response to draw the disaster from the realm of private loss to national catastrophe, and then capitalized on the national solidarity for his political agenda. Culture played an undeniable role: as I have already mentioned, Lugo's chronicles appeared side by side with Trujillo's emergency proclamations in the *Listín Diario*. It was from the response to the hurricane that this autocratic but collective Trujillan "culture of disaster" congealed, minimizing the influence of individual coping mechanisms such as denial, suppression, and fatalism that Anderson views as pathological (304–5).

Trujillo's creation of a culture based on the disaster, as effective as it may have been for collectivizing the disaster and installing a new normality, itself verged on the pathological. As we have seen, his regime ended up inscribing the entirety of Dominican history within a geography of recurring disasters, man-made as well as natural, and he viewed himself as the only possible response to this disastrous history. The culture of disaster that Trujillo and his collaborators constructed turned out to be all too effective, perhaps: the tragic view of Dominican history as catastrophe did not disappear with the regime's transformative efforts as planned but lived on far beyond Trujillo and his nightmarish take on modernity.

The Enduring Disaster

Tellingly, while it was Trujillo's regime that developed and exploited the perspective of Dominican history as a perennial disaster of which the hurricane was just the latest episode, many of his opponents ended up appropriating this same discourse for their own ends, with only minor modifications. Indeed, Juan Bosch, one of Trujillo's most vocal opponents and the first elected president following his demise, reproduced uncritically this vision of a disastered Dominican history in his book criticizing the dictator, calling his rule in one moment a "tempest" (60). The divergence, of course, is that he saw Trujillo as a product or even as the incarnation of the nation's catastrophic past, rather than as its remedy. Likewise, Juan Isidro Jimenes Grullón refers to morality under Trujillo as a hurricane-like "vortex of abominations" (249). This perspective of the "Era of Trujillo" as the greatest disaster to befall the Dominican Republic in all its cataclysmic history later became commonplace in academic as well as popular circles. As Ignacio López-Calvo points out in his study of the literary production on the "Era of Trujillo," Dominican evocations of the regime reveal a collective, national trauma comparable historically only to that of the omnipresent threat of Haitian occupation during the nineteenth century, which the regime had used so effectively to construct its own legitimacy (8). Paradoxically, López-Calvo also shows that the uncritical repetition of the tropes of trauma in these works has the unintended effect of desensitizing the reader to the patriarchal violence that they invoke, thus subverting their therapeutic function for coping with the trauma itself. Perhaps it is the persistence of this unmitigated trauma that has perpetuated the view of Dominican history as disaster far beyond the disappearance of the regime.[41] Ironically, the regime has become yet another symptom reinforcing the diagnosis of disaster that it itself had made.

As occurs so often with poignant symbolic expressions that enter common usage, the tragic perspective of Dominican history as disaster has abandoned to a great degree its contextuality. The historical specificity of the discourse, with its roots in the Trujillo regime's legitimization of its power, became subsumed to its abstract connotations in such a way that it has now come to form a localized cultural paradigm. This is to say that its meaning for Dominicans has become ubiquitous in such a way that it forms part of a general worldview. As a case in point, many Dominican intellectuals continue to use this metaphor even today, with only tangential or no reference to Trujillo at all. Seven-term president Joaquín Balaguer, perhaps not surprisingly given his affinities with the Trujillo regime, referred repeatedly to a disastrous Dominican history ("cúmulo de desastres") in the speech that he gave upon accepting membership in the National Academy of History (212–13). Likewise, Pedro Troncoso Sánchez wrote in a 1968 history textbook that many of the "negative manifestations of the Dominican psyche" were consequences of the "social trauma" of the nation's "catastrophic" history (7). More recent examples include Federico Henríquez Gratereaux's *Un ciclón en una botella: Notas para una teoría de la sociedad dominicana* (Cyclone in a Bottle: Notes toward a Theory of Dominican Society; 1996), a self-critical collection of essays on Dominican culture in the "Era of Globalization," and Miguel Ángel Fornerín's *La dominicanidad viajera* (Traveling Dominicanness; 2001), which in one vignette uses disaster and recovery as a Sisyphean metaphor for development.[42] In a similar vein, conservative commentator Manuel Núñez laments the "collapse" of Dominican nationality amid the "tempest" of Haitian immigration, in his *El ocaso de la nación dominicana* (The Twilight of the Dominican Nation; 2001).[43] The continuity of disaster imagery in Dominican concepts of nationality beyond the Era of Trujillo reminds one yet again of the power of discourse to outlive its context and to adapt to new circumstances.

Even foreigners who spend time in the Dominican Republic are susceptible to this phenomenon, as a close reading of Mario Vargas Llosa's historical novel on the Trujillan dictatorship, *La fiesta del chivo* (*The Goat's Feast*; 2000), reveals. Vargas Llosa, who spent several months in Santo Domingo researching his novel, picks up on this disastered view of Dominican history, reflecting it metaphorically and directly in his work.[44] Strangely enough, Vargas Llosa pays short shrift to the hurricane itself in his novel, even stating in one moment that the "storm" caused by a letter written by the Dominican Republic's Catholic leadership criticizing the Trujillo regime wreaked much greater havoc than did Cyclone San Zenón (241). In spite of the novel's minimization of the importance of the 1930 hurricane, however, it is replete with disaster imagery, and it repeats frequently the trope of Dominican history as disaster (296). Taking a leaf from Bosch's book, the majority of *La fiesta del chivo*'s disaster metaphors deal with the regime's actions, but it is an impartial rather than an associative metaphor, and it works for Trujillo's supporters as much as for his opponents. If Agustín Cabral's fall from grace or the capture and torture of the conspirators in the plot to assassinate Trujillo are described using disaster imagery, so too is the Organization of American States' blockade and the dictator's death.[45]

Furthermore, cyclones, hurricanes, and storms are not the only disaster images that Vargas Llosa invokes: the rape of a young girl by Trujillo's son Ramfis is described as an "earthquake" (137), while a generalized lexicon of terms such as "cataclysm," "disaster," "catastrophe," and "calamity" appears throughout the book.[46] The decontextualized polyvalence of Vargas Llosa's disaster vocabulary indicates that it most likely was not taken directly from Trujillan discourse, particularly since textual clues indicate that the majority of his sources were anti-Trujillan historians such as Crassweller and Galíndez, who avoided reproducing the regime's justifications for its policies. On the other hand, given the relative predominance of disaster imagery in this novel versus his other works, it seems reductive to assume that such images simply form part of the author's personal idiomatic expression. Rather, it seems clear that they derive from a Dominican worldview that had become generalized by the time in which he came into contact with it, even when this worldview had its origins in the specifically Trujillan construction of the New Patria.

Notably, few works that deal with the Trujillato, whether Dominican or foreign, reference the 1930 hurricane at all, and those that do downplay its importance altogether. One might surmise a variety of reasons for this omission: a desire to minimize one of the regime's most powerful discursive justifications; a feeling that natural disasters are neither here nor there, since they cannot be controlled by human means, while the recurrence of an authoritarian regime could be; or an avoidance of attributing agency to natural rather than human actors. Whatever the cause for sidestepping a discussion of the role of the hurricane in Trujillo's disaster politics, these works nevertheless employ the disaster imagery that the regime implanted in its rewriting of the national psychology, which used the hurricane and Trujillo's response to it as a powerful collective symbol for the rebirth of the Dominican subject. The persistence and proliferation of this discourse reveals simultaneously a success and a failure of Trujillo's rewriting of the Dominican Republic: his regime was able to revise national history (partially, but in a lasting way), but its project of rescripting the Dominican subject died along with its model citizen. Ironically, Trujillo continues to embody Dominican history, but no longer in the role of new founder as he envisioned. He now incarnates the catastrophe that he wrote, and the "Era of Trujillo," rather than pushing the nation forward into modernity, ends up retreating into the past to become the emblem of all that it had rejected.

2 Drought and the Literary Construction of Risk in Northeastern Brazil

> The Northeast is form and content that wound, that cut, that perforate, that cause pain and make bleed. It is an exposed wound in the nation's flesh.
> —Durval Muniz de Albuquerque, Jr., *A invenção do Nordeste*

> Everything could go lacking, except drought.
> [Tudo podia faltar, menos a seca.]
> —José Américo de Almeida, *Coiteiros*

THE SERTÃO, the arid interior of northeastern Brazil, holds a peculiar position in the Brazilian imagination. It is a mythical geography of contradictory fantasies, populated by honest-to-a-fault cowboys and corrupt politicians, Robin Hood–like *cangaceiros* who rape and pillage without conscience the poor as well as the rich, and penitent religious fanatics cohabiting freely in orgiastic abandon while sacrificing their children to Old Testament gods. Its figurative landscape evokes the uninhabitable abundance of an inclement paradise; it is an isolated wilderness located beyond the reach of history and capital but mired in a precise moment of European feudalism, a hermetic hinterland that exports workers and products to every region of Brazil. For Brazilians, the *sertão* is a paradoxical space of irrational cleverness and logical instincts, loyal bravery and bloody betrayal, family life and family feuds with no regard for life, animal sexuality and cloistered virginity, individualistic disorder and rigid patriarchal hierarchies, social solidarity and antisocial chaos, and racial and cultural uniformity rooted in diversity. And somehow all the contradictions hold true. The image is one of fragmented wholeness, a shattered mirror whose reflection is clearer than an unbroken one. Its loosely connected representations expose the remnants of a series of struggles over the control of discourse on the region, and yet, in spite of patent dislocation and incoherence, they configure an indivisible whole in the national imaginary that has outlasted fierce criticisms and frequent revisions.

Evidently, powerful centripetal forces converge to maintain the coherence of this symbolic system. On the one hand, processes of national identification generate cohesion through opposition. The *sertão* comprises a legendary landscape that embodies the national past at the same time that it conflicts violently with visions of a modern future. The *sertão* as conceptual geography was constructed largely from without, as the negative of modern Brazil. In this sense, the *sertão* carries out a double function, congealing everything antimodern while simultaneously serving as a national prehistory embodying traditional Brazilian values slated to disappear with the construction of the modern nation.[1] The ethnographic bent of cultural representations of the region aimed to conserve the national traditions, while transforming them from lived reality into a historical object on display in a textual museum. At the same time, these typically external representations were themselves internalized, often by proxy, into the real *sertanejos'* self-images, thus forging an inclusive regional identity that lives both within and outside concepts of national citizenship.[2] In a paradoxical strategy of incorporation and resistance, locals absorbed into their self-image literary tropes of *sertanejo* identity that had been modified from popular representations in oral traditions and *literatura de cordel* in the first place.[3]

A close look at the processes of identity and identification in the *sertão* reveals the sutures that bind together the *sertanejo* body, both wounded and reconstituted by cultural politics into a functional Frankenstein or *Invunche* figure, to borrow from the Chilean cultural lexicon.[4] This chapter examines those threads, which I argue are spun from one material: drought and its management. Drought recurs with such frequency in the region that it is not surprising to find that it forms an integral part of local social and political practice, economics, popular and high culture, and even religion. It does not simply paint a backdrop for life in the *sertão*, however; its role is much more complex. Researchers such as Durval Muniz de Albuquerque, Jr., and Alfredo Macedo Gomes have shown that drought and the Northeast itself are socially constructed symbolic systems as much as geophysical realities.[5] This to say that an "inventory of myths and stereotypes" has been created around the geography of drought, leading to the "invention" of a discourse that functions as a Derridean supplement to the reality, restructuring the phenomenon in its image. The discourse on drought ties together the disparate components of the *sertão*'s cultural geography into a single legible corpus. But that corpus is disembodied, phantasmagorical, for the process of coming into being signified its severance from the earthy bodies of the *sertanejos* themselves.

Historical records and travel accounts show that the cycle of drought and flooding that characterizes the interior of the Northeast has been occurring since before the first Europeans set foot there during the sixteenth century, although desertification due to the massive importation of European cattle has intensified the phenomenon.[6] The interior *sertões* of northeastern Brazil experience around a dozen droughts per century on average, with drought defined as insufficient rains for adequate agricultural production during what is normally the wet season (January to April). The effects of drought for the region's inhabitants vary drastically, however, according to their degree of vulnerability, with subsistence farmers and landless workers bearing the brunt of the disaster. The rapidly increasing population in the region during the late nineteenth through the mid-twentieth centuries, together with the consolidation of arable land in the hands of large landowners, among other causes, led to mortality rates running into the hundreds of thousands during "great" droughts such as those of 1877–1879, 1915, 1931–1932, and 1951–1953.[7] The majority of the victims died of starvation and/or epidemics. On the other hand, the gradual onset of these disasters meant that many people were able to flee in time to survive, leading to massive migrations to coastal cities and southern Brazil that have come to be known as *retiradas*. The repetition of such dire circumstances over generations could not fail to stimulate cultural production, creating narratives to explain the disaster and its social and political consequences.

My examination of the cultural tradition of Brazilian drought narratives scrutinizes its relationship with the demarcation, in a national context, of the interior *sertões* of northeastern Brazil as a danger zone or permanent disaster area, denominated by technocrats "O Polígono das Secas" (The Drought Polygon) in 1936. I argue that this demarcation was carried out through the layered political construction of risk; over a fifty-year period, the nation undertook a process of assessment that classified the Northeast and its residents as a security risk, a threat to its program of modernization, and an economic liability. To a large degree, the nation constructed its perception of risk discursively, via a poetics of risk rather than the actual statistic computation of probabilities that one typically associates with risk calculation. Literature played a key part in this process: since statistics were frequently unavailable, contradictory, or adverse to the political programs at stake, risk analysis was performed qualitatively through the use of literary tropes and symbolic abstraction, rather than through the quantitative analysis or "number crunching" that dominates in the appraisal of risk today. On the other hand, local culture also used a type of risk assessment to weigh its strategies for survival during drought years, as well as to calculate expected losses. This chapter discusses the social and political mechanisms and ramifications of the cultural construction of risk in the Northeast.

It is relatively simple to trace a genealogy of drought narratives in the Northeast: the cultural production dealing with drought is by no means limited to the fringes of national culture, as is often the case with cultural works dealing with regional ecological concerns. Of course, many people have argued that the centripetal thrust of Latin American literary regionalism in general belies its localist façade; though purporting to decentralize power, regionalism actually reinforces the center through essentialist legitimizing strategies and the incorporation of marginalized areas into the national cultural geography.[8] As the case may be, literary texts such as José de Alencar's *O sertanejo* (1875), Franklin Távora's *O Cabeleira* (1876), Francisco Gil Castelo Branco's *Ataliba, o vaqueiro* (Ataliba, the Cowboy; 1878), José do Patrocínio's *Os retirantes* (The Refugees; 1879), Rodolfo Teófilo's trilogy of drought novels (*A fome* [Hunger; 1890], *Os Brilhantes* [1895], and *O paroara* [The Rubber Migrant; 1899]), Manoel de Oliveira Paiva's *Dona Guidinha do Poço* (written in 1891), Euclides da Cunha's *Os sertões* (*Rebellion in the Backlands*; 1902), Domingos Olímpio's *Lúzia-Homem* (1903), four novels by José Américo de Almeida (*Reflexões de uma cabra* [Reflections of a Goat; 1922], *A bagaceira* [Trash; 1928], *Coiteiros* [Accomplices; 1935], and *O boqueirão* [The Big Hole; 1935]), Rachel de Queiroz's *O quinze* (*The Year '15*; 1930), Amando Fontes's *Os Corumbas* (1933), Graciliano Ramos's *Vidas secas* (*Barren Lives*; 1938), Jorge Amado's *Seara vermelha* (Crimson Harvest; 1946), José Lins do Rego's *Pedra Bonita* (1938) and *Cangaceiros* (Bandidos; 1953), João Cabral de Melo Neto's epic poem *Morte e vida Severina* (*Death and Life of a Severino*; 1955), Candido Portinari's paintings of *retirantes*, or drought refugees (1930s–1960s), and films such as Nelson Pereira dos Santos's adaptation of *Vidas secas* (1960), Ruy Guerra's *Os fuzis* (*The Guns*; 1963), Glauber Rocha's *Deus e o diabo na terra do sol* (*Black God, White Devil*; 1963), Andrucha Waddington's *Eu, tu, eles* (*Me, You, Them*; 2000), Walter Salles's *Abril despedaçado* (*Behind the Sun*; 2002), and Marcelo Gomes and Karim Ainouz's *Viajo porque preciso, volto porque te amo* (*I Travel Because I Have To, I Come Back Because I Love You*; 2009), among others, all deal with drought in the Northeast and employ similar tropes and thematic concerns, conforming a powerful discourse that simultaneously complements and rewrites the social reality of the phenomenon. The situation that has developed in the *sertões* of northeastern Brazil is quite unique: it is one of few in the world in which the majority of cultural works depicting the area deal with a recurring natural disaster, forming a comprehensive cultural tradition rooted in catastrophe. Tellingly, many of these works have been integrated into the national and even Western cultural canons as Brazilian classics, playing a powerful role in the formation of concepts of cultural citizenship and politics and highlighting the centrality of drought in the national imagination.

Historians of drought in the Northeast frequently cite literature directly in their works, giving a nod to the inextricable ties that bind symbolic production to perceptions of drought.[9] Marco Antonio Villa, in his comprehensive history of the phenomenon, notes that in the popular mind the disaster has apparently become a closed matter, exhausted by the literature of the 1930s, Cinema Novo, and the music of Luiz Gonzaga (14). On the same note, politician Lúcio Alcântara remarks emphatically in his introduction to Villa's book that by the mid-twentieth century, drought was "untouchable," its stereotypical representations and political implications set in stone after a century of repetition (7). Villa's and Alcântara's statements illuminate a key fact: drought in the Northeast is visible to the rest of the nation only when it is mediated through cultural production. Furthermore, as Alcântara hints, the remarkable consistency of representations of the *sertão* and its inhabitants proffered by writers, politicians, sociologists, and even "hard" scientists spans even apparently irreconcilable political differences. Though informed by close individual observations of nature and local culture, and presented through the filter of powerful, often conflicting ideological discourses, diverse authors nevertheless converge in their unvarying representations of drought, creating a potent master narrative of the disaster.[10]

Taken as a whole, these representations have been incredibly effective in establishing a uniform discourse of drought that emanates unassailable, self-evident truth and objectivity. This owes much to the typically realist or essentialist modes of representation that they employ, as well as the existence of an effective consensus across the political spectrum as to the tropes and themes they emphasize, even if for mutually antagonistic ends. Despite this uniformity, however, a closer look at the consensus discourse reveals a meticulous process of selection that emphasizes certain (typically negative) tropes as the essence of life on the *sertão*. This powerful discourse, rooted in the legitimacy of uncritical

repetition, overwhelms completely in the national imaginary more positive views of the region voiced by its residents in popular poetry and
song and by homesick writers living in cultural or economical exile outside the region—among them less canonical authors such as Afonso Arinos, Bernardo Elis, and Antonio Salles, whose works eschew drought
for nostalgic depictions of daily life in the *sertão* rife with images of cultural richness and natural abundance.[11] Given the existence of contestatory discourses on the region, it seems paramount to scrutinize the prevalence in the national imagination of the negative view of the *sertão* as a
disaster area, as well as its political uses.

The issue of the "otherness" of the *sertão* has already been examined
extensively in recent Brazilian studies. Researchers such as Célia Aparecida Ferreira Tolentino, Durval Muniz de Albuquerque, Jr., Nísia Trindade Lima, and Candice Vidal e Souza coincide in recognizing that the
sertão, beyond a geophysical landscape, forms a political and cultural
construct created by specific actors for political purposes. For many intellectuals, it became a symbolic space useful for expressing the contradictions that they believed threatened Brazil's project of national integration and modernization. As Trindade Lima points out, the term (*de*)
sertão arose during the Portuguese colonization of Africa, when it was
used to designate uninhabited spaces in the interior slated for future conquest (57). It evoked dichotomies that had developed during the millenary history of Western colonization, such as civilization/barbarism and
metropole/colony, but it also sparked connotations of "*terra ignota*,"
unknown lands, and questions of human habitability. From the beginning, *sertão* was the mark of environmental and human otherness; a
blanket term for describing the unexplored and the unknown, it could
only be inscribed as the negative of that which was known and dominated. In subsequent years, the concept was transferred to Brazil in the
same capacity, as *sertão* became the other of *litoral*, the more heavily
colonized and developed coastal regions.[12] Not being limited to any specific region or environment, it continued to indicate indeterminacy: there
were the jungle *sertões* of the Amazon and Mato Grosso, the mountainous *sertões* of Minas Gerais, and the southern *sertões* of São Paulo, as
well as the arid *sertões* of the Northeast. In the colonial mind-set, *sertão*
simply indicated distance from the colonial centers of political and economic power (Trindade Lima 50).

This all changed following independence in 1822, however, when Pedro I's assertion of Brazilian autonomy from Portuguese authority resulted in a shift in the geographical perception of Brazil from periph-

eral colony to modern nation. Brazil's borders gradually ceased to be conceived of as open frontiers on the fringes of empire and became the limits of nationality. Consequently, the presence of a great number of regions existing in political and economic isolation became a national concern.[13] The Brazilian Empire sponsored several scientific expeditions to catalogue the "unexplored" regions and inventory their potential for development.[14] The Empire did not view them as a particular risk, however, although it occasionally fretted over the possibility that Spanish American neighbors or European colonial powers might attempt to pilfer sparsely inhabited regions. With the overthrow of the monarchy and the founding of the Republic in 1889, however, the question became much more pressing. The ideologues of the Republic measured Brazil's potential for national unity and democratic governance by the yardsticks of western Europe and the United States. Basing themselves on concepts of nationality rooted in ethnic homogeneity and cultural uniformity, Brazilian intellectuals such as Capistrano de Abreu, Eliseo de Carvalho, Euclides da Cunha, and Francisco José de Oliveira Vianna became increasingly disturbed by the prevalence of largely unmapped, isolated regions of Brazil that they viewed as existing within Brazil but not forming part of it.[15]

On the other hand, the issue of border security became paramount with the War of Paraguay (1864–1870) in the South and the end-of-the-century rubber boom in the Amazon Basin in the North. The Republic sponsored a series of expeditions to demarcate as well as reassess the *sertões*, judging both their potential and risks for modern economic and political development. The final result of this process, which in the Northeast necessarily took into account drought and social unrest such as the 1897 War of Canudos, was the relative restriction of the word and the concept of the *sertão* to a single region that embodied the greatest risk to the nation. As the outlying regions of the nation were mapped, colonized, and modernized, the multiplicity of interior *sertões* collapsed into a single, symbolic space and meaning: they became Euclides da Cunha's *sertões*, the *sertões* of the Northeast. *Sertão* was divested of its colonial connotations as an unexplored reserve of future wealth and expansion, becoming limited to a single zone of high risk to the national enterprise.[16]

Not coincidentally, the implementation in Brazil of risk assessment as a framework for the objective appraisal of danger accompanied the process of the nationalization of formerly uncharted lands. As Niklas Luhmann has revealed in his seminal *Risk: A Sociological Theory*, the European shift toward capitalism based on colonial expansion and global trade during the seventeenth and eighteenth centuries led to the gestation of risk assessment as a method for investors to link the micro and macro economies through the probabilistic calculation of potential profits and losses arising from known and unknown events (1). Beyond economics, however, Luhmann postulates that risk implied a transformation in worldview from medieval deference to danger as the territory of the divine to a modern mechanism for "binding time" through endowing the future with the security of probabilities.[17] During most of the nineteenth century, Brazil's transition into capitalism was carefully controlled by the emperor and the Brazilian oligarchy, which guarded jealously its rights and privileges, while the hefty influence of the Catholic Church maintained intact religious notions of danger and time. In such a rigid economic environment, capitalistic investment and the need for risk assessment were minimal. When the Empire was overthrown in 1889, however, the new Republic's technocrats looked initially to European and US models to renovate nearly every aspect of national life, including the economy. Desirous of replacing the semifeudal *fazenda* economy that continued to prevail throughout Brazil despite the abolition of slavery in 1888, the Republic sought to liberalize economic policies, to attract foreign investment and immigration, to modernize agriculture and industry, and to globalize trade. The drive to synchronize development with the Western world also implied synchronizing Brazil's watches with a future measured in increments of risk rather than divine danger.

Throughout the nineteenth century, European colonial powers had developed models of economic analysis to maximize profit and minimize losses in their colonial enterprises. Though adorned with statistics, these analyses often took the form of narrative and did not rely on the complex formulas and mathematical probabilities of today's risk assessment. As Elaine Freedgood points out, they served more as tools of public relations than actual decision making, controlling and limiting discursively dangers inherent in the colonial enterprise by naming and quantifying them, as well as justifying the enormous expenses (13). In this usage, risk assessment became a way of managing potential trauma, of revealing and materializing the negative, of putting a price on hidden fears and dangers.

Influenced by pseudo-Darwinist views of nationality in which imperialism was the guarantee of future survival, many of the Brazilian Republic's ideologues viewed the "civilization" and nationalization of the interior as a project akin to the European colonization of Asia and Africa. The construction of the democratic nation and economic progress conflated into a single project of expansion into the *sertões*: the continued isolation of the *sertões* evoked traumatic fears of the apocalyptic regression into a subsistence economy and the disintegration of the national body politic. The European colonial tool of risk analysis became the instrument by which to calculate Brazil's potential for economic development and national consolidation in the project to incorporate the *sertões* into the nation. As these regions were by definition "terra incognita," statistical analysis was simply not a viable approach to this process of assessment: little or no data was available. Literary abstraction, on the other hand, could serve in its stead to construct a formula for conceptualizing the regions' potential for incorporation into the national economy and political structure.

Literary Geographies of Risk

The *sertão* acquired an early textual presence in the accounts of colonial travelers to northeastern Brazil, but more substantial literary treatment of the area only emerged after independence, when nationalistic authors searched in the isolated expanses of Brazil's "backlands" for a national essence ostensibly outside the detrimental influence of European cultural colonialism.[18] Perhaps not surprisingly, Brazilian romantics such as José de Alencar and Francisco Gil Castelo Branco were among the first to find literary merit in the *sertão*, whose very name evoked the solitary landscapes and unadulterated local customs for which they quested as the foundations of cultural autonomy. Likewise, the *sertanejos*' reputation as fiercely independent frontiersmen appealed to capitalistic notions of nationality as the sum of individual prowess that were in vogue in the nineteenth century due to the rapid westward expansion of the United States and its accompanying ascension onto the world stage.[19]

In keeping with previous works such as *O guaraní* (1857), *Iracema* (1865), and *O gaúcho* (1870), José de Alencar's *O sertanejo* (1875) deploys the allegory of romantic love and integration with an idealized vernacular nature to postulate a model for inclusive Brazilian citizenship.[20] Although *O sertanejo* takes place long before independence (in 1764), it constructs a view of its exemplary protagonist, Arnaldo, as a freedom-loving, individualist prototype of the Brazilian citizen. By rejecting the patriarchal order of the ranch that he manages as foreman, Arnaldo allegorizes mixed-race, middle-class Brazil's struggle to democratize the paternalist hierarchy of the Brazilian Empire during the late nineteenth century. The allegory finds an ending compatible with Alencar's contradictory desire to see Brazil progress as a modern nation without altering the social order; there is no symbolic consummation of Arnaldo's platonic love for the ranch owner's daughter, Dona Flor. Instead, each is free to go his or her own way; the only change in the status quo is the ranch owner's recognition of Arnaldo's independence and equality.

Although Alencar's *sertanejo* is shaped by his environment, and indeed blends seamlessly with it, he is also its master. In one moment he literally roars his position at the top of the food chain: "From his vigorous chest erupted the formidable bellow that no words could translate, a human roar with which the *sertanejo* proclaimed throughout the desert his reign as king of creation" (77). In this world of manly self-assuredness, natural disasters are not a threat to human dominance, merely an inconvenience. The only real victims of drought in Alencar's romantic *sertão* are the cattle and the land itself, which becomes a "vast bone yard" of denuded trees that he describes as the "tomb of creation" (15). In *O sertanejo*, drought is merely a precondition; it is the promise of the rainy season, with its connotations of material progress and integration into the national model of Brazil as abundant paradise.

Francisco Gil Castelo Branco's *Ataliba, o vaqueiro* (1878) tells a different story. This brief novella opens with a bucolic scene in which innocent, nymphlike Terezinha sighs her love in poetic verses while drawing water from a well. She is enveloped by sympathetic flora, invoking the romantic symbiosis of nature with feminine beauty. Ataliba, a ranch foreman described as a magnificent bronze statue, disturbs her reverie to ask her hand in marriage before her mother. Before the wedding can be celebrated, however, drought brutally interrupts the romantic collage, initiating an abrupt stylistic transition into a naturalistic narrative of the ravages caused by the disaster. Suddenly, the *sertão* ceases to embody the romantic ideal of wild beauty: the pastoral paradise rapidly transforms into an ashen wasteland, its inhabitants forced to abandon their homes and fields in order to survive. In keeping with naturalist causality, Terezinha's mother dies from pneumonia contracted while attempting to reinforce an emergency water reservoir. Ataliba and Terezinha eventually share her fate; only a short distance from salvation, Terezinha succumbs to hunger and fever, while Ataliba is bitten by a rattlesnake from which he attempts to protect his chaste fiancée's body.

Ataliba initiates the transition away from the *sertão* as an idealized repository of national identity toward a danger zone that threatens the construction of the modern nation. Drought crushes Alencar's romantic fantasy and with it the idealistic allegory of integration through individual prowess. Here Ataliba is helpless before the terror of nature, and the balking of his and Terezinha's union can only symbolize the frustration of nationalistic integration by drought. Given this drastic change in direction, which catches the reader quite by surprise, one might ask what led to such a stark divergence in the way in which the two romantic authors represent drought and its consequences? The timeline clues one in: *Ataliba* was first published by chapter in successive editions of Rio de Janeiro's *Diario de Notícias* in 1878, at the height of the Great Drought of 1877–1879. Clearly, disastrous reality had impinged on the domain of nationalistic fantasy. In fact, during the same year, Alencar was reprehended by his compatriots from the northeastern state of Ceará for his incongruous literary representation of drought in the interior, following comments in which he downplayed the gravity of the situation as a political ploy of the liberal opposition (Greenfield xi). In any case, Castelo Branco's novel marks the *sertão* as a contested site in the national imagination and as a danger zone rather than the scene of pastoral romance. *Ataliba*'s portrayal of the disintegration of the family due to disaster initiates a key trope in the literature of drought, with lasting implications for the position of the *sertão* in the national imaginary. With no union, there can be no reproduction, and the *sertão* becomes a threatening space, uninhabitable by modern man.

The shift toward literary naturalism, with its emphasis on the novel as a case study in the dynamics of what its practitioners considered social pathologies, had significant implications for the construction of the *sertão* as a danger zone. As a transitional text, *Ataliba* stopped short of serious evaluation of the implications of drought for the nation; the disaster simply signifies the undoing of the national project of integration. However, more overtly naturalistic texts inspired by the Great Drought of 1877–1879, such as José do Patrocínio's *Os retirantes* (The Refugees; 1879) and Rodolfo Teófilo's *A fome* (Hunger; 1890), explored the social and economic dynamics of drought in greater precision. These texts reformulated the vague notion of drought as a purely natural phenomenon of incalculable destructive force into a refined system governed by the interaction of classifiable variables, including social and political factors not formerly considered. More than impartial ethnographies, these novels' meticulous descriptions of local economic contexts, cultural customs, and political and social orders correspond to the calculated objectivity of risk assessment, with its aim of assigning contingent values to unknown quantities.

The 1877–1879 drought itself occurred during a time of massive political and social turmoil. The nation was undergoing the transition from monarchy to republic, and the power struggle between monarchist conservatives and republican liberals had reached the boiling point. Fueling the fire were such issues as centralism versus federalism, the individual rights of the middle classes, including democratic political participation, and, of course, slavery (although the positions toward slavery were not divided cleanly by party lines). The middle and upper classes of the Northeast pondered which way the lower-class *sertanejos'* loyalties would lie, especially when social inequalities had been exasperated to the extreme by drought. At the same time, the proponents of democracy wished to judge the prospects for *sertanejo* self-governance, worrying that the lack of material progress in the region betrayed deficiency in rational function, thus placing in question the *sertanejos'* suitability for participation in the democratic political process. Lacking the resources for large-scale polling of their objects of inquiry, and perhaps wary of ceding political agency to the subaltern *sertanejos*, who due to historical mistrust of authority figures might not answer reliably in any case, they opted for creating a literary formula for appraising the situation. They recurred to representative sampling, examining exhaustively the circumstances of one family or village to formulate theories applicable to the whole. To this end, they borrowed the typified figures pioneered by realist narrative to represent specific variables in the social equation, while counterbalancing the symbolism with a wealth of ostensibly factual stories that first appeared in newspapers or were transmitted orally, stories that would be easily recognizable by contemporary readers as "real," not fictitious events. In this way, these authors created a systematic collage that purported to account for all the variables and causes that converged in the frightening mortality and suffering that occurred during the colossal disaster.

The Brazilian naturalists' use of literature for practical purposes of risk assessment was wholly in keeping with Émile Zola's formulation of naturalism, which he defended in "The Experimental Novel" (1880) following the publication of several novels that had attracted criticism for their claims to scientific objectivity. Using Claude Bertrand's approach to experimental medicine as a guide, Zola argued for the incorporation into literature of the experimental method, with the goal of arriving at a scientific knowledge of human psychology and behavior. His proposal involved not only observation and data collection through assiduous note taking but also analysis, the formulation of theory, and finally "modification," or achieving mastery over both human and nonhuman nature (11, 25). His thrust exceeded the bounds of empiricism, penetrating into the realm of application: the novelist worked to isolate the "natural laws" governing human behavior in order to control it more efficiently. The parallel he drew with medicine was key: he outlined an organismic view of society in which the novelist masters social maladies in the same way that doctors conquer physical illness (25). Although he viewed the novelist primarily as an "experimental moralist" rather than a practitioner, he envisioned that his works would stimulate legislators to act based on criteria of social utility (31).

Notably, Zola insisted emphatically on limiting the novel's scope to positive epistemology, which he summed up as "how," rather than straying into the ontological terrain of "why" that he labels disdainfully as "philosophy." The role of the novel was to eliminate the space "left to conjecture," establishing a roadmap of determinism based on Darwinist thought (heredity and the natural environment) but also on what he calls the "social condition" (20). In other words, the novel constituted a utilitarian tool for determining the behavior of previously unpredictable components of social systems, with the practical goal of providing a formula for decision makers to act on. In this way, literary naturalism outlined a set of procedures for assigning values to social unknowns and assessing the risks posed to society and political order by pathological "social ills" such as prostitution, criminality, gambling, and alcoholism. Naturalism from its inception was conceived of as a tool for risk assessment that would inform state policy.

Aluísio Azevedo is most often credited with inaugurating naturalism in Brazil with his novel *O mulato* (1881), perhaps due to its chronological relationship with Zola's 1880 "Experimental Novel." Nevertheless, Patrocínio's 1879 *Os retirantes* undeniably reflects the empiricist precepts and focus on public policy laid out by Zola in his essay, even though it predates Zola's work by one year. This apparent anachronism is easily explained, as Zola and other theorists associated with the rise of naturalism, such as Hippolyte Taine, had already published a sizeable body of work in the 1860s and 1870s, before Zola felt obligated to defend the naturalist aesthetic in "The Experimental Novel." In fact, a number of structural considerations in *Os retirantes* that diverge from orthodox naturalism, including the greater weight it assigns chains of causality over determinism, reflect its position in this early or formative stage of naturalism, in contrast with Teófilo's 1890 *A fome*, which seems written by the (Zola's) book.

It is noteworthy that both Patrocínio's *Os retirantes* and Teófilo's *A fome* concentrate their gazes on the fates of middle- and upper-class families, analyzing the factors that contribute to their dissolution. Like Alencar's *O sertanejo*, these texts posit the middle and upper classes as the constitutive members of the Brazilian citizenry, somewhat to the exclusion of the lower classes. *Os retirantes* details the process by which an entire village disintegrates, using as focal points the families of prominent landowner Rogério Monte and middle-class schoolteacher Francisco Queiroz. Other iconic characters include the virginal daughters of the two families, Irena and Eulália, malefic village vicar Paula (whose feminine name plays off tropes of female wiles despite his very masculine sexual drive), bandit Virgulino, and corrupt local politician Antão Ramos. A substantial cast of lower-class characters is also present, but it is largely represented en masse, alternately as a faceless multitude of debased, hapless *retirantes* (drought refugees) and an uncontrollable mob manipulated unscrupulously by other characters. Using these characters as representative samples of *sertanejo* society, Patrocínio constructs a model of the circumstances that lead to the annihilation of both families, the village, and metonymically, the nation.

Tellingly, drought alone is not responsible for the disaster: it simply exacerbates the situation, providing the *retirantes* as unwitting henchmen of the dastardly local priest, whose seduction of Eulália Queiroz and attempted murder in a fit of misplaced jealously of the village's most important landowner, Augusto Feitosa, results in the death of several characters, the complete disbanding of the social order, and the subsequent abandonment of the village. Unjustly accused of the failed homicide attempted by Paula, even benevolent patriarch Rogério Monte and his blond-haired, blue-eyed daughter Irena eventually become *retirantes*, forced to eke out a living on the streets of Fortaleza, where Rogério succumbs to starvation and humiliation. Likewise, after Eulália's "perdition" at the hands of the priest, she gradually allows herself to be coerced into prostitution in order to support her family during their agonizing migration to the coast. Trapped within the rigid patriarchal morality, her family turns their backs on her despite her sacrifice, and she eventually dies alone in the street in front of the governor's palace, where her death becomes a morbid spectacle for passersby and cynical liberal politicians lunching with the governor. Her family will most likely run the same fate, as they board a foundering ship with hundreds of other refugees bound for Rio de Janeiro.

Ironically, the only character unscathed by the disaster that he created is the cynical parish priest Paula, whose impunity is underscored by his reassignment to another, more prestigious parish. The novel's sole spark of hope is the marriage of Irena Monte to Augusto Feitosa: the union of two historically antagonistic families hints at the reconciliation of bitter rivals such as the two dominant political parties, and thus at the possibility of a future of national integration despite tragedy. *Os retirantes* carefully lays out a formula that accounts for each of the social ills associated with drought: the travails and suffering of the *retirada* (journey to refuge), incredible mortality from starvation, epidemics due to unhygienic conditions, the total disruption of the local economy, mass unemployment and indigence, material and moral corruption at every level, rampant male sexuality and the prostitution of "honorable" women, criminality including banditry and looting, and even cannibalism.

Rodolfo Teófilo's *A fome* creates a similar model, although the catalyst of the catastrophic dissolution of upper-class landowner Manuel de Freitas's family is not the machinations of an unscrupulous priest but, rather, vice. With the family's having lost all their cattle to drought and not possessing sufficient provisions or currency to wait out the disaster, Freitas determines to sell their last remaining belongings, their cherished slaves (some of whom raised his children and to whom he had promised freedom) to predatory traders on the coast, who will ship them off to southern coffee plantations. His ill-fated cousin, Inácio do Paixão, is assigned the task of transporting the slaves to the coast and selling them. Paixão, overcome by his addiction to gambling, fritters away his family's last hope for survival in a few nights' gaming, quite literally wagering with the lives of his relatives. The disgraced cousin contemplates suicide but, beholden to his debt to his family, decides to redeem himself through work. He embarks to the Amazon to toil in the rubber boom until he recovers the money. The victim of exploitation himself in the rubber fields, he is only able to rectify his misdeeds when he conveniently wins a lottery. Meanwhile Freitas's and Paixão's own families are forced to partake in the lower-class *retirantes'* sufferings on the journey to Fortaleza, where they undergo further humiliations and several succumb to hunger and disease.

Not all is lost, however. As in *Os retirantes*, a marriage in the final pages symbolizes the possibility of a brighter future. In this case, Freitas's daughter, Carolina, is able to fend off the crude advances of the imperial drought commissioner, Simeão de Arruda, and she marries the young, stereotypically vigorous but poor student Edmundo da Silveira, who had loved her from afar since their shared childhood on the *sertão*. Paradoxically, it is only due to drought that their love comes to fruition: the disaster has had a leveling effect, making possible the integration of the middle and the upper classes. As the narrator states, "The drought, in a tremendous blow, destroyed fortunes and annihilated prejudices, and social positions vanished, making all equal" (183).[21] Furthermore, contrary to the ignominious end of Patrocínio's patriarch Rogério Monte, Manuel de Freitas survives the drought, though four of his children have died, and he and his wife return to the *sertão* in a powerful locomotive that one imagines will freight modernity to the interior. Likewise, a ray of justice absent from *Os retirantes* illuminates the ending: the villainous drought commissioner Simeão de Arruda gets his just deserts, perishing beset by remorse in a fit of delirium tremens induced by his alcoholism.

If *Os retirantes* endows social and moral considerations with primacy, *A fome* focuses to a greater extent on the economic consequences of drought. As the narrator makes clear from the outset, "The losses suffered in the drought by individual fortunes were enormous" (96). Suggestive images of the *sertão* as a cattle cemetery drive home the extent of the losses of the cattle barons of the interior, contrasting violently with descriptions of reproductive abundance during the rainy season. *A fome* delineates meticulously the disastrous consequences that drought entails for the local and regional economies, severely disrupting the chain of production; commercial transportation, which depended almost exclusively on draft animals that could not function without feed or water; and the labor environment, leading to massive unemployment and the dispersion of the workforce due to exodus (a phenomenon that Teófilo returned to in much greater detail in a later novel, *O paroara*). The economic analysis is fundamental. As the only investors in the local economy, the local landowners' losses and the paralyzed infrastructure render development in the *sertão* nearly impossible. A dual liberalist maxim follows, one that remains in vogue even today: the funereal consequences of drought are due to underdevelopment, and only development can remedy drought.

Not everyone loses with drought in *A fome*, however. Unscrupulous slave traders are quick to take advantage of the misfortune of the "benevolent" patriarchs of the *sertão*, buying and reselling their slaves for enormous profits. The novel recounts an economic disaster that results in a shift of commercial power to the South, to the tragic detriment of the traditional industries of the North: "The majority of businessmen in Fortaleza dedicated themselves to the slave trade, shipping them off to the South, in the same way they once exported cotton, coffee, and sugar to foreign ports" (96).[22] The mainstays of the northern economy are thus replaced by the morally reprehensible commerce in slaves, whose high profits are due exclusively to the disaster victims' desperation to sell and cannot be expected to sustain the general economy once the disaster ends. This disaster profiteering comes in addition to the corruption of government officials, symbolized by drought commissioner Simeão de Arruda, who receives his position due to party loyalty rather than personal merits and who believes that "*furtar do governo não é furtar*" (to steal from the government is not stealing; 159). Furthermore, Arruda abuses his position and government resources to seduce young *retirante* women, among them Carolina. The ill-gotten ostentation of the slave traders and corrupt government officials contrasts brutally with the rags and hunger of the honorable *sertanejos*, on whose shoulders rests the economic future of the region (139). Tellingly, the corruption is described as a lack of patriotism, thus constituting not merely a hindrance to the effectiveness of emergency aid but also a threat to the nation (362).

Os retirantes and *A fome* transparently postulate drought as a threat to the regional economy and social structure but also to public order and national security. Both novels cite statistics of over one hundred thousand abject, diseased refugees overwhelming Fortaleza, which according to estimates cited by Villa, had a permanent population of only about twenty thousand inhabitants at that time (70).[23] These rough estimates likely have their origin in local newspaper articles from the period and, although unsubstantiated, acquire legitimacy through repetition in a variety of sources, journalistic and literary. In any case, the quantities do not require precision: they are as effective symbolically as the poetic descriptions of the abjection and indigence of the refugees. In reality, the statistics represent a measure of the fear the local populace feels when confronted by the miserable masses of *retirantes*, more than an objective census of the refugee population, although they also lend credence to the novels' practical function as tools of risk analysis based on fact, not fiction.

Particularly in Patrocínio's novel, the masses of refugees become a faceless force of destruction, contrasting with the carefully problematized humanity of even the most corrupt villains. The clouds of social uprising hang heavy in the air: though instigated by the Machiavellian priest Paula, the *retirantes* plunder and set fire to the village in the first part of the novel, and fears of a recurrence are reiterated throughout the text. As one character, describing the refugees as "*canalha*" (worthless parasites), proffers, "*Eles eram capazes de fazer voar isto tudo*" (they are quite capable of destroying everything; 2:104). In another episode, the political opposition in Quixada instigates the *retirantes* to a *saque*, or looting of food stores, which the author describes as a near revolution (2:93). Likewise, both novels portray the *retirantes* as a threat to the rule of law: they form irrational lynch mobs whose bloodthirsty yearnings for misdirected justice are barely averted by the unerring impartiality of local judges.

The prevalence of the view of *retirantes* as a threat to political order is confirmed by Villa, who found a high incidence of similar tropes in newspaper articles throughout the nation from the time period, as well as a wealth of editorials whose authors voiced their fears that the drought would catalyze communist revolution (46). As an example, he cites a letter written by the governor of Rio Grande do Norte, who declares that the increasingly common disturbances in the streets of local cities were accompanied by a clamor for *"farinha ou revolução!"* (flour or revolution; 75). The threat of social revolt and descent into anarchy weighed heavily on the fate of the nation, exacerbated by the suspension of aid in the interior in 1878, which forced the masses of *retirantes* to make the harrowing journey to the coastal capitals to receive assistance, thousands succumbing to starvation and sickness on the way.

Somewhat in contrast to *Os retirantes*, the refugees in Teófilo's *A fome* do not conjure directly the threat of violent political upheaval; it is their contagious abjection, unemployment, and propensity to vice that become risks for the state. There is no overt mass action: the refugees are passive victims of their conditions. Their passivity does not necessarily translate to innocuousness, however, for their predilection and vulnerability to vice is contagious and threatens the decay of the social organism. In Teófilo's novel, vices such as prostitution, gambling, and alcoholic debauchery lead to irrational behavior that threatens the stability of the social order. The text includes minute medical descriptions of the physiological effects of addiction alongside those of starvation and illness, and the author makes no real distinction between physical sickness and "moral maladies" capable of undermining the patriarchal order. For the naturalist author, governability equated to systematic predictability, and unpredictable behavior due to addiction implied the threat of dissolution.

Tellingly, both *Os retirantes* and *A fome* posit moral decay as a worse disaster than starvation. As one character states in *Os retirantes*, "In times of calamity, it is very difficult for poverty to remain pure" (2:34). Confronted with this conundrum, the patriarchal mores univocally prefer death to dishonor. It is certainly not coincidental that the general exodus of the village in *Os retirantes* does not occur because of drought but ultimately traces to the vicar's unholy sexual obsession with Eulália. The disaster in this novel is thus posited as a kind of moral drought that can be brought to an end by eliminating sexual corruption in the clergy. In this way, these naturalist texts transparently postulate a moral component to risk analysis. In keeping with Zola's views, they conceive of the social codes of patriarchal morality within the framework of natural laws governing human behavior, and, naturally, any deviation from these norms is deemed pathological.

On the other hand, one must take into consideration the patriarchal moral order's role not only in preserving the social hierarchy but also in structuring the economy. Although in recent times there is a shift to divorce economics from morality, so that the only ethic of capitalism becomes profit, no such perspective existed at the end of the nineteenth century. The moral order was inextricably bound up with the economic order in a way that reached far beyond the sexual economy in which virginal daughters were pledged in marriage by their parents, with or without their consent, in order to consolidate commercial and political alliances. Both the internal and export economic structures were organized around the notion of male heads of extended households (read: *fazendas*, or plantations) dealing exclusively with each other, and the web of close personal relations and contacts was the only way to do business. For this reason, any disruption in the patriarchal order, moral or otherwise, constituted a threat to the economic structure. Of course, drought interfered with the sexual economy as well, converting potential model *sertanejo* brides such as Eulália and Carolina into candidates for prostitution, a blanket term that refers to the perceived loss of virginity due to any real or rumored sexual contact, not only sex in exchange for food or money. These novels' heavy emphasis on morality undeniably had economic as well as social implications, and their assessment of the risks posed by drought would be incomplete without analysis in this area.

The Nature of Violence: The *Cangaço*

I have outlined several key aspects of the naturalists' assessment of the risks posed by drought and drought victims. On the one hand, the dissolution of middle- and upper-class families threatened the national allegory of integration and the patriarchal moral order, as well as regional economic development. On the other, the masses of classless *retirantes* represented a risk to private property through looting, to political order due to potential for social revolution, and to social well-being because of their contagious physical and moral infirmities. Nonetheless, these novels typically discount the *retirantes'* possibilities to act as a disruptive force except in cases in which they are instigated by outside agents. There is one exception to this rule, however. Both Patrocínio and Teófilo establish a link between drought and the rise of *cangaceirismo*, or banditry, in the *sertão*. This connection is explicit in *Os retirantes*, in which one drought refugee, Virgulino, is forced into banditry by social marginalization. Though guilty of the cruelest acts against his fellow *sertanejos*, Virgulino is not altogether evil: he also aids several drought victims, including Eulália and her family, with his takings.

In contrast, *A fome's* feared Calangro bandits appear only peripherally, simply embodying another facet to the disaster that is making the *sertão* uninhabitable. Nothing if not thorough, however, Teófilo does not abandon the topic to such cursory treatment. Like a good naturalist, Teófilo prefers to isolate his objects of study: if *A fome* is dedicated almost exclusively to the figure of the *retirante*, he analyzes the social phenomenon of the *cangaço* in much greater detail in another novel, *Os Brilhantes* (1895). Unlike Patrocínio's Virgulino, who had been a laborer on a *fazenda* before becoming a *retirante* and eventually a bandit, Teófilo's novel depicts the *cangaceiro* as an upper-class victim of political intrigue. The protagonist, Jesuíno Brilhante, is described alternately as generous hero and schizophrenic madman suffering from a mental disorder: "The beatific air of his appearance, which accentuated the deep melancholy of his gaze, suddenly transformed into such a ferocious expression that it horrified one to look at him. These eclipses, altering at moments his placid physiognomy, were announced by a series of tensings of the facial muscles" (33).[24]

Even before Brilhante's descent into criminality, these sudden shifts in expression reveal that he is the latent "bearer of a homicidal neurosis," which is awakened when he witnesses his uncle's murder at the hands of the rival Calangro family. After handily doing away with his rivals and government soldiers sent to aid them by their political allies in a bloodbath, Brilhante turns his hand to righting wrongs. In the absence of real justice, since the governmental judicial procedures have become tools of corrupt politicians, he becomes a local law unto himself, defending the weak and unprotected against the predatory strong in the Darwinist environment of the *sertão*. His revenge on the breakers of traditional *sertanejo* social mores, however, is often heavy-handed, as the rational mind-set needed to dole out justice impartially is overcome by his homicidal genetic predisposition.

Notably, the drought of 1877–1879 appears only midway through the book, although it occupies the bulk of the second half. The chronology reveals that its author avoids establishing direct causality between drought and Jesuíno Brilhante's slide into criminality, which depends instead on genetic predisposition and political factors. In fact, the drought represents a saving grace for Brilhante, who, like Patrocínio's Virgulino, transforms from homicidal avenger into a kind of Robin Hood, doling out food supplies and justice to drought refugees whom the government has failed to aid. There is nevertheless a sense that the harsh environment of the *sertão* informs his behavior, at the least aggravating his tendencies toward savagery. Indeed, one of Brazil's most prominent literary critics of the time, José Veríssimo, summed up the underlying environmental determinism present in the novel:

> The land of drought, which is that whole land, is also the land of crime, of violence, and of carnage, not of crime like that which you find anywhere, but of crime assuming the special characteristics of a struggle among races, or castes, and producing criminals that remind one of outlaws, of those primitive banditos, whether esteemed for the terror they inspire and living within society, or truly outside its laws, banished from it, and pursued and harassed by it. (262)[25]

Veríssimo's reading of Jesuíno Brilhante makes clear the connection between the *cangaceiro* and the drought-plagued environment in the mind of the reader, even if it is not explicitly developed in the text.

This reaction reveals the power and persistence of prior discourse, and particularly the influence of the self-described founder of "northern" regionalism, Franklin Távora. Although his work does not ascribe the centrality to drought that the later novels by Patrocínio and Teófilo do, Távora glossed over the social effects of the disaster in his novel *O Cabeleira* (1876), initiating the construction of the *sertanejo* as a violent, barbarous figure wrought by fire in the hellish, drought-plagued environment of the interior. In fact, the titular bandit becomes the human complement to drought, "a scourge no less fatal than that of the plague and starvation that subjected [the people] to extreme suffering" (125). Távora's concatenation of the natural disaster and banditry converted the *sertão* irrevocably into the land of "drought and criminality," as Veríssimo would have it.

More complex a figure than Távora's caricature of the *cangaceiro*, Teófilo's Brilhante, simultaneously "saint" and "satanic," embodies the contradictory representations that were to plague the *sertanejo* in subsequent literary treatments, especially following Euclides da Cunha's rewriting of all *sertanejos* as potential *cangaceiros* in his masterful *Os sertões* (1902), although Cunha trades the word for *jagunço*, with only marginal differences.[26] As Muniz de Albuquerque, Jr., points out, the figure of the *cangaceiro* marks northeasterners as potential murderers, a connection rationalized through the chain of causality in *Os sertões* (126). The *cangaceiro* is not a faceless force of destruction, however: Teófilo's Brilhante exemplifies heroic qualities of impartial justice and largess as well as cruelty and vengefulness, and even Távora's bloodthirsty Cabeleira is reformed through love in the end, although his crimes must be repaid through his willing execution. In any case, Cunha's revision of the figure rewrote this fundamental tension through the lens of nationalism: the enterprising, if murderous, *sertanejo* became simultaneously the undoing and the foundation of the nation.

The analysis undertaken by naturalist authors such as Patrocínio and Teófilo of the risks posed by drought rewrote the disaster from a natural phenomenon into a deterministic roadmap of social pathologies. Their evaluation of the disaster was informed by their training in medicine and Teófilo's role in treating drought victims as a pharmacist, as well as the influence of Zola's formulation of literary naturalism. In their works, naturalism's emphasis on the pathological was transferred to the *sertanejos*, who came to be classified as a pathological culture living in a diseased environment. Paradoxically, upon marking *sertanejo* culture as pathological, they converted the worst-case scenario into the norm. To an observer outside of the situation, an empirical failure in their logic of drought becomes immediately visible: they themselves constructed the literary simulacra of the disaster, thus limiting circularly the results of their assessment to an epistemology of their own construction, which happened to be pathology.

As theoretician Sven Ove Hansson has noted, risk assessment necessarily involves simplification, as the complexity of the real world overwhelms mathematical models. Calculation can only be made by reducing the equation to knowables, a conscious process of reduction based not on arbitrary decisions but on rational assessment: "If a decision problem is treated as a decision 'under risk,' this does not mean that the decision in question is made under conditions of completely known probabilities. Rather, it means that a choice has been made to simplify the description of this decision problem by treating it as if it were a case of known probabilities" (Hansson). Drought literature performs this important function, creating a calculated, essentialized view of drought that allows a much clearer equation to be formulated. The phenomenon of drought in the Northeast is much too expansive and complex to detail statistically; therefore, a qualitative analysis based on a kind of "realism of the essences," to borrow a phrase from Mexican author Julieta Campos (144), or "symbolic realism," as geographer J. B. Harley would have it ("Deconstructing" 10), becomes necessary to get at the heart of the problem. Unfortunately, as Luhmann points out, risk assessment invariably ends up replicating the blindness inherent in rational traditions: it can only see what it formulates; everything else is beyond its field of vision (14). And the way problems are formulated, whether through risk calculation or other means, both limits and constructs possible solutions.

In any case, naturalist drought narratives worked within the consensus view that emerged from the Great Drought of 1877–1879. As Villa points out, both *Os retirantes* and *A fome* relied heavily on journalistic sources for their plotlines and interpretative framework (69). The congruity of journalistic and literary sources ends up constructing an effective consensus as to the causes, effects, and interpretation of the disaster that, given the agreement on both sides of the political spectrum, appears apolitical. The only real points of divergence are where the governmental response went wrong and what role the church played in the disaster. The collusion of sources indicates an important point: these drought novels do not dispute the newspapers' versions of events. And with newspapers proclaiming the ravages of drought throughout the nation, these novels were hardly necessary to draw attention to the disaster. The disaster was already in the public eye. Nor could one claim that the novels were directed toward a distinct readership: the relatively limited lettered audience was one and the same. In this light, it becomes clear that the novels had a separate function, which I have argued was to assess the risk that drought posed to the local and national economy, social structure, and political order, as well as to put in motion the process of the institutionalization of the disaster as a national problem requiring sustained attention from the federal government.

Patrocínio's and Teófilo's seminal naturalist texts set the foundations of both "drought literature" as a subgenre and of literature as a vehicle for risk assessment in Brazil. Creating a causal hierarchy, they developed specific categories of narrative that corresponded to what they saw as the greatest threats in the equation: forced migration, including the possibility of mass disorder and epidemics, and criminality. From this process of assessment arose two prime modes of representation: the narrative of the *retirada* and the *cangaceiro* novel. These two modes did not always form distinct texts, however: they overlapped as components of a single causal system.

The novel of migration based its plotline on the *retirada*, typically focusing on the displacement of upper- and middle-class families from the economic structure as well as the effects of massive waves of migration to urban centers. Tellingly, there are no migration success stories: all these novels end in various degrees of failure and the disintegration of the family, which metonymically symbolizes the nation. In spite of the history of economic and political interdependence between *sertão* and *litoral*, the narrative of the *retirada* situated the *sertão* in diametrical opposition to the coast, constructing the interior as a danger zone that contrasts starkly with the relative safety and ease of life in coastal cities. In this geography, migration represented a threat to order and hygiene in the urban centers, as the problems that plagued the *sertão* poured over into the idyllic coastal environment.

The novel of the *cangaceiro* was the second narrative mode that emerged from this initial process of risk assessment. These novels postulate the *sertanejo* as a marginal figure who is genetically, socially, and/ or environmentally predisposed to violent criminality. As potential outlaws, *sertanejos* are revealed as ungovernable beings living beyond the reach of political order and the national judicial system. Contributing to the chain of causality in these works are a host of smaller threats, ranging from prostitution, the negative influence of depraved clergymen, local political corruption, and environmental degradation to predatory male sexuality, the resultant fall into prostitution of *sertanejo* women, and a host of other vices. Each of these threats conforms a variable in these novels' analysis of the risks posed by drought to social, political, and economic order. Even though these naturalist drought narratives focus primarily on calculating the potential for losses posed by drought, however, their hopeful endings also turn an eye toward profit, which is contingent on the potential for modernization of the region, political progress and stability, and national unity symbolized by marriage.

At the same time, the unrelenting repetition of tropes of hellish nature, victimization, depopulation, pathological abjection, criminality, governmental corruption, and vice throughout this body of works set the discourse of drought in stone, conforming a unique and persuasive mode of representation from which later works rarely diverged, particularly following the spectacular success of Cunha's *Os sertões* and its consolidation of all the tropes into one text. The uncritical repetition of the tropes of drought led to the formation of a "concrete abstraction," to borrow

Henri LeFebvre's words, in the national imaginary, in which it became very difficult to make any distinction between the discourse and the experience of the disaster. Legitimated by consensus across genres and the political spectrum and consolidated through accumulation, the tropes function in a way similar to the statistics in risk assessment, which are themselves often assigned arbitrarily according to the parameters of the analysis. More specifically, the repetition of tropes, character types, and themes in literary assessments of the risks posed by drought fulfilled a role akin to that of frequency in statistical probability calculation, with greater repetition indicating higher probability.[27] Furthermore, theorists of risk, such as Hansson, recognize that risk by definition must be assigned through consensus. In the case of drought in the Northeast, accumulated literary discourse both substituted for and created consensus: the repetition of tropes and images in a variety of genres and contexts took on the redundancy of statistics, imitating the irrefutability that is claimed by both statistical analysis and social consensus. In this way, the discourse on drought became a powerful self-reproducing system of self-evident meaning.

Canudos: A Time for Revision

Although the almost unimaginable social consequences of the Great Drought of 1877–1879 were acknowledged throughout Brazil, most observers viewed the catastrophe primarily as a one-time event, an exception evident in its denomination as the "Great Drought." As Euclides da Cunha criticized in *Contrastes e confrontos* (Contrasts and Confrontations; 1907), drought remained "an eternal and monotonous novelty" (80). No institutional response was developed, in spite of the efforts of Teófilo and others to motivate the government to establish effective disaster plans and, primarily, to modernize the infrastructure in order to better the local economy and thus avoid the mass exodus of *retirantes* to the coastal cities.[28] Indeed, aid remained unorganized and sporadic up through the first years of the twentieth century. Even the first major drought of the Republican era, from 1898 to 1900, did little to convince the government to act: President Campos Salles did not respond to calls for drought aid, arguing that any extraordinary expenses would interfere with his program to implement fiscal stability. Instead, he suggested the relocation of the *sertanejo* workforce to other regions of Brazil that were in need of manpower, a policy that had already been implemented during the drought of 1877–1879, when thousands of northeasterners were channeled to the Amazon Basin to work in the booming rubber industry under deplorable conditions (Teófilo, *Seccas* 219; Villa 91).

The effects of the massive displacement of refugees and disruption of the economic system in the Northeast were still highly visible throughout the nation, but a decade later the Great Drought of 1877–1879 was largely viewed as a closed book, a freak event whose risks had been sufficiently accounted for by the naturalist authors and whose effects, in any case, had largely played out. It is revealing that no new extensive literary explorations of drought were published until 1899, although Manoel de Oliveira Paiva's *Dona Guidinha do Poço* (written in 1891) uses drought as a backdrop in its postulation of the dangers of the inversion of gender roles for the patriarchal society, and Teófilo included drought in his analysis of banditry in *Os Brilhantes* (1895). Many Brazilians saw the establishment of the Republic in 1888 as a key step in mitigating the political and moral corruption that the naturalist authors had singled out as the prime contributor to the drought victims' suffering as well as to the rise of banditry in the *sertão*. This optimism was not immediately challenged, as the first serious drought of the Republic did not occur until 1898.

Another event shook things up considerably, however. The 1897 War of Canudos precipitated a reevaluation of the risks posed by drought, the *sertanejo*, and the *sertão* as a whole. Canudos was a boomtown founded by religious fanatics in a sparsely populated area in the *sertão* of Bahia. Scholars estimate that within a few years the town grew to nearly thirty thousand people before it was attacked by government forces, ostensibly for protecting bandits and preaching against the Republic, although many have suggested that the case was greatly overstated by local landowners and the Catholic Church, who were zealous of losing political power and ecclesiastical authority (Nogueira Galvão, "*Rebellion*" 154). The government failed in its initial attempts to police the city, however, and repeated defeats of its troops led to a national panic in which it was feared the government would fall to monarchist rebels. Following nearly a year of conflict, the government troops succeeded in razing the city, leaving few survivors.[29]

The violence of what was viewed as a *sertanejo* uprising could not be accounted for adequately using the models developed by Patrocínio and Teófilo, particularly since the rebels were religious zealots rather than drought refugees. A new threat would have to be taken into account: religious fanaticism. While the naturalist drought narratives certainly touched on religion, albeit in a cursory manner, they did not present the *sertanejos*' religious beliefs as a risk. Corruption in the clergy had played an important role in the formula for social disaster developed in *Os retirantes*, but the author marked the behavior of the clergymen as a clear aberration from Christian mores. In Teófilo's novels, on the other hand, the church appeared as a benevolent force that played a central role in maintaining social order and controlling vice. With the Rebellion of Canudos, however, religion suddenly became a divisive political factor, threatening the very sovereignty of the nation. The naturalist formula for risk assessment clearly begged revision, and although a wide range of journalists and authors scrutinized the phenomenon, Euclides da Cunha's analysis in *Os sertões* (1902) acquired the greatest circulation, becoming one of Brazil's first bestsellers and cementing in the public imagination the view of the *sertanejo* as the product of a hostile environment and a national security threat.

Cunha's literary assessment of the risks that the *sertanejo* posed to the nation, which though framed in scientific discourse uses literary tropes rather than statistical analysis to back its arguments, both catalyzed and formed part of the institutional response to drought in the first years of the twentieth century. I have argued elsewhere that *Os sertões* posited drought not as a local problem but rather as a threat to the entire nation and that Cunha sought to quantify that risk by creating a formula based on Hippolyte Taine's theories of environmental determinism, in which the drought-stricken environment, history, and race all conspired to create the rebellious, ungovernable *sertanejo*.[30] (Mis)informed by the nineteenth-century racialist theories that dominated the intellectual panorama of the time, Cunha concluded that all *sertanejos* were potential troublemakers who had genetically adapted or even deevolved for survival in drought conditions in such a way that they could not form part of the rational, modern nation without substantial revision. Cunha's assessment apprised him not only of the risks that drought and the *sertanejos* posed to the newly formed Republic but also of the threat that they presented to themselves according to the positivist paradigm of human progress. Their inability to deal with drought in a "civilized" manner led to their extreme vulnerability to its effects, and their failure to tame the harsh environment resulted in a degenerative society that, left to its own devices, would soon go extinct. Indeed, Cunha believed that the *sertão* bred neurosis, which in turn led to religious fanaticism (Castro-Klarén 367). For Cunha, the only way to control the contagious risk of national dissolution posed by the *sertanejo* was to transform the *sertão* itself: the technological modification of the environment would end the ravages of drought and thus make unnecessary the *sertanejo*'s admirable but barbarous adaptations to his ecosystem. In this way, the *sertanejo* would be transformed as well and could be integrated into the national concept of citizenship.[31]

Yet, disillusioned with the government's brutal treatment of the people of Canudos, Cunha ended up revising his earlier prejudices against the *sertanejos* toward the end of his book. Indeed, *Os sertões* provides a complex representation of the *sertanejo* simultaneously as the nation's other and its future—condemned to disappear as a distinct geographic type, he becomes the building block or cornerstone of a new, integrated, *mestiço* society. Stripped of his distinguishing characteristics, he transforms into a model of both integration and erasure: Cunha reluctantly accepts the *mestiço* phenotype but vigorously rejects cultural difference. Upon disappearing into the nation's melting pot, the *sertanejo* symbolizes the nation itself.

Leopoldo Bernucci notes that Cunha envisioned himself as the official historian of the Canudos conflict (55); as such, his assignment was to develop a procedure for assessing the political risk that the Canudos rebels and *sertanejos* in general posed to the nation, as well as a model for integration. His analysis was not limited to cultural politics, however; he also engaged the economic dimension of risk assessment. *Os sertões* provides both a framework and the justification for economic development in the *sertão* in the nineteenth-century liberal model. The book undertakes a process of mercantile, if eloquent, enumeration of the region's geographical resources, with civil as much as military uses. And his analysis clearly postulates drought as the impediment to political stability and economic profit. On the other hand, he also endows his study with a political bent. The outmoded monarchy had failed to deal adequately with the problem of drought, and it was now up to the highly educated technocrats of the modern Brazilian Republic to reverse the situation and to incorporate the *sertão* into the national culture and economy.

Cunha's assessment of the risks posed by the *sertão* incorporated two new variables into the equation: religious fanaticism and racial miscegenation. In reality, he saw the two as inextricably related, as racial miscegenation led to the mental imbalances that allowed religious extremism to take root. Cunha was hardly the first to suggest race as a factor in the problems of the Northeast: although Patrocínio sidestepped the issue, possibly due to his own mixed-race background, Teófilo alluded to it several times throughout his works, without making it a prime focus. Cunha diverged from his precursors, however, in granting race equal weight with environmental and social factors in his formula of risk assessment. His paradoxical description of the *sertanejo* as the mixed-race but ethnically homogeneous *caboclo* postulated racial miscegenation as a threat both to the psychology of modernity and national unity, reversing Alencar's fantasies of racial integration through sexual union. In any case, Cunha's incorporation into his analysis of religious fanaticism induced by racial imbalances completed the triad of factors that were to dominate drought discourse for years to come: migration, criminality, and fanaticism.

Cunha and the Institutionalization of Drought

Cunha's analysis of the Canudos conflict institutionalized drought as a national problem, one that required the state-sponsored transformation of the environment to mitigate the economic and political threats that it posed to the government. Although *Os sertões* does not specify the way in which this transformation will be carried out, Cunha provides a detailed plan for combating drought in a later essay entitled "Plano de uma cruzada" (Plan for a Crusade), first published in three parts in the *Estado de São Paulo* in 1904 and later anthologized in *Contrastes e confrontos* (1907). This engaging piece proclaims a "One Hundred Years War against the climate," bringing to bear all fields of science and culture in the battle of civilization versus barbarism in the interior of northeastern Brazil (81). Reacting to the enormous social, political, and economic repercussions of the Great Drought of 1877–1879, Cunha's primary complaint is the lack of a systematic approach to the transformation of the environment, which he sees as the basis for the powerful expansionism of successful nations. In his trademark mixture of poetics and science, he describes nationalistic expansionism as part of a physical order: Brazil must civilize its interior, for "nature abhors a vacuum," and if Brazil doesn't occupy these lands, another power will (89). In keeping with the environmental determinism on which he bases his arguments in *Os sertões*, he constructs a view of international power relations intimately tied to the possession and transformation of nature.

The matter is urgent, for he envisions a breakdown of the nation if drought remains uncontrolled. As in *Os sertões*, nature is by no means benign; he equates drought with an almost military expansion of the desert: "The desert invokes the desert. Every drought that appears seems to attract another, greater and less remorseful, leaving the land with a growing receptiveness to the catastrophe" (82).[32] In fact, drought threatens even the lush South, as desertification, provoked both by the climate and human activity, will eventually invade the states beyond the São Francisco River, bringing climactic modifications with it (93).

Cunha's arguments did not go unheeded. During the drought of 1903, barely five years after the Canudos conflict and only months after the publication of *Os sertões*, the Republican government decided to take a hand in drought management, creating various disaster-planning and relief agencies charged with elaborating public works projects and disaster-response strategies to mitigate the cataclysmic effects of the disaster.[33] In 1906, these various organizations and commissions were placed under the authority of the Superintendência de Estudos e Obras Contra os Efeitos das Secas (Superintendency of Studies and Works to Combat the Effects of Drought), and in 1909 the Inspetoria de Obras Contra as Secas (Inspectory of Works to Combat Drought; IOCS) was created to supervise the efforts. The model for IOCS was US President Teddy Roosevelt's Reclamation Service, which had transformed arid areas of the US Southwest into an agricultural powerhouse. Notably, in a speech made at the National Library in 1913, the first director of the IOCS, Miguel Arrojado Lisboa, linked drought to the Canudos Rebellion, revealing the influence of Cunha's thought in policymaking (Villa 94).

In fact, Cunha himself formed part of the group of intellectual advisers assembled in 1907 by President Alfonso Pena to steer the modernization of the nation, using fellow positivist Porfirio Díaz's transformation of Mexico as its model. It was during this period that Cunha penned the essays in *Contrastes e confrontos*, two of which are dedicated to remedying drought through the technical modification of the environment. Rabello notes that many of Cunha's recommendations in "Plano de uma cruzada" were adopted by the IOCS, although it generally failed to put them into practice (227). In any case, the liberal ideologues of the Republic viewed development as a strategy both to mitigate the effects of drought and to reduce the need for federal emergency aid; ideally, the development projects would lead to the modernization of the regional economy, which would, in turn, produce tax revenue for the federal government.

Even with the institutionalization of drought beginning in 1903, aid remained sporadic, as the changes in governments affected funding for the Northeast enormously. The massive drought of 1915, in which Villa estimates more than thirty thousand died just in Ceará, revealed the insufficiency of the government actions (120). President Venceslau Brás's inaction led to the perception of the government as the "República do Café" that catered to politicians from the southern states of São Paulo,

Minas Gerais, and Rio Grande do Sul, to the detriment of northeastern interests. This situation was reversed under the administration of Epitácio Pessoa (1919–1922), who was from the northeastern state of Paraíba. Unfortunately, the detailed blueprint for development that he put into place was deactivated when his southern successor, Artur Bernardes, discontinued funding for the projects, a shift in policy satirized in northeastern author and politician José Américo de Almeida's *O boqueirão* (The Big Hole; 1935).

Following the publication of Cunha's *Os sertões*, literary production on drought rapidly tapered off, perhaps underscoring the relative unanimity with which Cunha's analysis was received. A number of serious droughts with funereal consequences for the inhabitants of the *sertão*, including those of 1888–1889, 1898–1900, 1903–1904, 1915, and 1919, sparked very little immediate literary response to speak of, although Rodolfo Teófilo continued his lifelong project, publishing a compendium on the droughts of the nineteenth century and an essay detailing the ravages of the drought of 1915 that reiterated his views in earlier texts. In any case, Teófilo by now had become a lone voice in the wilderness. The downturn in literary production on drought was due in part to *Os sertões's* success, which as I have argued, drastically modified public policy toward the disaster, catalyzing the process of the institutionalization of aid with the creation of a number of federal agencies. Once again, drought appeared to have become a closed book.

On the other hand, the Old Republic was preoccupied with several other pressing matters during the first two decades of the twentieth century. The rubber boom in the Amazon Basin led to border conflicts with several nations and the annexation in 1903 of the formerly Bolivian province of Acre, following a war that, paradoxically, was won primarily through the prowess of *sertanejo* migrants to the region. Likewise, there were multiple threats to the political stability of the Republic, many stemming from the politics of "*café com leite*" (coffee with cream), in which politicians from the states of São Paulo and Minas Gerais alternated in power. Both the extreme South and the North resented the exclusion, leading to local uprisings and military revolts. One of the most famous was the 1911 rebellion led by Padre Cícero in Juázeiro, in which the renegade priest, allied with the conservative oligarchy headed by the Acioly family, rose up in arms against the federal government. Although Padre Cícero's rebellion occurred in the *sertão*, it did not inspire revisions in the existing model for risk assessment; it was largely written off as the aftershocks of Canudos, which had already been analyzed amply by Cunha. The only addition was increased scrutiny of the role of the local oligarchy in politics, particularly that of the famed "*coronéis*" (coronels), who began to appear in literature as *coiteiros*, the unscrupulous protectors, allies, and even kingpins of the *cangaceiros*.

The Revolution of 1930 and the Reassessment of the Northeast

It was not until the late 1920s that literature returned to drought. The revisiting of the issue was partially a response to the horrifying mortality of the drought of 1915, which rivaled that of the Great Drought of 1877–1879.[34] More than the suffering of the northeasterners, however, the winds of political change motivated the return to the issue. It is revealing that none of the novels that deal directly with the 1915 drought appeared immediately afterward, as had been the case with Patrocínio's *Os retirantes* and a host of other texts during the drought of 1877–1879. Nearly fifteen years passed before the disaster retook its central position, in a novel by the man who was to rival Rodolfo Teófilo as the most prolific author of Brazilian drought narratives: José Américo de Almeida. Tellingly, Almeida penned his iconic *A bagaceira* (*Trash*; 1928) only two years before the overthrow of the Old Republic during the Revolution of 1930.

As Muniz de Albuquerque, Jr., has pointed out, the so-called Romance de 30 (Novel of the 1930s, loosely associated with the Revolution of 1930), more than a cohesive literary movement with a fixed aesthetic or social agenda, represented a shared reaction of northeastern authors to southern political and economic dominance during the Republic (106–19). While northeastern writers associated with the Romance de 30, such as Almeida, Jorge Amado, Rachel de Queiroz, Graciliano Ramos, and José Lins do Rego, all agreed on the need to update regionalist fiction through dialogue with the literary aesthetics pioneered by European and North American novelistic experimentation, on the one hand, and the Brazilian avant-garde, on the other, they diverged widely in style and, more to the point, politics.[35] Almeida was intimately involved with Getúlio Vargas's populism, although he later challenged him for the presidency, while Queiroz and Ramos adhered in varying degrees to the Communist Party line, and Lins do Rego allied himself with the conservative regional oligarchy, whose cultural branch was headed up by sociologist Gilberto Freyre. Despite their differences, all these authors rejected what they viewed as the purposeful marginalization of the Northeast from national politics and culture and the technocratic, paternalist attitude toward development held by southern politicians, who rarely visited the Northeast but made all the decisions about its future based on what northeasterners believed to be flawed theories, many of them unapologetically racist.

Almeida, more than any other author of his generation, worked from within the system, turning prior discourse to his own ends. From the very beginning, he conceived of a political role for his literary works, seamlessly integrating literary production with his political career. His first novel, the satirical *Reflexões de uma cabra* (Reflections of a Goat; 1922), attacks the politics of depopulation of the Northeast and the brain drain of northeastern intellectuals to the southern cultural centers of Rio de Janeiro and São Paulo. The protagonist renounces his roots as a middle-class northeastern *retirante*, figuratively selling his soul to the South for monetary and political gain. Although drought took a backseat to satire in Almeida's first incursion into fiction, the disaster became the centerpiece of both his politics and his literary production shortly after. The following year he penned an influential, seven-hundred-page essay entitled *A Paraíba e seus problemas* (Paraíba and Its Problems; 1923). This work, written while he was secretary of the interior and justice of the state of Paraíba under governor João Pessoa, lays out the philosophical orientation and factual bases of nearly all his future works and political undertakings. Partially a response to pessimistic analyses of the Northeast by southern authors such as Euclides da Cunha and Francisco José de Oliveira Vianna, both of whom he engages directly, Almeida's essay discounts environmental determinism, with its emphasis on race and climate, as a factor in the underdevelopment of his state. Unable to discard completely the racialized discourse of development that continued to prevail when he was writing, he nevertheless refutes the trope of the tropical depression of rational function in his examination of the historical intermixing of races in Paraíba, arguing that any lack of intellectual development in the region is cultural, rather than racial. He postulates that this failing can easily be remedied through education, a thesis that was sustained earlier by Graça Aranha in *Canaã* (1902) and that was further developed by authors such as José Francisco de Araújo Lima in defense of the Amazon.[36]

Almeida concurs with Cunha on one point, however: that drought is largely responsible for impeding development in the region, although a much greater factor is neglect from the central government. He constructs a history of drought and development in Paraíba in which the central government continues uninterruptedly the tradition of Portu-

guese colonialism, taxing the state's economy without investing anything in the local infrastructure. To aggravate matters, catastrophic
drought routinely destroys the inroads in development made through
private initiative without federal assistance. He deeply resents the Republican government's failure to address drought and development in
the region, writing that "it was in the name of the interests of the nation
and collective well-being that the political institutions were transformed.
But in the government of the people by the people, the population of the
Northeast, precursor of the liberal cause, continues to be destined to die
of hunger" (317). He blames the southern technocracy for the problem;
their prejudices and lack of knowledge of local conditions has led them
to abandon the region to its own devices. He points out that despite the
creation of organizations such as IOCS, there were only three pluviomet-
ric stations in Paraíba, none of them in the *sertão*. How could the southern technocrats claim to understand drought when they lacked even the
most preliminary data to study the phenomenon? His essay purports to
rectify this scientific neglect; it is replete with graphs, statistics on rainfall and population growth, and historical background that contextual-
ize his arguments.

By subordinating all of Cunha's and Oliveira Vianna's arguments to
drought, and posing drought exclusively as a problem of development,
Almeida's essay coalesces all the threats into one: a simple lack of development. He reclassifies drought as an economic problem rather than one
of environmental, moral, or racial degradation. In fact, drought is secondary in his analysis; providing specific precipitation statistics, he dis-
putes the classification of the region as arid, and he points out that even
in drought years rain falls, though sparsely or unevenly. He argues that
the problem is not therefore a lack of water but, rather, insufficient distribution, a problem that could easily be remedied through the creation
of a system of reservoirs and irrigation. As no private party could possibly raise sufficient capital to undertake such massive projects, the duty
falls to the central government. In this way, Almeida rewrites earlier risk
assessments of drought in purely political terms: the Republican neglect
of drought has become the prime threat to modernization in the region.

Although fellow Paraíban Epitácio Pessoa attempted to remedy this
ignominious history of ignorance and abandonment upon assuming the
presidency in 1919, his reforms and development initiatives were discontinued by his successor, Artur Bernardes, a Mineiro who represented a
return to the Republic's standard *"café com leite"* politics. The discon-
tinuation of Pessoa's policies led to massive disillusionment with the cen-

tral government in the Northeast. This, coupled with the economic disaster heralded by the worldwide Great Depression and the assassination of northeasterner João Pessoa, who accompanied Getúlio Vargas on the ticket as candidate for the vice presidency in the elections of 1930, resulted in the region's overwhelming support for the revolutionary overthrow of the Old Republic, following what was seen as the fraudulent election of Paulista Júlio Prestes. Tellingly, Almeida formed a key part of the new regime: he was named civil "Chief of the Revolution" for the northern states during the movement to depose the government, and once the new regime was consolidated under Vargas's leadership, he assumed the central position of minister of transportation and public works. From this post he put into practice his plans for the modernization of the Northeast, adhering closely to Epitácio Pessoa's blueprint for development.

In the lulls between his political duties, Almeida penned two novels that examine the failure of institutionalized development in the Northeast: *A bagaceira*, which forms a prelude to Epitácio Pessoa's initiative, and *O boqueirão*, a bizarre novel detailing the hurdles that Pessoa's project faced in the region slated for development as well as its tragic abortion by Benavides. In the vein of realist narratives such as Eça de Queiroz's *A cidade e as serras* (*The City and the Mountains*; 1901) and Spanish American regionalist contemporaries such as Rómulo Gallegos's *Doña Bárbara* (1929), *A bagaceira* employs symbolic characters to allegorize the national disconnect between modern urbanization and the persistence of seemingly reactionary rural traditions. The novel focalizes on Lúcio, an enlightened young "son of the countryside" who has received a cultural education in the metropolitan centers of Brazil, to highlight rural underdevelopment. As usual, a beautiful but wildly uncivilized young woman, Soledade, symbolizes the solitary land, and her domestication coincides with the modernization of the agricultural economy. In Almeida's novel, however, things are decidedly more complex than in the average regionalist allegory of development, as disaster and regional politics muddy the waters.

To begin with, Almeida constructs a geographic opposition not simply between the countryside and the city but between three conflictive spaces: the *brejo*, or lush mountainous highlands of coastal Paraíba, is placed in opposition to the drought-prone *sertão* as well as to the metropole, which appears only in allusion. By no means a third mediating space, the *brejo* represents a morally and racially degraded area in which the feudal economy of the *engenho*, or sugar plantation, prevails and individual initiative is smothered by patriarchal egoism and animal instinct. In a snub to Gilberto Freyre's nascent thesis of an integrated Northeast based on the coastal "sugar civilization," Almeida describes the sugar plantation as a moral and economic wasteland inhabited by "the dregs of miscegenation," whose variegated pigmentation reflects their disordered mentalities (57).[37] As Manoel Cavalcanti Proença notes in his introduction to the novel, Almeida inverts Cunha's assertion that *sertanejos* live in "unconscious servitude" to the land owners (xxii). Here it is the variegated coastal *mestiços* who are mental slaves incapable of even minimal affectivity: "Pariahs of the sugar mill, victims of an entrenched organization of labor and a dependence that dehumanized them, they were the most insensitive to the martyrdom of the *retiradas*" (8).[38] In a notion of nationalism based on social solidarity and modern human rights, a lack of affectivity indicates inability to participate in democratic governance, as the novel's ending makes clear. In any case, Almeida redirects attention away from Cunha's view of the *sertanejos* as modernity's antagonists, rescripting the inefficient sugar plantation and its inhabitants as the real threats to economic progress and political democracy.

In contrast, the *sertão* reverts to its idealistic representation in Alencar's romanticism: beyond the stifling grip of the coastal master/slave dichotomy, it becomes a frontier of individual enterprise and wild freedom that is paradoxically upheld by an implacable moral code. Refuting Cunha's representation of the *sertanejos* as innate outlaws, the novel reframes them as the most law-abiding citizens of the nation, who, despite the absence of institutional justice in the *sertão*, adhere strictly to their own code of conduct from which any divergence is strictly punished. All violence committed by *sertanejos* in the novel is attributable to the enforcement of this code, in sharp contrast to the immorality and criminal lack of discipline that are the norm in the *brejo*. This double perspective of the *sertanejos* as rugged individualists and strict moralists allows Almeida to resolve the contradictions in the national images of them simultaneously as blood-thirsty murderers and passive drought victims. As Almeida himself writes, with a somewhat revolutionary bent, "The history of drought was a history of passivities" (9).[39] The implication is that if the *sertanejos* actively took things into their own hands, the disaster would end. In any case, Almeida's representation of the *sertanejos* as law-abiding, enterprising individualists suggests that they would make far better candidates for modernity than would the *brejeiros* that he criticizes so roundly.

On the other hand, despite Lúcio's education in the cultural centers of Brazil, the metropole does not embody modernity in the way one might expect. It appears only abstractly as the seat of the central government, and the state, in the few instances when it appears, merely represents the arbitrary, often misdirected exercise of power. As the narrator states, referring to the *sertanejos'* perception, "For them, the government was solely this notion of violence: the reinforcement of local powers, illegal imprisonment, party conflict. . . . They had never experienced any tutelary manifestation from it" (50–51).[40] In fact, the novel ends up literally putting the government on trial. In a chapter entitled "Judgment," Lúcio, in his eloquent defense of a venerable *sertanejo* refugee who killed the sugar-plantation foreman for seducing his daughter (although it turned out the foreman was only acting as the agent of Lúcio's father, the plantation owner), turns the tables on the prosecution, asking, "Who is more criminal—the prisoner who killed one man, or a society that, having the means to prevent it, allows thousands of men to die?" (134).[41] He concludes that Brazilian society, which is well aware of the ravages of drought and has the means to mitigate it, is the guilty party. Although the judge clamors for order, Lúcio's arguments eventually carry the day: the *retirante* is released, and the *sertanejo* code of justice is exonerated.

This scene verbalizes the message that the novel carries implicitly: governmental neglect is the real disaster in both the *sertão* and the *brejo*. Tellingly, Lúcio succeeds in converting his father's sugar plantation into a model of industrialized agriculture, in the process transforming the abject *brejeiros* into modern workers by providing them with fair pay, production incentives, education, and modern housing. Yet his success comes at a price: he is forced to renounce his passion for wild Soledade, who rejects him in favor of his father, and to marry the daughter of a sugar-mill owner. The union of Lúcio and Soledade, which would have symbolized the integration of the *sertão* into the modern nation, is aborted, and there is no reconciliation of the two Brazils. Instead, Soledade undomesticates Lúcio's father, returning with him to the wilds of the *sertão*, where he is killed by a rival. The novel ends with her reappearance on Lúcio's doorstep as a *retirante* of the drought of 1915, in the same way that she had materialized years before, thus highlighting the circularity of drought and its lack of resolution. Likewise, Lúcio's transformation of the sugar plantation into a utopia of capitalist progress is belied by his inability to indoctrinate his *brejeiro* workers in the human values that he ascribes to modernity. The callousness that they display toward the *retirantes* of the 1915 drought reveals that material gain has not led to the profound social transformation from a psychology of dependence to a mentality fit for democratic self-governance based on utilitarian principles. The conclusion thus becomes a question mark interrogating the methods and viability of uniform, decontextualized modernization.

A bagaceira posited the Republican government and the reactionary local oligarchy as the prime causes of underdevelopment and the suffering of drought victims in the Northeast. The Revolution of 1930 claimed to have solved the first problem, and, according to the novel, generational change would solve the second. As Almeida's report *O ciclo revolucionário do Ministério da Viação* (The Revolutionary Cycle of the Ministry of Transportation; 1934) made clear, he saw himself as Epitácio Pessoa's successor in the project to modernize the Northeast. With the southern opposition forcibly removed from the government, he believed that development would be a cinch. Unfortunately, he ran into many unforeseen obstacles, not the least of which was staunch opposition to change from the regional oligarchy, which feared that economic reform would loosen its vice grip on the local economy and politics, and that of the *sertanejos* themselves, who did not necessarily wish to relinquish their traditional way of life.

These were topics that Almeida addressed in his next two novels: *O boqueirão* and *Coiteiros*, both published in 1935. The first returns to the Republic's neglect of the region and the abortion of Epitácio Pessoa's initiative to modernize the Northeast at the hands of his successor, Artur Bernardes. As in *A bagaceira*, Almeida takes a nuanced look at the cultural and psychological implications of excessive and abrupt modernization of the rural environment. *Coiteiros* completes the obligatory triad of *sertão* themes in its examination of the phenomenon of the *cangaceiros* and its indictment of the politicians that protect them. This novel is largely a reaction to conflicts with local politicians that he experienced while attempting to carry out his "revolutionary" reforms in the northeastern economy as the minister of transportation, conflicts that led him to resign the position in 1934. He insinuates that the conservative, corrupt politicians of the local oligarchy are responsible for holding back change and destabilizing the government by sponsoring what can only be described as the terrorism of the *cangaço* in the interior.

Realizing that Getúlio Vargas's Revolution of 1930 had failed to break the power of the oligarchy or to bring about revolutionary change, Almeida challenged Vargas for the presidency in the elections of 1937, using his tenure as minister of transportation and public works as his political platform. His disillusionment with the lack of funding for drought projects led him to make the most iconic statement of the campaign, which chilled the hearts of his oligarchic antagonists: "Eu sei onde está o dinheiro" (I know where the money is). When Getúlio's supporters realized that Almeida was likely to beat him at his own populist game, they sponsored the coup that inaugurated the Estado Novo dictatorship, and Almeida became embittered with politics, not returning until 1945, when he gave an influential interview criticizing Vargas that contributed to the downfall of the regime.

Almeida's reassessment of drought in the Northeast discarded the environmental determinism (or geographic fatalism, as Araújo Lima called it) that had characterized naturalist constructions of risk in the region. He also discounted the influence of religious fanaticism that Cunha had incorporated into the formula. Almeida's construction of risk in the Northeast demystified development, positing it as a social and political problem that could be solved through education, individual initiative, institutional support, and political reform. Strangely, however, his works endowed development with its own brand of mysticism, binding together inextricably modernization with transformative love and human compassion. In any case, Almeida completed the labor of the "rehabilitation" of the *sertanejo*, rescuing this cultural figure from the determinism of earlier works, a task that had actually been initiated by Euclides da Cunha decades earlier in his self-critical reassessment of his own work.[42]

Not all of the writers of Almeida's generation agreed wholeheartedly with his reassessment of the *sertão* and the *sertanejo*, but they coincided nevertheless in inscribing drought primarily as a social and political phenomenon rooted not in racial or environmental abjection but, rather, in inequality and injustice, the central themes of Queiroz's *O quinze* (1930) and Ramos's *Vidas secas* (1938). In these novels, drought became a problem of fairness in the distribution of vulnerability and risk. Only Lins do Rego retains the older paradigm in *Pedra Bonita* (1938) and *Cangaceiros* (1953), which return to the tropes of irrational race-induced religious fanaticism and violence. Lins do Rego's departure is easily explained, however, by his adherence to Gilberto Freyre's postulation of the coastal sugar-cane plantations as the real heart of Brazil. After all, Freyre himself had voiced a similar disavowal of the *sertão* as that "other," degraded Northeast, in the introduction to *O Nordeste: Aspectos da influência da cana sobre a vida e a paisagem do Nordeste do Brasil* (The Northeast: Aspects of the Influence of Sugar Cane on Life and the Countryside in Northeastern Brazil; 1937). In any case, the Romance de 30 posited drought as a technical problem of social, political, and economic modernization, a view that was shared by Getúlio Vargas's provisional government.

The Drought Polygon

If Euclides da Cunha's work catalyzed the initial institutionalization of drought under the Republic in the creation of the IOCS in 1909, Almeida and the Romance de 30 played a similar role in Getúlio Vargas's disaster policies and, in particular, in his government's delineation of the "Polígono das Secas," or Drought Polygon, in 1936. Tellingly, Vargas placed Almeida in charge of drought works and aid programs as minister of transportation and public works, not once but twice: in 1930, following the revolution, but also when he was reelected democratically in 1950—this in spite of the years of enmity over the coup of 1937. Although Vargas and Almeida had parted ways by the time the law creating the Drought Polygon was passed in 1936, and the decree itself may have been an attempt to wrest Almeida's most persuasive theme from his hands during the election battle, there can be no doubt that the Romance de 30 influenced heavily in the renewed political currency of drought. Far before Getúlio's government decreed the legal boundaries of the Drought Polygon, they had been inscribed by regionalist literature—Ceará by Teófilo and Patrocínio, Pernambuco by Távora, and the interior of Bahia by Cunha. As federal aid came to be seen as the sole remedy for both drought and underdevelopment, inclusion in the government's geography of drought became a highly contested prize, and one literally needed to be "written in." Almeida was certainly aware of this necessity: his drought literature inscribed the state of Paraíba into the geography of disaster formerly dominated by Bahia, Ceará, and Pernambuco, and it was included in the original 1936 law decreeing the Drought Polygon. On the other hand, the state of Piauí, largely lacking novelistic representation, was excluded from the original decree, and its governor was forced to write a series of letters lobbying for inclusion when the law was revised in 1951.

The resemantization of the *sertões* of northeastern Brazil as the Drought Polygon capped the process of risk assessment and the institutionalization of drought that had begun half a century earlier during the Great Drought of 1877–1879. The naming of the Drought Polygon entailed official recognition of that "exposed wound in the nation's flesh" that Muniz de Albuquerque, Jr., perceived in the Northeast, setting in the stone tablets of the law the view of the region as a disastered geography existing in a permanent state of disequilibrium, threat, and emergency.[43] For, as Diogo Mainardi's grotesquely satirical novel *O polígono das secas* (The Drought Polygon; 1995) underscored in letters of blood (or the putrid unguent that its protagonist uses to spread infection throughout the region), the Drought Polygon constitutes a disastered space that invokes not only the natural disaster for which it was named but the entire discourse of drought, including its components of moral and physical abjection, extreme poverty, religious fanaticism, violence, banditry, political corruption, and even racial degradation—in short all the tropes written into drought by its literary assessors. No simple geophysical category, the Drought Polygon designates a permanent disaster zone populated more densely by symbols than by real people.

Disciplining Drought

Political action taken on the basis of literary risk assessment acknowledged, even if unconsciously, literature's role in the process. Policymakers continued to reference literary tropes directly and indirectly in speeches, as well as citing as authorities writers such as Almeida, Cunha, Queiroz, and Ramos, while simultaneously relegating them to the past. Once the necessary political structure had been created for dealing with drought, the disaster transformed from lay into technical problem. Although many of the initial literary assessments of drought were written by specialists, whether physicians, pharmacists, engineers, lawyers, or politicians, few of them wrote their treatises for specialized audiences. Their works had political rather than technical ends, and they were directed primarily at molding policy through public opinion.

Paradoxically, drought literature's success was its undoing. Political recognition and the institutionalization of its tropes signified the obsolescence of literary assessment of the risks posed by drought. Ultimately, the Romance de 30's postulation of drought as a social and political rather than a cultural problem relinquished control of the discourse to sociology and political science, which emerged as academic disciplines in Brazil during those same years. Influenced by the thought of John Dewey and Émile Durkheim, the group of educators that penned the 1932 "O manifesto dos pioneros da educação nova," prominent among them Fernando de Azevedo, Afrânio Peixoto, Anísio Teixeira, Roquette Pinto, Francisco Venâncio Filho, and Cecília Meirelles, were instrumental in transforming the academic panorama in Brazil, particularly in advocating higher education beyond the traditional "liberal professions" of engineering, medicine, and law.[44] The 1934 founding of Brazil's first modern university, the Universidade de São Paulo, put into practice many of this group's ideas, although ideological conflicts with Getúlio Vargas's regime forced many of them to abandon their transformative project during the Estado Novo period. Nevertheless, the 1950s and 1960s witnessed the drastic rebirth of Brazilian higher education, particularly in the institutionalization of fields such as anthropology, economics, and sociology. In fact, prominent French social scientists such as Claude Lévi-Strauss, Roger Bastide, Paul Arbousse Bastide, and Paul Hugnon lent a hand in founding programs at Brazilian universities similar to those created by Durkheim in France and Dewey at the New School for Social Research in New York.[45] The establishment of these programs cemented the professionalization of the social sciences in Brazil, taking over terrain that had been occupied until then by literature and spurring passionate debate over literature's relevance to social analysis in works such as Antonio Candido's *Literatura e sociedade* (1965).

As Nísia Trindade Lima reveals throughout *Um sertão chamado Brasil* (A *Sertão* Called Brazil), in the first half of the twentieth century, many of Brazil's first professional anthropologists and sociologists, among them Roquette Pinto, Belisário Penna, and Emílio Willems, studied the *sertão* and the role drought played in the formation of culture there. Subsequently, geographer Josué de Castro, economist Celso Furtado and his Grupo de Trabalho para o Desenvolvimento do Nordeste (Northeast Development Work Group), and countless other anthropologists, biologists, climatologists, ethnographers, and engineers applied their expertise to the problem of drought. The detailed studies compiled by these specialists redrew the vague literary geography of drought into a minutely detailed map of the problem. They did not, however, discard completely the literary discourse of drought that preceded them. In fact, it is surprisingly common to find references to literary sources in their works, and, tellingly, a disproportionate number of them claim Euclides da Cunha as precursor. Likewise, literary tropes of drought abound in their works, including many with little scientific basis, although they are often resemantized with more technical wording. In this way, the science of drought in the Northeast acknowledges its genealogy in literature even as it displaces it.

Literature, divorced from its role in risk assessment, had only two futures: it could dispute the new, technocratic version of events or accept its destiny and renounce its scientific pretensions. It did both: leftists such as Jorge Amado and Graciliano Ramos in the 1930s and the filmmakers of the Cinema Novo in the 1960s produced versions of drought that contradicted governmental assurances that the problem was nearing resolution, while a new folkloric aesthetics borrowed from northeastern popular poetry took root in the work of authors such as Ariano Suassuna and João Cabral de Melo Neto. Both tendencies were nourished by the brutal drought of 1951–1953, which thrust the disaster into the national consciousness once again, flooding southern cities with hundreds of thousands of *retirantes* transported on modified trucks known as *paus-de-araráss* because of the parrotlike way in which refugees perched on them. The ravages of the new drought led many intellectuals to question the efficiency of the governmental institutionalization of drought. In particular, journalist Antonio Callado shocked the nation with his reports on the northeastern oligarchy's manipulation of emergency funds and the public works projects of the DNOCS (Departamento Nacional de Obras Contra as Secas) for their own profit.[46]

On the other hand, the waves of northeastern migrants brought their traditional poetry and song with them to southern cities, where they were reframed as folk art and became immensely popular in a variety of media, from the voice of singer/songwriter/radio personality Luiz Gonzaga to literature, art, and television. The folklorization of drought culture clearly served a purpose in the ongoing search for national heritage: not coincidently, the I Congresso Nacional do Folclore (First National Congress of Folklore) was celebrated in 1951, accompanying the foundation of the Comissão Nacional do Folclore (National Commission of Folklore). Shortly after, in 1958, A Campanha de Defesa do Folclore (Campaign to Defend Folklore) provided an even greater impulse to the move to institutionalize popular culture. Undoubtedly, the classification of *sertanejo* culture as national folklore had both positive and negative implications: it represented a move to preserve cultural practices that were beginning to disappear under the onslaught of modernity, but it also signified a darker maneuver by the state to control and relegate to the past a live culture with a stubborn history of resisting modernization. Similarly, the rescription of literary representations of drought as folklore stifled any serious discussion of the questions they raised about the disaster, as folklorization reinforced the vision of the *sertão* as the constitutive negative to modernity. The subordination of more human, literary representations of drought to technical specialization—even when they had brought it on themselves, with their pretensions and deference to objectivity—signified the conversion of individuals into statistics and of human rights into bureaucratic politics. And the final step in the process, the folklorization of drought narratives, implied their relegation to myth, where they could no longer play a role in history.

The post-1930s stagnation of the dialogue on the causes and effects of drought that Villa and Alcântara noted in their comments (cited in the introduction to this chapter) was not simply a case of the exhaustion of lines of research or literary possibilities or, obviously, the eradication of the problem. Rather, the uncritical repetition of the tropes of drought over half a century created a master narrative from which there could be little or no deviance, effectively fettering the possibilities for wider literary exploration of the phenomenon. The roots of the genre of drought narratives in literary naturalism, combined with obligatory sensitivity in avoiding the reification of disaster victims, forced literature into a straightjacket of realist representation that left little room for self-reflection or sounding out other possibilities, which could have included exploring in greater depth the psychology of disaster through symbolism or fantasy, or more deconstructive approaches involving the use of language play, humor, or satire. As many critics have noted, drought narratives are often as desolate and desiccated as the disastered landscape itself, a fact that, while dazzling in Ramos's *Vidas secas*, impoverishes the genre as a whole. Tellingly, more penetrating narratives such as those of João Guimarães Rosa and João Ubaldo Ribeiro, though set in the *sertão*, deftly sidestep the issue of drought, freeing themselves to plumb the depths of human psychology and the metaphysics of modernity without hindrance from the overbearing weight of the prior disaster discourse. Perhaps the unique exception to this trend and one of the only recent novels to deal with drought, Mainardi's *O polígono das secas* (1995) does little to rectify the stagnation in the dialogue on drought: its narrator does his utmost to mutilate, defile, murder, and eradicate altogether (rather than to revise) the discourse of drought and *sertanejo* culture in general. In any case, the technification of the disaster during the first half of the twentieth century took drought off literature's hands in perpetuity. The literary assessment of risk had become outmoded, relegated to folklore, and though it still played a key role as point of reference in the national past, its days as an agent in the fomentation of dialogue and policy had come to an end.

Coda

Having dedicated this chapter almost exclusively to the role that literature played in assessing the risks posed by drought to Brazilian national projects of modernization and democratic rule, the reader will rightly wonder whether I have overstated the case. Was the perception and management of the disaster controlled completely by lettered outsiders who never suffered the effects of drought personally? Did the drought victims themselves and their hereditary disaster culture play no role in deciding their own destinies, taking no hand in risk assessment or the institutionalization of the disaster? Clearly, the authors of drought narratives had much greater access to the political system than did the *sertanejo* drought victims; nearly all the authors were from the middle and upper classes, and many were involved directly in the political decisions that shaped successive responses to the disaster. Undoubtedly, the great majority of these writers and politicians wished sincerely to mitigate the suffering of drought victims as well as to promote development in the region; however, local politics also entered into play, and many members of the oligarchy were loathe to cede economic or political power to the subaltern *sertanejos*. The testimonial mode of these authors' works— whether actual testimonial texts or fictionalized representations—became a way of giving a voice to the voiceless, but as myriad critics have pointed out, the testimonial process is imperfect at best. Although the testimonial is undoubtedly useful for raising awareness among middle- and upper-class readers, all too often the author or editor of the subaltern voice turns it to his or her own ends. Critics such as John Beverley have shown that in spite of testimonial literature's good intentions, it can actually end up reinforcing the subaltern position of the very people it purports to help.[47] The fact is that often as not, the people represented gain little or no direct political (or economic) agency from the testimonial process.

Without a doubt, local culture was an object of study of nearly all the authors of Brazilian drought narratives, but their views on the issue were readings from without, in even the most conscientious cases constituting classic reifications of the subaltern subject. Beyond common criminality, the capacity for popular agency was simply edited out of most of these stories. Even politically active, leftist authors such as Graciliano Ramos and Jorge Amado (in *Vidas secas* and *Seara vermelha*, respectively) found no potential for subaltern action or engagement in politics beyond emigration, which opened the possibilities for education and indoctrination in Marxist ideology. Nothing could be further from the truth, however: though often marginalized politically, socially, and economically, the inhabitants of the *sertão* have a long tradition of working consciously from both within and outside the system of risk assessment instituted by the state, assuming an active role in disaster response and management. Although I cannot enter into great detail here, I wish to raise at least some bare considerations relating to local risk assessment and popular agency in governmental policy on drought.

Far before the government took an interest in drought management, locals affected by the disaster developed an elaborate system for predicting and assessing the severity of drought based on the close observation of natural phenomenon. Collectively classified as *experiências* (trials or experiments), *sertanejos* learned to judge the probabilities of drought by carefully studying their environment over hundreds of years. Brazilian doctor and amateur folklorist Josa Magalhães, in his seminal article, "Previsões folclóricas das secas e dos invernos no Nordeste brasileiro" (Folkloric Prediction of Drought and the Rainy Season in Northeastern Brazil), groups the *experiências* into several general categories: those associated with Catholic rituals and the calendar of saints; the behavior of certain animals, insects, and birds; those related to plant life cycles; and a miscellaneous section including such diverse activities as breaking bread, numerology, astronomical observation, and dream interpretation.[48] As fascinating as the *experiências* may be, there is not space here to go into exhaustive detail, a project that has already been undertaken by Getúlio César, Magalhães, Alberto Galeno, and Alfredo Macedo Gomes in any case. Some brief examples from each area should suffice to provide the reader with a general sense of their importance in the drought culture of the *sertão*.

There are two primary religious dates associated with the popular prediction of drought. The first is the thirteenth of December, *Dia de Santa Luzia* (St. Lucy's day). The *experiência* requires that one set out six or twelve small salt crystals overnight, exposing them to the open air. Each salt crystal represents one of the months of the coming year; the amount of water absorbed from the air by each crystal foretells the amount of rain that will fall in the corresponding month. The second key date is the nineteenth of March, day of the *Santo das Chuvas*, São José (the Rain Saint, St. Joseph). It is widely believed that if precipitation falls on São José's day, the rainy season is assured, while if it fails to rain by or on this date, drought is inevitable. Galeno mentions that some *sertanejos* hold so much stock in this belief that they initiate the *retirada*, or journey to places of refuge, immediately following a negative *experiência* of São José (7). In any case, Macedo Gomes notes that this day, March 19, is the latest date by which farmers can plant their crops and still anticipate a full growing season, making the question of whether rain will fall after São José's day somewhat academic for a culture that traditionally depends almost entirely on local agriculture for its food supply (149).

The majority of *experiências* that rely on observing the behavior of animals, birds, and insects deal with reproduction, migration patterns, and abnormal activity. Likewise, the *experiências* that take plants as their subject typically employ criteria of abundance, although the out-of-season blooming of certain plants and trees is a sure sign of drought to come. Galeno provides an engaging example that uses rhyme as a memory aid, a key strategy in the oral transmission of disaster culture from one generation to the next: "matápasto florou, inverno acabou" (the Mata-Pasto plant bloomed, the rainy season's doomed; 14). A variety of astronomical and climactic phenomena serve as material for popular *experiências* as well, such as a pair cited by César that judge the probabilities for rain according to the colors and extension of the summer sunset: "vermelhão pro sertão, chuva no chão" (crimson above the *sertão*, rain on the ground; 16) and "vermelhão na baixa, é sol que racha" (crimson down low, the sun's burning glow; 17).

To these observations relying directly on natural phenomena one must add a host of more apparently arbitrary phenomena. Numerology plays a role in what Macedo Gomes calls the "logic of the eras," in which practitioners have inferred that years ending in 4 and 5 historically have good rains, while drought is much more probable in years ending in 1, 2, and 3 (142–46). Magalhães also describes a singular *experiência* based on the sound made when the priest breaks the Eucharist bread during the New Year's midnight mass (257). If the cracking noise is crisp and clear, drought is to be expected, but if it makes more of a dull sound, humidity is present and the rains are on the way.

Clearly, some techniques employed by the *sertanejos* to predict the probability of drought are more esoteric than others. At first glance from the modern eye, many appear arbitrary and even downright laughable. Nevertheless, even though they may be imbued with religious symbolism and superstition, the majority of the *experiências* reveal novel ways of measuring scientific phenomena using close observation and local materials. Brazilian researchers have shown that even seemingly outlandish *experiências* such as the salt crystals of Santa Luzia and the breaking of the Eucharist actually represent ways of measuring the relative humidity in the atmosphere without instrumentation, while biologists have long recognized that animals frequently sense changes in barometric pressure that humans rarely perceive without the aid of measuring devices.[49] As a practice, the *experiências* constitute a kind of "popular empiricism" that, while not always completely accurate, examine and collate a wide range of measurements to calculate the probability for drought in any given year. In this light the *experiências* reveal remarkable sophistication: they demonstrate a well-developed methodology of popular risk assessment that remains nearly autonomous from outside manipulation, even when its practice has declined with recent advances in climatology and modern skepticism of local knowledges.[50]

The popular response to drought is not limited to prediction, however, nor is it wholly autonomous from the institutional system. Traditional culture in the region amassed a host of strategies for responding to the disaster, ranging from forming social networks of assistance to eating *comida braba* (wild foods) to the *retirada*, or journey to places of refuge in the greener mountains or on the coast.[51] The advent of external emergency aid and the governmental institutionalization of drought did not mean that local residents abandoned completely these traditional survival strategies, particularly given the fickleness of successive government responses to drought.[52] Nonetheless, as the government put into place its strategies and networks of emergency aid, the *sertanejos* rapidly assimilated the political developments, creating new, highly effective strategies for interfacing with the system. Although literary drought narratives typically depict drought refugees as hapless beggars waiting passively for government handouts from corrupt officials who take advantage of them, such representations divulge only the part of the picture that served the authors' political agenda. In reality, *sertanejos* developed a variety of mechanisms for taking control of their situation through attracting aid and manipulating the system of emergency funding, even in the face of governmental inaction, corruption, or denial, as was the case in the drought of 1970, in which the military junta staunchly refused to declare a state of emergency.

A key strategy that *sertanejos* use to increase awareness of their plight during drought years involves making their suffering visible through public performance. No one would deny the very real suffering of those affected by drought and starvation; nevertheless, *sertanejos* have developed cultural formulas through which they communicate their victimhood and need for public assistance, modes of making their suffering known that have become, in lieu of a better concept, "canonical" due to their effectiveness. The act of taking on the collective identity of the *retirante* is a powerful step. The mass pilgrimage on foot or by bus or train to centers of public aid draws enormous attention to the plight of displaced persons, with all the connotations of mass homelessness and insecurity that their simple presence evokes. Upon arriving at their destination, the occupying of public spaces, plazas, parks, and streets confronts the public and political eye: it becomes impossible to ignore them. The lack of sanitation and adequate clothing makes all the more evident their abjection. Whether they garner reactions of anathema or compassion, emaciated, unwashed bodies draped in rags burn their image into the eye of the beholder.

At the same time, the *retirante* identity has become highly codified through its cultural representations, functioning almost as an icon of drought whose presence sets into motion the emergency response machinery. In this way, the mere arrival of *retirantes* in the state and federal political centers becomes a performance of subalternity that, paradoxically, results in the rekindling of collective agency as a method for forcing state action. In fact, the performance is so effective that it can even be carried out by proxy; self-representation of drought victims in popular music and the *literatura de cordel* has a similar effect in maintaining the disaster in the public eye, if somewhat diminished, stimulating the audience to take action. Through the public and literary performance of victimhood and need, *sertanejos* affected by drought are able to acquire a modicum of control over their destinies

Victimhood and passivity are not the only modes of performance employed by drought victims, however. Macedo Gomes has insinuated that the "*saques*," or collective raiding of government and private food stores, also constitute a powerful public performance that stimulates the government to action (185). Although the *saque* presents itself within the same framework of desperate need arising from victimhood, it also holds a veiled political threat, communicating the drought victims' potential for organized, even violent physical action. Indeed, throughout the history of drought in northeastern Brazil, authorities have read *saques* as possible preludes to social revolution, forcing them to act rapidly to mollify the masses and defuse tensions. Even though *saques* occasionally have the negative side effect of inducing state repression, they are particularly effective in communicating the gravity of the problem and its possible consequences, as well as the need for immediate resolution.

These brief examples, though far from complete, reveal that the residents of the Brazilian Drought Polygon, despite their typical exclusion from the political process of risk assessment and the institutionalization of drought, have exercised and continue to exercise a great degree of agency and autonomy. In fact, the actions of the drought victims themselves are the best indicator of the degree of interpenetration between the formal and informal systems of risk assessment and response. On the one hand, the *sertanejos* have become adept at reading and negotiating the public perception as well as the political machinery of drought. On the other, the government often puts off responding to the disaster until it receives indicators of its social effects, which are communicated to it by the drought victims themselves using the performative mechanisms I have described. A kind of informal, backdoor emergency "understanding" or arrangement between the government and drought victims depending on grudging collaboration has thus arisen, which, although far from optimal, retains a certain functionality. It has become a necessity due to the ever-increasing complexity of the national assessment of the risks posed by drought, which has become so entangled that it is nearly immobilized, having grown to envelope everything from allegations of institutionalized corruption known as the "Drought Industry" and the continued struggle over regional politics to the effects of massive migration on southern cities. In other words, risk assessment has become nonoperational due to the overabundance of variables. Only partial, politicized interpretations of the disaster are now possible, which do not achieve the consensus required for effective risk assessment and mitigation. Although the informal system of drought response fails to address the unequal distribution of risk and vulnerability that gives rise to the social disaster, it nevertheless acts with a certain efficiency: in crisis, the government grudgingly cuts through the bureaucracy surrounding drought to provide emergency aid, and the drought victims' suffering is mitigated to a sufficient degree that they do not explode in open rebellion against the government. Once the drought has subsided, they return to their traditional autonomy until the cycle repeats itself.

The case of drought in northeastern Brazil is highly unique in that it is a recurring natural disaster that has become canonical through repetition as well as cultural mediation, arriving at the point where it is seen as an integral trope in Brazilian national culture. Despite or perhaps because of its national primacy, the literary mediation of drought never ceded political agency to the victims it represented; therefore, those who were most affected by the disaster were forced to develop the alternate strategies for interfacing with power that I have outlined. Somewhat surprisingly, given the uniqueness of Brazilian drought culture, one finds parallels in cases throughout world history when disaster victims have had little or no access to channels of power and aid.

I would argue that more than contextual parallels, these similarities depend on the relationship between disaster victims and specific modes of representation, especially those of the media. In order to attract assistance, disaster victims must place themselves in the public eye, at times through physical presence as refugees but most often by becoming newsworthy. Mass news reporting developed as a genre in western Europe following the invention of the Gutenberg press and was subsequently exported throughout the world; it is therefore unsurprising that similar modes of representation reappear globally.[53] At the same time, journalistic modes of visual representation (interviews, panoramic shots, close-ups, etc.) configure the position of the reader/viewer in relation to the object of reporting. Educated in these genres due to prior experience as viewer, an imaged subject becomes conscious of transitioning into object and is able to stage the representation, presenting oneself in a way that communicates one's own message as much as that of the photographer (Barthes 11–12). In this way, the subject conserves a degree of agency in the midst of objectification.

3 Volcanic Identities

Explosive Nationalism and the Disastered Subject in Central American Literature

With a volcanic soul I entered this hard life.
— Rubén Darío, "Momotombo"

Oh, belatedness of fire, of the hurricane, of lightning!
— Miguel Ángel Asturias, "¡Salve, Guatemala!"

VOLCANIC ERUPTIONS FIGURE AMONG the most destructive natural forces conceivable in the human imagination. Memories of the incredible devastation wreaked by volcanoes on human populations from Pompeii, Italy, to Krakatau, Indonesia, and Paricutín, Mexico, linger on in the collective imagination and mythology far beyond the effects of the disasters themselves. Visions of silent cities immersed in stone and, in the case of Pompeii, unsuspecting humans converted instantaneously into monuments to human fragility give material form to millenary fears of an antagonistic nature. Far from the loving mother of human evolution, this vindictive nature stalks us from just beyond the walls of civilization, lying in wait permanently and impatiently for the chance to devour us in a single gulp. Before the nuclear era, at least, volcanic eruptions embodied the nearest thing to total annihilation that humans could envision.

For people living in volcanic geographies, however, volcanoes' looming presence means much more: dominating the cultural as well as the geological horizon, they play a wide range of roles in the construction of individual, social, and environmental identities, through both symbolism and lived experience. To be certain, those who live "under the volcano," to pilfer Malcolm Lowry's title, reside permanently in the awareness of potential doom; consequently, they must devise coping strategies for dealing with the psychological trauma that this implies. Many of these coping devices are cultural, ranging from local personification or deification of the agent of destruction (the residents of the flanks of Po-

pocatépetl in Mexico refer to the fitful giant intimately as Popo or Don Goyo, for example, while the association of volcanoes with deities such as the Roman god Vulcan or Tlaloc and Pacha Mama in the Americas abound) to myth making and its modern equivalent in music, literature, art, and film.

On the other hand, the shear power of volcanic eruptions translates into equally forceful metaphors in social and political discourse. Unlike other natural disasters such as hurricanes and earthquakes, the lasting physical presence of volcanoes scores the geographical and cultural landscape with inescapable reminders of the impermanence and violent mutability of the very element that grounds our conception of stability: the earth itself.[1] This constant, overshadowing physical presence endows volcanoes with cultural significance that cannot be matched even by recurring disasters such as drought in northeastern Brazil, in which decades may pass between catastrophic events. More than the disasters engendered by the volcanic eruptions themselves, it is the potentiality of eruption that inscribes volcanic geography with such powerful cultural symbolism and utility in the construction of individual, collective, and national identities.

Volcanic identities play off concepts of self rooted in the land; but paradoxically, volcanic land embodies the potential for explosive transformation rather than the immutable groundedness that one normally associates with emplaced identities. In volcanic identities, external nature and the nature of the self converge not through shared experience or human cultivation of the land, as in the Latin American regionalist novels, but because the environment and the self are seen as sharing as their essential characteristic the potential for violent eruption. Ironically, or perhaps purposefully given the political and economic instability that has historically plagued the nations in question, these volcanic identities anchor themselves in the enduring certainty of disruption, thus securing stability from a geography of instability. In this sense, they engage mathematician John Allen Paulos's maxim that "uncertainty is the only certainty that there is, and knowing how to live with insecurity is the only security" (v).

Clearly, identities rooted in the capacity for eruption are highly useful in projects of political transformation, but political actors who wish to engage them must also develop containing mechanisms if they hope to avoid being consumed by the flames that they fan. Harnessing volcanic imagery through historical narrative is one central strategy for containing explosive identities, particularly at the national level. For instance, the metaphor of volcanic eruption acquired historical centrality as a national trope in nations that based their political legitimacy on violent social struggle, as is the case with Spanish American colonies that framed their independence movements as popular uprisings against a foreign power. The use of volcanic imagery in foundational narratives creates the impression that the national geography itself joins the rebellion against external oppression, while simultaneously disciplining potentially explosive identities by inscribing them within frameworks of action mediated by the state. Similarly, in nations in which volcanoes dominate the geography, institutionalization transforms them into markers of political spaces rather than of geophysical processes. National imaginaries appeal to volcanoes as centripetal focal points in the construction and reproduction of national heritages and histories: the volcanic geography forms a kind of monumental landscape that inspires patriotic sentiments and memory as well as uniting the nation visually.[2]

The basing of national legitimacy on volcanic tropes is a highly volatile proposition, however, leaving it vulnerable to inversion and questioning of projects of internal colonialism. The volcanic metaphor of a nation forged by fire is often turned on its head by proponents of social revolution, coming to symbolize internal class warfare between the impoverished masses and the political and economic elite. In this revised version of the metaphor, the lower strata of society, that most closely tied to the land itself, erupts violently to overthrow the superficial, Europeanized or US-backed oligarchy. The national essence, forced into the substrata of the national soil by oppression from above, erupts forth to take its rightful place on the surface, purging with fire all nonnative elements. And clearly, this metaphor of social eruption has racial as well as social implications. As much as José Martí may have argued for a kind of postrace autochthony based on tilling the land figuratively and literally, the majority of Latin American social representations posit the "children of the earth" as the indigenous, and it is their culture that will burst forth from its bowels to remake the national landscape in their image.

It is no accident that Nicaraguan poet Rubén Darío's "A Roosevelt" (1905) employs volcanic imagery to describe what most Spanish Americans viewed as the disastrous politics of interventionism following the hand that the United States took in Panama's 1903 secession from Colombia.[3] If relatively infrequent in Darío's poetry, which tends to privilege intimate or abstract spaces over local landscapes, volcanic imagery is ubiquitous in Central American cultural representations. Nearly all Spanish American nations' geographies have been sculpted by the volcanic activity of the Pacific Ring of Fire that wells up between tectonic plates, but perhaps in none do volcanoes hold such a central position in the national imaginary as in the Central American nations of Costa Rica, El Salvador, Guatemala, and Nicaragua. This is partially due, of course, to practical considerations of scale: one is rarely, if ever, out of sight of volcanoes in any of these nations, and volcanoes constitute their most imposing geological features, orientating their viewers toward the heart of the nation and away from the dispersion and dependence on foreign shores that the equally omnipresent coasts symbolize. On the other hand, volcanoes have influenced nearly every aspect of life in these countries, from endowing their soil with the fertility of volcanic ash to affecting the climate, dictating the social geography, molding history, and occasionally sowing terror and death in eruptions and mudslides.

Rather than focusing on the political circumstances surrounding a particular disaster event, as did the previous two chapters, I scrutinize here the centrality of volcanic imagery to politicized Central American cultural identities at the local, national, and regional international scales. I am particularly interested in the way that volcanic imagery is used to mediate interactions between individual and collective identities and the state. As the first part of the chapter shows, volcanoes figure frequently as benign beacons of nationalism in official Central American iconography from independence on. I explore national iconographies of volcanoes in national heraldry and Rubén Darío's poem "Momotombo" (1907), analyzing the way in which volcanic landscapes are endowed with cultural and political memory and symbolism.

Nationalist concepts of landscape as heritage often lead to the exclusion of certain groups from the national conceptual geography, however, and the long history of conflict between ethnic groups and social classes in Central America led to competing claims to ownership of the volcanic landscape. The second part of the chapter focuses on the construction of identities that resist the imposition of nationalistic iconography over their lived landscape, turning volcanic imagery against autocratic symbolic orders and emphasizing the metaphorical potential of eruption as social revolution. I study the elaboration of a volcanic topography of the individual in the poetry of Guatemalan writer Luis de Lión, as well as the way in which he creates a collective identity of resistance based on the lived experience of the Volcán de Agua. I then turn to more negative associations in which volcanic tremors suggest the immanence of a traumatic schism in individual as well as social identities due to psychological trauma inflicted on the individual living under repressive regimes, re-

sulting in representations of what I call the "disastered" subject. In this
section, I base myself primarily on *Cenizas de Izalco* (*Ashes of Izalco*;
1966), a novel cowritten by Salvadoran Claribel Alegría and American
Darwin Flakoll. Finally, I continue with my discussion of *Cenizas de
Izalco* as well as Manlío Argueta's *Magic Dogs of the Volcanoes/Perros
mágicos de los volcanes* (1990), Roque Dalton's "Parábola a partir de la
vulcanología revisionista" (Parable Derived from Revisionist Volcanology; 1974), and José Coronel Urtecho's parodic "Oda al Mombacho"
(1931) to reveal how institutionalized representations of volcanoes were
rewritten as tropes of social revolution, which were in turn reincorpo-
rated into the national imaginary following the triumph of the Sandinista revolution in Nicaragua in 1979 and the peace accord that ended the
Salvadoran civil war in 1992.

The Volcanic Nation: Fiery Nationalism and Emblematic Landscapes

The concept of national landscapes incorporates both old and new visions of humans' relationships with our environment. Humans have always identified with the places we inhabit, but up until the rise of the
nation-state, territoriality tended to be delimited by the centrality of
presence rather than fixed borders. In the nineteenth century, however,
the expansion of colonial capitalism coupled with rapid advancements
in communications and transportation made territorial control possible in ways that had never before existed, turning the national eye out-
ward, away from the center toward its borders.[4] Controlling and patrol-
ling the borders between nation-states became the measure of national
territoriality. This centrality of the margins ran counterintuitive to the
way in which humans had related to their lived spaces up until that moment, however, leading to conflicting symbolisms in national imaginaries. On the one hand, borders were fixed symbolically through the use
of territorial signifiers such as national maps that blanked out or dis-
colored adjacent states and territories, thus creating conceptual separation where often no natural divisions existed. As Kenneth Olwig states,
"The tendency to see the shape of a nation as a body-like organic whole
is enhanced by the fact that many national maps simply leave out adjacent states, or represent them as empty space" (77). Furthermore, J. B.
Harley notes that maps have few genuinely "popular, alternative, or subversive modes of expression," as they are "preeminently a language of
power, not of protest" ("Maps" 301). In this sense, the mapping of borders expresses the political power of those who inscribe them, as well

as the subalternity of those who do not have access to the national symbolic landscape.

On the other hand, the national imaginary elaborated a cardinal vocabulary based on the human body and its relation to its surroundings in order to conserve the conceptual centrality of lived space: terms such as *homeland* and *heartland* abound in this discursive construction of the nation as an organic whole.[5] As Oliver Zimmer has suggested regarding the position of the Alps in Swiss nationalism, these central spaces in the national body were imagined as a physical dimension of the national past that had played a key role in determining the "national character" (243–45). In other words, the "heartland" was conceived of as the internal, geographical embodiment of national moral qualities and social values. This comforting conceptual geography offered stability and an inward orientation amid the uncertainty of rapidly changing political configurations and economic expansionism (Zimmer 243).

If the Alps came to represent the essence of the nation for the Swiss, volcanoes became national emblems for Central American nations constantly threatened by foreign intervention. As Allaine Cerwonka comments, citing Antonio Gramsci, the impulse to essentialize the national geography intensifies when a nation encounters "deterritorialization," or increased transnational flows, as a result of both colonization and decolonization, foreign interventionism, and global trade (6). The Central American volcano drew the national eye inward and upward, away from the coasts that had become sites of foreign penetration. Indeed, the volcano as symbol embodied the sense of mountains as natural fortresses and repositories of essential, even divine knowledge as well as the potential for eruptive violence in defense of the nation. This symbolism worked particularly well within national and regional Central American foundational narratives, which situated the legitimacy of the nation in violence against foreign aggressors, whether Spanish colonizers, Mexico (which attempted to annex Central America directly following independence in 1821), American William Walker and his army of filibusters, or US military, political, and economic intervention in the twentieth century. At the same time, Olwig notes that national identity is most often viewed as a natural rather than artificial phenomenon: *natural, national,* and *native* all share the Latinate prefix *nat-*, meaning "birth" (73). In the Central American imaginary, volcanoes exteriorize the native essence, dredging up national landscapes from deep within the earth.

Tellingly, the nationalistic use of the volcanic landscape was present in the earliest visual representations of Central American autonomy following independence. The official coat of arms of the ephemeral Provincias Unidas del Centro de América (United Provinces of Central America, 1823–1825) depicts five stylized volcanoes, each of which represents one of the five member provinces (El Salvador, Guatemala, Honduras, Nicaragua, and Costa Rica). This confederation existed on and off throughout the nineteenth century, changing names and members frequently. After 1825, it endured in a new form as the República Federal Centroamericana (Federal Republic of Central America), but a civil war from 1838 to 1841 resulted in its dissolution into separate nations corresponding roughly to the colonial departments delineated by the Spanish. Subsequent attempts at restoring regional unity, such as the Federación de Centroamérica (Central American Federation, 1851) and the República Mayor de Centroamérica (Greater Republic of Central America, 1898), were short-lived. Despite the drastic changes in political organization, however, successive coats of arms retained a similar composition, highlighting the volcano as a unifying symbol in the midst of political dissolution, civil war, and regional rivalries.[6]

The Central American federation's coat of arms first appeared on February 20, 1822, on a flag designed by Coronel Manuel José Arce that was presented to Salvadoran troops who went off to battle Mexico for independence.[7] Following the triumph of the Central American forces, the flag was adopted by the National Constitutive Assembly of the United Provinces on August 21, 1823.[8] The configuration of the coat of arms varied slightly in successive iterations, but it maintained the key elements of the five volcanoes (except for that of the 1851 Central American Federation, which had only had three member states) inscribed within an equilateral triangle. A wake symbolizing progress led across the sea to the volcanoes, which were illuminated from above by the red Phrygian cap, icon of liberty and equality during the French Revolution, and an overarching rainbow that united the five volcanoes in peaceful fraternity.[9] In the original coat of arms, the triangle was further bound by a circle bearing the words "Provincias Unidas del Centro de América."

The importance of the national landscape for Latin American nations anxious to establish territorial and cultural autonomy from colonial powers is well documented in the literature of the independence period. Poems such as Cuban José María Heredia's "A Emilia" (1824) and Venezuelan Andrés Bello's "Silva a la agricultura de la zona tórrida" ("Ode to Tropical Agriculture"; 1826–1827) sexualized local landscapes in terms of the female body, as the site of national economic production as well as the reproduction of the national subject. Like José Martí's "Nuestra

América" (1895), which was written in a similar mode three-quarters of a century later, these works deploy tropes in which the male patriarchal founder legitimizes himself as autochthonous (despite his European or mixed-race origins) by cultivating the native, female land-body. In this imaginary, sex as metaphor for the foundational act of nationality involves the intertwining of the masculine national subject with the archetypically passive, female landscape.

This trope becomes somewhat more complex when the national landscape is volcanic in origin, however. Passivity cannot be assigned uncritically to a landscape that threatens cataclysmic movement. The Central American nationalist imaginary engaged two primary strategies to domesticate the phallic violence associated with volcanic eruptions: the conceptual delimitation of threatening elements and incorporation of the volcano's masculine symbolism into the national cultural landscape. Artistic depictions were central in this process of transforming volcanoes into safe, national icons. In the coat of arms, the five volcanoes are rendered geometrically, made to resemble man-made pyramids in a heraldic motif rather than uncontrollable features of a threatening landscape. Furthermore, these volcanoes are inscribed within the formal perfection of an equilateral triangle, delineating figurative borders that contain the volcanoes' potential for violent eruption as well as converging the nation's physical geography with the ordered masculine, geometric logic of the Enlightenment. The positioning within the triangle of the volcanoes below, with the rainbow above, and the Phrygian cap as pupil in the center conforms the Freemason "Eye of Providence" symbol that appeared commonly in independence-era texts, engaging the trope of divine oversight of human and natural affairs to deposit yet another layer of safety over the volcanic imagery. In addition, the placement of the darker green volcanoes between the light blue of the seas on either side makes it appear as if the volcanoes themselves emanate light. Not only are they illuminated by the Phrygian cap, but they also become illuminating beacons of liberty and equality in their own right.

The conversion of natural geological features into ideological symbols results in the conflation of the volcanic geography with the national project: the volcanoes come to symbolize the masculine principle in a perfectly ordered, natural national foundation narrative. The prevalence of masculine elements does not mean that the trope of the feminine "*madre patria*" (literally "mother-fatherland") is abandoned entirely, however: the entire collage is inscribed within the circular border of the seal, suggesting the union of the masculine (triangular) and the feminine (circular) in the concept of nationality. Furthermore, the lush green color of the volcanoes together with the depiction of water, whose apparent passivity and enveloping properties are often associated with female sexuality in patriarchal societies, suggests a return to the tropes of feminine fertility invoked by poets such as Bello and Heredia. In this way, the coat of arms coalesces masculine and feminine tropes in its representation of the national landscape, depicting the volcano as patriarchal founder and protector of the fertile female landscape. The destructive potential of the volcano is harnessed in defense of the nation, serving as the counterpart to the female reproductive potential of the land, which is in turn fertilized by the emission of volcanic ash. Through this symbolism, the national political project roots itself in the natural authenticity of the volcanic landscape. Volcanoes become heritage, and the coat of arms becomes a geography of nationalism, a conceptual map of the nation.

Although the Central American union had a relatively brief and tumultuous existence, even after it disbanded, nations such as Nicaragua and El Salvador conserved versions of the original coat of arms on their flags, in part to dispute each other for political legitimacy as the direct inheritors of the original Republic. Costa Rica has abandoned the original coat of arms, but its seal conserves three stylized volcanoes, and Honduras's coat of arms also features a lone volcano, perhaps to emphasize its autonomy from its more politically prominent neighbors. Only Guatemala has eschewed completely the original coat of arms, which, when contextualized, must be seen as a conscious rejection of the political dominance of El Salvador and Nicaragua during periods of confederation as well as a rejection of symbolism that heightens ethnic divisions, as I study in depth further on in this chapter. In any case, it is evident that volcanic imagery became canonical in the construction of nationality throughout Central American history and that its centrality in the national imaginary continues unabated today.

Volcanic Subjectivity in the National Imaginary

Strangely enough, one of the first narratives that explicitly linked Central American volcanoes with nationalistic resistance to the colonial imposition of identities was not written by a Central American nationalist at all. In a burst of romantic exoticism inspired by a passage in E. G. Squier's *Travels in Central America* (1853), iconic French author Victor Hugo penned a fanciful poem entitled "Les raisons du Momotombo" (Momotombo's Reasoning) that narrates a verbal duel during the colonial period between a Spanish priest and Nicaraguan volcano Momotombo, personified as a wise indigenous chieftain.[10] The Spanish priest has been charged with baptizing all the pagan volcanoes of the New World in order to reduce the incidence of earthquakes in the region. Flame-crowned Momotombo, unique among his fellow volcanoes, refuses to allow himself to be baptized, alleging that the Spanish god is as demanding of human sacrifice as was the indigenous counterpart that he drove away. He refers repeatedly to atrocities committed by the Spanish Inquisition to back up his arguments, which explains why this poem was included in the section on the Santo Oficio (Holy Office) in Hugo's *La légende des siècles* series (1859). In any case, Momotombo's refusal to accept baptism gains additional significance in the colonial context, as baptism was associated with the erasure of indigenous identity and renaming, which implied acculturation. Similarly, the priest's stated motivation in reducing the frequency of earthquakes suggests a link between natural disasters and identities of resistance—Momotombo was only dangerous as an indigenous volcano. Once stripped of its indigenous cultural trappings, the volcano would become an innocuous natural curiosity.

Hugo's poem served in turn as inspiration for two works by Nicaraguan archpoet Rubén Darío: a brief chronicle of volcanic activity in Central America entitled "La erupción del Momotombo," which he published in the Chilean newspaper *El Mercurio* on July 16, 1886, shortly after his arrival in that nation, and the poem "Momotombo," which he included in *El canto errante* (The Roving Song; 1907). Although Darío alludes to Hugo's poem in both works, his perspective of the volcano, and of his homeland itself, shifts drastically in the later poem. "La erupción del Momotombo" tends toward the descriptive, reconstructing for his Chilean readers a lush but tragic Central American geography of volcanoes and lakes. Darío divides his chronicle in five sections corresponding to the five Central American nations (Panama did not exist as a separate nation until 1903), each of which links volcanic activity to tragic foundational myths and their literary representations.

In the section on Guatemala, he cites José Milla y Vidaurre's novel *La hija del adelantado* (The Governor's Daughter; 1866) in referring to how Doña Beatriz de la Cueva, wife of governor Pedro de Alvarado, perished in the mudflow from the Volcán de Agua that devastated the colonial capital in 1541. Complementing Hugo's poem, this reference underscores the symbolism of volcanic activity as a visceral reaction of the land to the colonial enterprise, although it establishes no direct causality. The section on El Salvador continues to elaborate the link between volcanism and political identities, but again, Darío draws no clear connection beyond parallelism. He describes El Salvador as the "most volcanic" of all the Central American nations, and he cites the Volcán de Izalco in particular, but he glosses over particular eruptions, stating only that the capital has been destroyed more than once by volcanic activity. He then writes, not without irony, that although there have been several attempts to move the capital to safer ground, they have been frustrated: "The valiant children of the Salvadoran homeland are stubborn and strong, and they wouldn't care even if it were Vulcan with his Lipari and Mongibelo. Unfortunately, they are as disdainful of seismic revolutions as they are of others, that are highly detrimental to the progress of those nations" (Los valerosos hijos de la patria salvadoreña son testarudos y fuertes y no se les daría un ardite del mismo Vulcano con su Lípari y su Mongibelo. Para las revoluciones seísmicas tienen tanta altivez como, por desgracia, para otras, que son harto fatales al progreso de aquellos pueblos; 2).[11] Once again, volcanic activity poses a challenge to political authority and the domestication of what is now the national landscape. Darío purposefully employs an ambiguous and stilted sentence structure in which it is not at all clear whether "detrimental" (*fatales*) refers to the volcanic and "other" revolutions or to the disdainful Salvadoran policymakers themselves.

Darío was not known for political activism, a fact I believe owed more to childhood entanglements in the political strife between conservatives and liberals than to the apolitical, escapist attitude that critics often attribute to him. Nevertheless, there certainly seems to be a veiled political message in these lines, and he condemns outright the fratricidal civil wars that have plagued the Central American nations since independence: "A sad reputation, that of all my Central American countrymen: not even a few years can go by without shedding the blood of brothers!" (2).[12] The volcanic eruption and political infighting pose equally catastrophic threats to the well-being of the nation. In contrast, he concludes by lauding Costa Rica for its more "sane" (*cuerdo*) political history. The following section remarks that the Costa Ricans have not suffered greatly from volcanic upheaval, thus linking, again if only by parallelism, political stability with a lack of volcanic volatility.

Darío continues the concatenation of the national geography and politics with volcanic activity in the section on Nicaragua. Momotombo reprises his symbolic role in Hugo's poem, which Darío incorporates in prose translation. He describes Momotombo as the most imposing but also most beautiful Nicaraguan volcano, postulating an aesthetics of power and indomitability to which he returned in the poem in *El canto errante.* Citing the recent eruption of October 11, 1886, which "half-destroyed" León and also affected seriously Managua and Chinandega, he personifies Momotombo as a "militar de alto rango" (high-ranking military official) who refuses to abandon his warlike ways (2).

Tellingly, the preceding paragraph refers to the 1550 "Contreras Conspiracy," in which two sons of governor Rodrigo de Contreras were implicated in the brutal murder of Bishop Antonio Valdivieso. Motivated by concerns of social justice or petty politics, depending on who tells the tale, the bishop had denounced their father for refusing to enforce the 1542 Nuevas Leyes de Indias that were designed to protect the Spanish Crown's indigenous subjects against exploitation by unscrupulous *encomenderos.* According to legend, the day the bishop was killed, Lake Managua boiled and Antiguo León was flooded in divine retribution (Darío, "Erupción" 2). Instigated to action by followers of Gonzalo Pizarro, who ironically proclaimed Hernando Contreras the inheritor of the Incan empire with the title "Príncipe de Cuzco y Capitán General de la Libertad" (Prince of Cuzco and General Captain of Freedom), the brothers led an initially successful uprising against the Crown, sacking Panama. When confronted by royal troops, however, they fled into the jungle never to be heard from again. It is said that Hernando was devoured by a caiman. In any case, the narrative order links Momotombo's 1886 eruption to political strife even if there is no apparent direct connection. And although Darío could hardly be considered a champion of the rights of the dispossessed, particularly given the scorn in which he held socialism, one needs little imagination to associate the excesses of landowners during the colonial period with those of the "coffee barons" in Darío's present. Furthermore, by tying together a colonial eruption associated with divine retribution against political repression and that of Momotombo in his present, Darío establishes a genealogy of volcanic heritage in which the nation's destiny and political legitimacy (which, though questioned, is at issue) are linked intimately with the national landscape.

Darío's poem "Momotombo," written nearly twenty years later, further develops the connection between the volcanic landscape and national identity, using it to anchor the subjectivity of a poetic voice adrift in an ocean of cosmopolitan indeterminacy. Tellingly, "Momotombo" is a travel narrative, a meditation on Darío's exodus from Nicaragua as a teenager, but it also represents a nostalgic, literary return from decades of exile that anticipates the literal repatriation retold in *El viaje a Nicaragua* (Journey to Nicaragua; 1909). The opening lines of the poem juxtapose images of displacement and permanence: "The train rolled along its rails. It was / in the days of my golden springtime / and it was in my native Nicaragua" (El tren iba rodando sobre sus rieles. Era / en los dias de mi dorada primavera / y era en mi Nicaragua natal). The contrasting images of the train in movement, with its connotations of linear progress and modern development, and the nostalgic longing for a return to youth and nature suggested by "golden springtime," together with the assertion of national origins, converge in a portrait of the exiled subject as a conflicted being, disoriented, torn between distant spaces and imaginaries. But "Suddenly, between the treetops, I saw / a gigantic cone, 'bald and nude,' and / full of ancient, triumphal pride" (De pronto, entre las copas de los árboles, vi / un cono gigantesco, "calvo y desnudo," y / lleno de antiguo orgullo triunfal). Not only does Momotombo's sudden apparition orient the poet's vision, drawing it up and away to the heights of sublime contemplation from the dizzying spectacle of the landscape in movement, the perspective of exile, but it also roots him in national authenticity. The allusion to Hugo's lines "bald and nude," which are also included in French in Darío's epigraph, suggests venerable age (historical legitimacy) and natural authenticity, a complete lack of human artifice. Of course, this nudity represents an artifice of its own: as Anthony Pym notes, Darío redresses the volcano's nakedness with ornate linguistic garb that includes the use of Hugo's original French (187). Indeed, Darío uses references to Hugo's poem, here and in "La erupción de Momotombo," to revalidate his own cultural background as well as that of the nation: as a key writer in the Romantic renovation of the Western aesthetic, Hugo's interest in the Nicaraguan landscape and cultural history amounts to an acknowledgment of Nicaragua's cultural sovereignty and legitimacy as a nation, particularly given the anticolonial drift of the poem.

Indeed, Darío reads Momotombo through Hugo: "I had already read Hugo and the legend / that Squire taught him." His individual experience of the landscape is clearly mediated by culture, and by one that emphasizes volcanic identity as a marker of resistance to the colonial imposition of identities. For Darío this would resonate not only with Hugo's indictment of Spanish colonialism in the sixteenth century but also with that of the United States in the nineteenth and twentieth centuries. It can hardly be coincidental that Darío returned to Hugo's poem after two decades, directly following the scathing attack on US imperialism that he proffered in "A Roosevelt" in *Cantos de vida y esperanza* (*Songs of Life and Hope*; 1905).

Darío's affirmation of Hispanic identity and cultural autonomy necessarily extended to the nation. It is true that Darío's vague political writings tended to champion Hispanic unity in the Bolivarian model, particularly when it came to the project of restoring the aborted Central American Republic, which one could take as a rejection of the nation-state model. However, Bolívar's followers rarely advocated the dissolution of the nation; they were more concerned with uniting the existing nations in an international superstructure to counteract US and European neocolonialism. In this sense, there is no contradiction for Darío in affirming simultaneously his Nicaraguan heritage and his desire for a united Spanish America.

Darío's "Momotombo," with its *silva*-like structure, harks back to the early nineteenth-century Romanticist poetry of fellow Spanish Americans José María Heredia and Andrés Bello that exalted the landscape as the foundations of national originality as well as the source of sublimation of nationalist sentiments. At the same time, the incorporation of modernist elements such as the alexandrine provides greater rhythmic precision. This mixture of styles allows Darío to fuse his personal aesthetics, with its emphasis on individual genius and the mystical quest for the Ideal through formal perfection, with the looser theoretical bounds of nationalist sentiment. In fact, "Momotombo" is rife with a nationalistic rhetoric of origins and emblems. In the first lines, Darío has already marked the volcano as a beacon of identity and origins, as a memorial to his childhood in Nicaragua. The second stanza reinforces the paternal relationship between the national landscape and the exiled subject, establishing a direct genealogy: "Ancient father / who duplicates himself in the harmonious mirror / of pearly, emerald, pale green water" (Padre viejo / que se duplica en el armonioso espejo / de un agua perla, esmeralda, col). One need not belabor the Lacanian imagery, with the paternal role in the constitution of identity suggested by duplication and the mirror. This initiative function is reiterated later in the poem when Darío writes,

> Father of fire and stone
> I asked you that day
> for the secret of your flames, your arcane of harmony
> the initiation that you could give;
> because of you I meditated on the immensity of Ossa and Pelion,
> and that there are Titans above in the constellations
> and below inside the earth and the sea.[13]

In this case, the initiation into (poetic) language provided by the father leads to the formation of a national, not solely individual, identity.

Momotombo takes on a role equivalent in Nicaraguan mythical origins to that of Mounts Ossa and Pelion in Greek mythology. He becomes an indigenous Titan, epic hero, and patriarch of the nation:

> And I arrived and I saw in the clouds the prodigious head
> of that cone of the centuries, of that volcano of *gesta*
> which was a revelation before me.
> Lord of the heights, emperor of waters
> at his feet the divine lake of Managua,
> with islands of pure light and song.
> Momotombo!—I exclaimed—Oh, epic name![14]

Darío represents Momotombo as a conquering emperor from the dawn of history, and the poetic voice locates itself as the founder of a national discourse rooted in the medieval tradition of *gesta*, or epic poetry. Indeed, he has already traced his intellectual genealogy to the Spanish conquerors. He admits freely his affinity for the exoticized past, writing,

> I was already nourished by Oviedo and Gomara
> and my blossoming soul dreamed of strange stories,
> fables, fictions, romances, love
> of conquests, victories of fierce horses,
> Incas and priests, prisoners and slaves,
> feathers and gold, audacity, splendor.[15]

In keeping with the early nineteenth-century Romantic notion that national histories should be rooted in mythic origins, he weaves a vision of Nicaragua's past in which Momotombo becomes a fabled hero memorialized in the cultural landscape, a national symbol of liberty and illumination.

Darío is not known for nationalism—just the opposite. He reiterated tirelessly throughout his poetic career his belief in a somewhat mystical universalism under the banner of Western culture, in which national divisions appeared almost as wounds in the organic body of humanity. Consequently, the specific emphasis on the Nicaraguan landscape and cultural history make this poem unique among Darío's literary production. Building on Hugo's representation of Momotombo as a symbol of indigenous resistance to the colonial imposition of identities, he underscores Momotombo's national significance by linking him to the foundational narrative of independence, with its tropes of Enlightenment: "One might say that you were a barrier to shadows, / ever since the white man heard your chief's tongue / and its declarations of liberty" (Dijérase que fueses para las sombras dique, / desde que oyera el blanco la lengua del cacique / en sus discursos de libertad). Furthermore, playing off the common trope of mountains as places of refuge and bulwarks against attack, Momotombo defends the nation against the specter of foreign invasion:

> When the Babylons of the West
> in purple catastrophes pursuing immensity
> circled the august pride of your forehead,
> you were like an icon of Serenity.
> In your incessant furnace I saw perpetual war
> in your stone, military units without end.
> I felt in your earthquakes the bellow of the land
> and the immortality of Pan.[16]

Darío describes an inspirited, national nature in which the land itself rises up against foreign occupation, which remained a very real threat given the history of Spanish colonialism, William Walker's 1855 foray into Nicaragua, and repeated US interventions in Panama and Honduras. Indeed, the United States occupied Nicaragua as well only three years later, in 1910. In this nationalistic imaginary, the volcano Momotombo becomes a virile father, progenitor and protector of the national heritage.

Furthermore, as this fatherly imaginary suggests, the relationship between the land and the nation is also internalized, allowing the poet to emplace himself within the national geography despite exile. As he proclaims, "With a volcanic soul I entered this hard life / my heart suffered hurricane and Aquilon [the north wind] / and hurricane and Aquilon move the burning chimera / of my mind."[17] Through volcanic imagery, Darío is able to resolve the apparent contradictions between feelings of suffering and alienation, the search for national origins misplaced during the experience of exile, and his desire for wider recognition as part of the Western artistic canon and as an initiate into this mysterious "Ideal" that he frames as a kind of universal consciousness.

Building on imagery from Hugo's "Les raisons du Momotombo," Rubén Darío's poem marks Nicaragua's volcanic topography as an originary site for both individual and national identity. Not coincidentally, by this time Darío himself had come to be considered a national fixture in Nicaragua, despite the fact that he had barely set foot in the country for nearly twenty years. The issue of his exile was immaterial, however, as Darío's poem only reinforced nationalist sentiments that were already commonplace, although he theorized these connections in greater depth than did his predecessors in the visual arts. Darío's use of volcanic imagery reflects what Brian Graham and Peter Howard, citing Laurajane Smith, call "authorized heritage discourse" (Introduction 2). The continuity of Darío's imagery with the national narrative of volcanoes as emblematic landscapes serves to connect the national past with his present, reinscribing the role of volcanoes as repositories of national sentiments and memory. And heritage is canon (Graham and Howard, Introduction 6).

As any scholar of literary studies is well aware, the construction of a canon necessarily implies processes of negotiation and exclusion. As Graham and Howard point out, "The creation of any heritage actively or potentially disinherits or excludes those who do not subscribe to, or are embraced within, the terms of meaning attending that heritage" (Introduction 3). In Central America, the canonical foundational narrative paradoxically rooted its concept of national territorial stability in a highly unstable geophysical phenomenon. Perhaps the volcanoes' perennial instability made them attractive as a symbol of permanence amid enduring crises in national identities due to political and social instability and the constant threat of foreign intervention: the only certainty was uncertainty. Paradoxically, the volcanoes' potential volatility kept their symbolism open despite canonization as themed spaces.

In the national imaginary inscribed by the elite founding fathers, volcanoes had been stripped of danger and overwritten with national heritage, becoming monuments to nationality. As Sarah McDowell points out, the state is the "official arbitrator of public commemoration and, therefore, of national heritage" (40), a custodian relationship that becomes highly problematic when the state maintains a repressive relationship with its citizens. For those who were excluded from concepts of nationality and citizenship, often the majority during the tumultuous politics of the twentieth century, volcanoes remained a contested landscape inscribed by conflicting spatial codes and inhabited by identities of resistance. These identities of resistance establish an alternate genealogy in which the descendants of the volcanoes were not the nationalistic oligarchy but, rather, those who threatened their hegemony. In this alternate imaginary, the ruling class was associated with internal colonialism based on foreign models, while the true "children of the volcanoes" were the marginalized indigenous and revolutionary fighters who took refuge on the volcanoes' flanks to escape political persecution. For the latter, volcanic eruption entailed the uprising of the oppressed "children of the earth," who would purge all traces of foreign influence and local oppression in a bath of fire.

Identities of Resistance: Igneous Individuals and the Volcanic Race

Guatemalan indigenous poet Luis de Lión's opens the first poem of his *Poemas del Volcán de Agua: Los poemas míos* (Poems of the Volcán de Agua: Poems of Mine; 1980) with words that echo the role that Rubén Darío assigned "Momotombo" in the formation of individual and collective identities in Nicaragua: "he lives in the arms of the Volcán de Agua, / because he is a child of that father" (vive en los brazos del volcán de agua, / porque es hijo de ese padre).[18] The scope of Lión's poem is rather more limited, however: he uses the third person here to refer exclusively to his birthplace, a Kakxikel Mayan village at the foot of the Volcán de Agua named San Juan del Obispo. The emphasis on geographic specificity precludes the elaboration of a national synecdoche, which would be unavailable in any case due to the subaltern position of Mayan identity in Guatemala at the time in which Lión was writing. Nevertheless, the landscape becomes emblematic of another identity: that of its indigenous inhabitants, marginalized from social, political, and economic citizenship.

Lión advances the connection between the landscape, its inhabitants, and their organic social organization by juxtaposing consciously the twin meanings of *pueblo* as site and social corpus in his poem. He personifies the town as "dark-skinned, pacific, sweet" (moreno, pacífico, dulce), "semi-Indian, semiliterate, and semi-ingenuous" (semiindio, semianalfabeto, semiingenuo), and good at soccer and birdcalls. With this introduction, he puts into play the complex European trope of indigenous innocence and proximity to nature, but with a twist: he views himself and his people not as "children of the earth" but as "children of the volcano," adding volatility to an expression that typically communicates a passive relationship with the land to the detriment of the modern emphasis on development and human modification of the environment. On the other hand, his identification of the children of the volcano does not depend exclusively on race: they are only "semiindio." Of greater importance is the experience of life under the volcano.

Poemas del Volcán de Agua: Los poemas míos is a meditation on the constitution of the poet's identity; and as the title indicates, it is an identity constructed in relation to the lived experience of the landscape in contrast to the abstract symbolism of volcanoes in the nationalist imaginary. These are poems not "on" but "from" the Volcán de Agua. The second poem, "Poema para mi cielo," recounts how the poetic voice's horizon was shaped on one extreme by the Volcán de Agua and, on the other, by the Volcán de Fuego. He repeatedly emphasizes this connection with the volcanoes as an inseparable part of his identity, even when his *cielo* (which embodies connotations of utopian social projects as well as cultural horizons) expanded through his travels and knowledge, on the one hand, and the cultural encroachment of neocolonialism, on the other. Indeed, the shared experience of subalternity within a globalized economic framework transforms his *cielo* into the international "prolongation of other skies/heavens" (prolongación de otros cielos) united through "these blues of us all / the whole world" (este azul de todo el mundo), thinly veiled references to the contestatory ideology that characterizes the book.

In "Poema a mi niño," the volcano has been internalized, promising a violent future: "underneath this hide / is the tender skin of a child / who barely sleeps / who bears burdens / and trudges even while asleep: / his feet are two peeled fruits, / his burden is a volcano, / his path is of stone" (abajo de este pellejo / está la suave piel de un niño / que apenas duerme / que carga / que camina hasta en el sueño: / sus pies son dos frutas sin cáscara, / su carga es un volcán, / su camino es de piedra). The child in this poem becomes a polyvalent symbol used to refer alternately to Lión's own childhood, the repressed Guatemalan peasantry as a whole, and the infancy of a growing social revolution. The poem proceeds to detail the daily hardships of life on the volcano, as the child rises with dawn, climbing with his mother upward to their "private property, their bit of volcano" (su propiedad privada, su pedazo de volcán) with its "semisterile soil, / like a mother near menopause" (tierra semiestéril, / como una madre próxima a la menopausia) to gather their meager harvest for sale in the markets of the city in the valley below. He describes the child alternately as a warrior armed with slingshot and machete, a nascent poet equipped with the empowerment of words, and a slave bearing the mark of the *mecapal*, the cord used to carry heavy burdens, branded into his forehead as if he were cattle.

Although the poem focuses on the poet's own experience, the emphasis on social inequality posits the "children of the volcano" as a collective identity of resistance, a rejection of the imposition of a uniform national identity from without. As the final lines of the opening "Poema para el niño del Volcán de Agua" (Poem for the Child of the Volcán de Agua) make clear, Lión holds a negative view of the nationalization of a territory of resistant individual and group identities: "he still has a chunk of land in which / to stand, / but tomorrow . . . / well, soon it will all be / the color of this flag" (ahora todavía tiene un pedazo de tierra donde / poner el pie; / pero mañana . . . / bueno, ya no tarda en ser todo / del color de esta bandera). The emphasis on color is key: the overlaying of the white and blue stripes of the Guatemalan flag on the local physical and cultural landscape evokes images of *"blanqueamiento,"* or whitening of indigenous populations through *mestizaje*, which in Guatemala is an extremely volatile trope. Furthermore, throughout *Poemas del Volcán de Agua*, Lión associates the color blue with domination and the melancholy of the colonized, that "azul de todo el mundo" from "Poema para mi cielo." This concept appears more explicitly in "Los héroes," which opens with the lines, "they were tall / and they bragged of the green / or / the blue / through which they saw us" (eran altos / y presumían del verde / o / del azul / con que miraban), describing within the framework of imperial gaze the eyes of the well-shod, white local landowners' sons over whom the barefoot, indigenous local boys triumph in a soccer match. When Lión describes his relationship to the nation, it is always through the prism of disenfranchisement and failure, a trope that reaches full force in "Poema del que pretendió ser novio" (Poem about the guy who tried [and failed] to be a groom). In Lión's work, the national romance can never be consummated, as the "madre patria" rejects integration with the indigenous subject despite his amorous intentions.

Tellingly, the volcanic geography represented in "Poema a mi niño" reflects the social hierarchy in reverse: as in the *favelas* and shantytowns that proliferate on the fringes of Latin America's urban geographies, only the most destitute peasants inhabit and work the highest reaches of the volcano. The landscape shifts as one descends from the poorest fields and villages at the highest altitudes to the political and economical urban center far below, waiting indolently, "with its toothless mouth of a master who awaits" (con su boca desdentada de patrona que espera), in the fertile valley for the boy to deliver the fruits of his labor. Tellingly, the town is described in terms of patriarchal authority—in the colonial organization of labor, the "patrón," as the *pater*, heads up the local social and economic hierarchy. Yet here the master is toothless, the virile authority of the "patrón" decayed by age and distance from the means of production, and it is feminine, "patrona," which, as much as one would like to read as a female subversion of the masculine order, only makes sense here within the traditional, phallocentric trope of feminine weakness.

Returning to the poem, in a direct inversion of the metaphor of "climbing the social ladder," the poetic voice describes how the boy and his mother "will descend and leave the volcano behind, / but they will descend as two beasts of burden" (descenderán y dejarán el volcán atrás, / pero descenderán como dos bestias de carga). In the shadow of the volcano, geographical descent implies social ascendancy, but not in this case: the boy and his mother's journey downward is only a temporary pass to serve the city's elite. Despite the economic abjection of those who inhabit the upper reaches of the volcano, however, they hold the higher moral ground, for they have the unfettered vision of the horizons. Harmonizing with indigenous associations of volcanoes with divine power and the sacred, Lión repeatedly emphasizes the sublimity and sanctity of life on the volcano, even when confronted with poverty and exploitation. In fact, the misery that Lión describes engages the Catholic trope of the expiation of sin through suffering. Doubly sanctified by suffering and geographical proximity, the volcano's residents are only a step from heaven.

The volcano's social geography undoubtedly reflects issues of vulnerability: although the Volcán de Agua has not erupted since the sixteenth century, those who are closest to the cone are more exposed to the devastating lahars, or debris flows, that rumble periodically down its flanks, destroying everything in their path. The geographical hierarchy is also related to ease of life and economic value; the valley floor has greater fertility and access to water and infrastructure. On the other hand, as the Spanish seized indigenous urban centers on the valley floors during the conquest, the displaced were pushed up the volcanoes, whose slopes became simultaneously places of refuge and focal points for rebellion against the Spanish overlords. The volcanoes became natural fortresses as well as repositories of cultural knowledge; they were beacons of resistance to the imposition of identities amid the specters of forced acculturation, religious conversion, and assimilation into an economy of near enslavement. Though the indigenous were forced there by the Spanish, their continued occupation of the volcanoes led to their identification with volcanoes by all sides: the indigenous see themselves as "children of the volcano," while those in power view the volcanoes and the indigenous as equal threats of eruption. In this way, the physical geography became a cultural landscape endowed with meanings that reflected the nation's social divisions.

The association of the national landscape's most prominent features, the volcanoes, with threats to the nation gave rise to national histories rooted in the fear of disaster, both geophysical and social. There were certainly grounds for these fears: during the sixteenth century, La Antigua Guatemala, the colonial capital of the Capitanía General de Guatemala, was ravaged repeatedly by Luis de Lión's Kakxikel Mayan ancestors during successive uprisings, as well as by a massive mudflow from the Volcán de Agua in 1541 that effectively razed the city. Following a series of devastating earthquakes in the seventeenth century, the capital was finally moved to its present location in Guatemala City. In any case, successive elites in Guatemala, but also in El Salvador and Nicaragua, frequently exploited the trope of a national history permanently on the verge of disaster to justify repressive measures in a manner akin to the way in which Trujillo turned the 1930 hurricane in the Dominican Republic to his advantage. The nation lived in a permanent state of emergency or exception in which the rule of law was perpetually suspended.

Lión's poetry engages intimately with his own childhood, but he collectivizes the individual experience of life on the volcano by inserting his personal memories into a shared history of marginalization and economic exploitation. For Lión, memory, like the landscape from which it cannot be extricated, is a social, not an individual, space. This construction of social space through personal memory does not claim embodiment, however. He has no pretensions of speaking "for" all the children of the volcano, instead availing himself of an ingenious strategy for side-stepping the ethical conundrum that Gayatri Spivak outlined in "Can the Subaltern Speak?"

By the time Lión published his works, he had undoubtedly become a *letrado*; he lived in the capital, and he became a university professor and labor-union leader who used the "high-culture" genre of written poetry to communicate his message. He had necessarily abandoned his subaltern status as a condition for speaking.[19] He does not disown himself from his indigenous past, however, or from the moral authority of the experience of subalternity. Instead, he brings into play the mechanism of memory to create a distance or schism between the lettered speaking subject in the present and its former subaltern self in the past. The use of the third person to talk about his own past is no simple parlor trick to collectivize the child as a mythical archetype or collage of the volcano's residents; Lión's child is not figurative but rather autobiographical, as the book's subtitle, "Los poemas míos," and the frequent use of the first person in more intimate poems indicates. On the contrary, the use of the third person is an honest recognition of the changes and empowerment that he has undergone, as well as of the persistence of the inequalities and injustices that he himself suffered as a child and that his people continue to endure in the present. Through narrative doubling, Lión's poetic voice is able to maintain its subaltern status in the past without extending it to the present, when his own exceptional circumstances might undermine claims of collective representativity.

Lión's meticulous literary mapping of the local geography uncovers a struggle not only for control over local identities, land distribution, and access to the means of production, all topics that he engages explicitly, but also for custodianship of the volcano as a collective cultural symbol. The careful descriptions of the *campesinos'* relationship with the local environment validate their claims to ownership of the land but also to the symbolic interpretation of the landscape. As his evocation of the attempted imposition of the Guatemalan national flag over the local cultural landscape made evident, volcanic symbolism is disputed territory, one that must be defended in word as much as in deed. Lión's poetry uncovers the competition for cultural control of volcanic landscapes, in the process revealing that all spaces, whether geographical or social, are defined by the relationships that they mediate.

Lión's "Poema a mi niño," for all its volcanic allusions, concludes rather innocuously, possibly due to the threat of censorship or reprisals. He nevertheless warns that "in spite of time and having learned another profession, / inside, / in the deepest depths, / this child always accompanies him" (a pesar del tiempo y del aprendizaje de otro oficio, / adentro, / en lo más hondo, / ese niño siempre va con él), and with him his memories of oppression and volcanic origins. A future eruption would seem a distinct possibility.

Tragically, Lión was kidnapped and murdered in 1984, at the height of Guatemala's decades-long civil war (1960–1996). Nothing definitive was known about his whereabouts for more than a decade, but in 1999 his name and photograph surfaced in the infamous "Diario Militar," a file the Guatemalan military kept on the persons that it had "disappeared." As a leftist university professor at the Universidad de San Carlos de Guatemala and a leader in the socialist Partido Guatemalteco de Trabajo (Guatemalan Workers' Party), he had become a political threat to the military government headed by General Óscar Humberto Mejías Victores. On the other hand, his cultural works disputed the nation's official iconography of volcanoes as part of the national cultural patrimony, and, of course, the patrimony is the legacy passed on by the *pater*, evoking the historical conflation of *patria* with *patrón* that so many Central American authors have decried. In any case, Lión's killers evidently recognized that the war was over control of not only the nation's physical geography but also its ideological underpinnings and the cultural iconography that sustains them.

There was clearly an important racial component to Lión's postulation of the indigenous as "children of the volcano"; however, this trope is not limited to the indigenous or to Guatemala. In both El Salvador and Nicaragua, associations of indigenous identity with volcanoes continue to be important, if somewhat less so than in Guatemala; however, racial considerations take the backseat to social and political divisions. The volcano maintains its role as the refuge of identities of resistance, but in cultural representations from these two countries, the "children of the volcano" are most often revolutionaries engaged in guerrilla warfare against repressive regimes. In this twist on the metaphor, volcanic eruption comes to symbolize the potential for revolutionary change, but volcanic imagery also appears in many texts as a trope alluding to the emotional trauma of "disastered subjects" living under the shadow of governmental repression, social alienation, and individual anxiety.

Volcanic Sociality and the Disastered Subject

Luis de Lión's poetry puts a positive spin on an identity constructed from a landscape of domination and disaster. The shared individual experience of social inequality and life on the volcano led to the formation of a common social identity that holds within it the potential for eruptive social change: it is that boy carrying a volcano within. This social eruption implies a process of reverse colonization in which the volcano retakes the valley below, annihilating the restrictive social and racial hierarchy and allowing for a new social order to appear. Not all representations of volcanic identities are so positive, however.

Claribel Alegría and Darwin Flakoll's *Cenizas de Izalco* (*Ashes of Izalco*; 1966), considered by some critics the only Central American novel of the Boom, also scrutinizes closely the relations between place and identity.[20] Based to a large degree on Alegría's childhood in El Salvador, this novel combines three plotlines to examine closely concepts of local, national, and class identity. It is framed by the narrative of Carmen, who returns home to El Salvador from the United States for the funeral of her mother. While sorting her mother's things, she comes across the diary of American Frank Wolff, a writer who suffered from depression and alcoholism. The diary recounts how Wolff, in El Salvador on a desperate quest for lost innocence, falls in love with Carmen's married mother, Isabel, who in turn dreams of nothing more than leaving her hometown and traveling to Paris. Meanwhile, the area's indigenous population, most of whom toil in miserable conditions on the coffee plantations of wealthy landowners known as "coffee barons," has been growing increasingly discontent, and open rebellion eventually explodes when hardliner general Maximiliano Hernández Martínez deposes sympathetic president Arturo Araujo. The resulting chaos ends in the arrest and subsequent execution of local hero Agustín Farabundo Martí, one of the founders of the Communist Party of Central America, and in what has come to be known as "La Matanza" of 1932, in which up to thirty thousand indigenous persons as well as dozens of local landowners died. Local Volcán de Izalco accompanies the increasing agitation with minor eruptions of steam and ash, finally exploding violently just as the indigenous rebellion breaks out.

The novel uses a fragmented chronology that intersperses Carmen's present with her childhood memories and passages from Frank's diary in order to emphasize historical causality: she comes to grips with her own personal and social identity through reconstructing that of her mother as well as the events that led to the 1932 massacre. As in Lión's book, the centrality of the volcano is established in the novel's title and in references throughout the work. In keeping with the novel's focus on the construction of multiple layers of identity, however, the volcano is not relegated to mere symbol of the social explosion that unites all the narrative threads in a single climax; it plays different roles in the construction of identity by each of the novel's characters. Although the indigenous residents of the flanks of the Volcán de Izalco are again posited as "children of the volcano," and the eruption itself is described as the awakening of the god Tlaloc, which constitutes yet another metaphor for the indigenous peasants' consciousness of their oppression, the volcano's symbolism becomes highly contested by different characters. In fact, the social subtext of the novel, like the substratum that lies just under the surface, is subsumed to the plotline focusing on Frank and Isabel until it finally explodes in the dénouement.

Until this final eruption, when the significance and magnitude of the social unrest finally become patent, the volcano has distinctly individual meanings. For instance, upper-middle-class Carmen's nostalgic reminiscing about picnics with her father and brother on the crater's green rim decades after the 1932 eruption reveals a bucolic dimension to the volcano that contrasts starkly with its earlier association with the indigenous uprising. Nonetheless, one could make the case that her enjoyment of the view while her father recites poems by Rubén Darío relates directly to her position near the top of the social hierarchy; she disposes of leisure time, the means to travel to the volcano, and, more than anything else, the tourist eye that exoticizes natural landscapes. In fact, in the narrative order, her visit to the volcano mirrors Frank Wolff's exoticist imaginings of El Salvador a few pages earlier, when Carmen's uncle Eduardo, at that time a young Marxist bohemian, takes him to task for viewing poverty and underdevelopment as picturesque. As Frank is compelled to admit, "Since coming here, I've accepted the disparities around me as so many exotic elements of a pleasing picture painted for my benefit" (94). Eduardo forces Frank to read the Salvadoran landscape through a different lens; unfortunately, the removal of this mechanism for coping with difference only exacerbates the American writer's already tenuous mental state.

Frank Wolff embodies what Robert Kastenbaum has described as a "disastered state of being" (71). In his study on the psychology of disaster victims, Kastenbaum notes that "many of the individuals whose inner state most closely conforms to our notion of a disaster victim may have experienced no 'official' disaster at all" (71). Frank suffers from a sense of the wounded self, but he is unable to trace the source of the trauma to a specific moment beyond a vague loss of childhood illusion and the failure to develop a viable self-image despite his success as a writer. He takes refuge in alcohol as a coping mechanism. He claims that his alcoholism began as an act of rebellion of a pastor's son against the national ethos manifested in the Volstead Act, but it rapidly escaped his control and morphed into a mechanism for isolating himself from society (47). Notably, Frank's alienation is existential rather than social. Furthermore, as an outsider in El Salvador on a whim, Frank has little or no investment in the social order that leads to the peasant uprising. Given the explicit parallels the novel draws between the volcanic eruption and social rebellion, Frank's association with the Volcán de Izalco becomes particularly poignant: his psychological suffering is not the result of his experiencing a volcanic or even a social disaster; rather, the volcano and its destructive potential become expressions of the trauma that he carries within.

In part, this trauma is chalked up to sexual repression: his passion for Isabel builds to a crescendo on a par with the increasing violence of the Volcán de Izalco's eruptions. He abandons Santa Ana on a bus that is hijacked by the indigenous rebels, after he has dictated an unanswered ultimatum that Isabel leave her husband and join him in traveling the world. The insurgents force him to take the wheel of the bus after decapitating the driver, ordering him to steer for the headquarters of the uprising in the town of Izalco. As the bus descends the final hill toward the town, Frank puts the gear in neutral and leaps out, leaving his kidnappers to their fate. He contemplates the eruption of Izalco as he drags himself toward town, nursing a broken leg and a bottle of whisky. Forced into immobile contemplation and endowed with the lucidity of acceding to his addiction, he realizes that his Isabel was only a fantasy he created so that when the inevitable rejection came he could give in to his alcoholism. He passes out upon attaining this epiphany, waking the next day to stumble into Izalco, where the indigenous rebels are turning in their arms to government officials in exchange for amnesty. Shortly after, he witnesses them being massacred by soldiers with machine guns. This horrifying spectacle provides the final *tiro de gracia* to Frank's long descent into self-pity, and his story concludes on a positive note hinting at transformation: he sends his diary to Isabel with a final letter explaining what has happened and that she will never see him again.

Frank Wolff represents a genre of character pioneered by British author Malcolm Lowry in *Under the Volcano* (1947). Like Wolff, Lowry's protagonist, Geoffrey Firmin, sometime British consul in fictional (but Cuernavaca-like) Quauhnáhuac, Mexico, is a traumatized individual who conceives of life in terms of disaster, who self-medicates with alcohol, and whose alienation is expressed in expatriation. Indeed, *Ashes of Izalco* dialogues transparently with Lowry's novel: in both works, living "under the volcano" evokes connotations of unrelenting fear and anxiety, permanent psychological trauma, disrupted identities, and the sensation of circling precariously the rim of self-destruction. Disaster, in its association with these characters, symbolizes a schism in identity, marked by temporal and spatial fragmentation, displacement, and discontinuity. These individuals embody the negative, the counterpart of the Utopian whole, their identities unified only in disjunction. In them, trauma becomes a permanent rather than a transitional state of being.

The disastered self carries out the function that Kirby Farrel associates with trauma as a trope, that of "an enabling fiction, an explanatory tool for managing unquiet minds in an overwhelming world" (x). Indeed, clinical psychologists such as Peter Hodgkinson and Michael Stewart emphasize the importance of constructing a narrative of traumatic experience in order for patients to achieve "cognitive completion," allowing them to integrate the traumatic experience into enduring models of the world and their relationship with it (24). Both the consul's and Wolff's alcoholism become therapeutic if unsuccessful narratives, recounted in the consul's conversations and letters and in Wolff's diary, that attempt to piece together the shattered knowledge of their own lives. In Wolff's diary in particular, the chronology of his struggle with addiction serves a unifying function in lieu of more cohesive life meaning: the succession of dates provides narrative coherence rather than plot. In this reading (and writing) of one's own experience, disaster becomes the unifying narrative of a life disjointed by fear and failure.

Tellingly, the disastered subject in *Ashes* has a social dimension distinctly absent from Lowry's novel. Although both novels associate the trauma of colonized groups with volcanic imagery, drawing attention to the volatility of the disastered lower classes and their potential for explosive rebellion, the climactic uprising in the final chapters of *Under the Volcano* is absurd, senseless. Geoffrey's grotesque death at the hands of paradoxically dark-skinned, Mexican Nazi sympathizers does not resonate with the discourse of human rights or social justice: it is the irrational, xenophobic explosion of delusional locals against a self-destructive foreigner. Entirely without social connotations, Geoffrey's ignominious end only highlights the pathetic trajectory of his solitary life, even if there is a fleeting sense of redemption in that he sacrificed himself in order to save his half brother Hugh. In any case, more than social eruption, the novel ends in an individual implosion. As Geoffrey lays dying, he imagines that he is falling into the crater of Popocatéptl: "Now there was this noise of foisting lava in his ears, horribly, it was in eruption, yet no, it wasn't the volcano, the world itself was bursting, bursting into black spouts of villages catapulted into space, with himself falling through it all" (391). Social concerns are given short shrift before individual suffering, and Geoffrey's descent into his personal inferno has few implications beyond himself.

In contrast, disaster is a generalized state in *Ashes of Izalco*. Frank Wolff is by no means the only disastered subject to grace the novel. In fact, nearly all the characters bear the marks of trauma. In Isabel's case, for example, her longing to escape Santa Ana's suffocating small-town atmosphere reveals a schism in her social identity, a sense of the alienated self that she vocalizes explicitly: "Sometimes when I look at my sisters, at friends I've known all my life, they seem to be from another country and to speak a language I don't understand" (52). Her husband, Manuel, seems to be the only one who is immune to life's misfortunes, although he always regrets having left Nicaragua as a child, and he loses vitality with the tragic death of one of their children in infancy. Eduardo, Isabel's brother, appears equally stable emotionally, but he has

become an ethical disaster, having renounced his youthful revolutionary idealism for middle-age cynicism and cronyism with the repressive
government.

Furthermore, all of Manuel and Isabel's children conceive of their
lives within the framework of disaster in one way or another. Alfredo, in
particular, comes across almost like a Salvadoran Frank Wolff. An alcoholic himself and perennial failure, he flirts repeatedly with suicide. His
revolutionary ramblings seem to hint at some possibility of redemption
through social action, but the fact that he never puts them into practice
only highlights his degradation. And though Carmen, the narrator, is
not as destructive as her brother, she is dealing with her own problems
springing from the experience of exile and displaced identities. She realizes that she has become the inverted reflection of her deceased mother,
who always wished to escape the suffocating social atmosphere of Santa
Ana. Carmen fled Santa Ana's stagnation on the margins of history only
to find herself trapped in the rigid chronometry of life at her husband's
side in the United States, leading her to muse, "Maybe I'm going dead
too, dying a little more each day with Paul" (72). Adding the personal
disasters of other minor characters such as Frank's evangelist friend Vir-
gil and the horrifying social disaster embodied in the massacre of indigenous people, *Ashes of Izalco* reads like a meditation on genres of failure and trauma.

The coincidence of the indigenous uprising with the eruption of the
Volcán de Izalco should not be interpreted as a case of ingenuous Romantic patheticism, since it is matter of historical record and there is no
blanket meaning assigned to it: the readings of the eruption's symbolism
vary by character. Neither should the volcano's association with a generalized state of trauma be read within the framework of environmental
determinism, as the novel clearly emphasizes the particularity of each
case of trauma as well as its roots in social rather than environmental
phenomena. It is indicative that the volcano itself is named after the indigenous town at its foot: *Izalco* means "city of obsidian" in Náhuatl.
The "Volcán de Izalco" is thus denominated in function of its human inhabitants, rather than the inverse; yet the city is also described as volcanic in origin, as made of obsidian. In this concatenation of volcanic identities, the characters' psychological trauma fuses with natural disaster to
create a national geography of disaster, a bruised, traumatized cultural
landscape that extends beyond the individual to encompass the collective, and beyond the collective to the nation. Indeed, Frank Wolff summarizes this view when he describes the nation's capital as a disastered

city: "The entire city has the improvised air of a refugee camp thrown together by survivors of some great catastrophe" (79). San Salvador has been laid low by a series of volcanic eruptions and earthquakes that have left the city in ruins, but Frank's description is also a commentary on the state of the nation as a social and political entity. It is a nation of persons displaced by a series of disasters, social and political as much as geophysical, and Izalco is the common symbol that conjoins them.[21] And displacement is the antithesis of citizenship.

Ashes of Izalco ends with a cut back to Isabel's funeral in the present. As Carmen watches her mother's burial, she realizes that Frank's diary has allowed her to discover another face of her mother and of herself (173). In another play on the "ashes of Izalco," she muses that "earth keeps falling, covering her, covering us all" (173), and that soil is the black ash of the volcano. Santa Ana becomes a modern-day Pompeii: time is immobilized under the ashes, and no social change has occurred. Despite the social and natural disasters, life continues uninterrupted. As Ramón Luis Acevedo has noted, "nada ha cambiado" (nothing has changed) becomes the operative leitmotiv in *Ashes*—there is no resounding resolution to any of the novel's plotlines (118). Yet consciousness of the ongoing social disaster, of forming a nation divided by class and ethnicity, results in a schizophrenic view of the national subject as a divided self. El Salvador, like the foreigner Frank, has become a disastered nation unable to trace the roots of its trauma to its source, because there is no sole causality. The nation is united through shared discord: all are blanketed equally with the ashes of Izalco.

Fortunately, *Ashes of Izalco* ends in medias res, unlike Lowry's novel, in which only the final descent into the absolute abjection of death (the last lines detail how Geoffrey's body is tossed down a ravine, a dead dog thrown after) can bring peace and rest. Although all the characters in *Ashes* have been altered irrevocably by the experience of disaster, the novel does not frame that experience as wholly negative. In both Frank's and Carmen's cases, the traumatic experience brings about an epiphany, leading the reader to believe that positive life changes may result. The process of narrating their experiences has allowed them to create some sense of coherence, to draw together the shattered pieces of their lives in a meaningful manner. In this sense, disaster has the potential for positive transformation.

Likewise, the volcanic and indigenous eruption of Izalco forced El Salvador's social tensions into the open. As is often the case with natural disasters, the indigenous rebellion resulted in the violent rupture of barriers between the private and the public. On the one hand, the sacking and raiding of private homes by both sides smashed down doors and walls, strewing personal objects in public view, opening them to outside readings and interpretations. On the other hand, formerly private citizens became refugees and victims, generic public figures symbolizing disaster. The collapse of the barriers between the public and the private reached an extreme in the abjection of the cadavers of the indigenous people massacred by government troops in the central plaza of Izalco. The indigenous victims' insides were violently exposed to public view through the bullet holes and wounds riddling the fragile barrier of the skin. Yet worse, this horrifying violation of corporeal integrity was purposefully enacted in a public space in order to communicate a warning to future rebels. Despite, or perhaps because of, this violent intrusion of institutional power into the private sphere, the story of the Matanza of 1932 became an enduring narrative of resistance that revolutionary groups accessed throughout the rest of the century to legitimize their struggle against injustice. The centrality of the volcanic eruption to this narrative is key, as the national geography joins in with the human rebellion against a tyrannical regime capable of such inhuman, unnatural acts.

Under authoritarian regimes, dissenters cannot often construct official monuments to their cause due to repression and censorship. They can, however, ascribe alternative meanings to official iconography. Sites of repression such as Tiananmen Square in China or the Plaza of the Three Cultures in Tlatelolco, Mexico, take on alternative symbolism as shrines to the memory of repressive acts, confronting the symbolic order inscribed by the state. The Volcán de Izalco served this function in Salvadoran society; it became an unofficial monument that evoked an inherited memory in young generations of Salvadorans who did not live the experience of the Matanza of 1932 but who identified it with a linear genealogy of repressive regimes.[22]

Volcanic Revisionism

As in the case of Luis de Lión's and Claribel Alegría's rooting of indigenous identity in the volcanic landscape, the association during the 1970s and 1980s of revolutionary activity with volcanoes in El Salvador and Nicaragua depended partially on lived experience. Whether to avoid capture or to follow the successful model set by Fidel Castro's Cuban revolution, Central American guerrilla fighters often hid out in rugged, unpopulated areas on the flanks of volcanoes. At the same time, the material association of revolutionaries with volcanoes converged with symbolism in which volcanic activity (such as that of Izalco) had become associated with popular uprisings against autocratic political orders. This trope had developed from independence-era iconography in which volcanic eruption signaled the complicity of the native land in the project to overthrow Spanish colonialism, but in the twentieth century this institutionalized symbolism was turned against the postindependence political order by authors sympathetic to revolutionary movements.

In the 1970s and 1980s, large numbers of works appeared that used the volcanic trope as a metaphor for social revolution, from poetry written by guerrilla fighters on damp scraps of paper in jungle bivouacs to official party publications and anthologies edited by leftist foreign sympathizers. I refer to works such as Miguel Huezo Mixco's anthology of poetry written by guerrilla fighters, entitled *Pájaro y volcán* (Bird and Volcano; 1989), the Partido de la Revolución Salvadoreña's *El Salvador: Un volcán social* (1980), which provides justification for the armed conflict in El Salvador, the exposition of the history and political platform of the FMLN (Frente Farabundo Martí para la Liberación Nacional) in *El volcán en guerra: El Salvador, 1979–1987* (The Volcano at War; 1988), edited by Iosú Perales, and Alejandro Murguía and Barbara Paschké's bilingual anthology of leftist poetry, *Volcán: Poems from Central America* (1983), whose introduction insists forcefully, "This is not an anthology at all, but a contact bomb, a volcano ready to erupt" (xii). Clearly, by the 1980s the volcanic discourse had been successfully appropriated by leftist revolutionaries, who turned it against the inheritors of the oligarchic state that had first developed it as a trope of cultural autonomy during the struggle for independence.

This cultural imaginary was cemented for future generations in books such as Manlío Argueta's bilingual children's story *Magic Dogs of the Volcanoes/Los perros mágicos de los volcanes* (1990). As Argueta has stated in interviews with Linda J. Craft, he wrote this book in order to educate the children of Salvadorans who were forced into exile during the civil war (Craft 109). He imagines a role for this work in civic education, as an alternative to official textbooks that minimize the divisions that led to the civil war in favor of national unity. In keeping with several of his earlier works, Argueta eschews the official title of "El Salvador" for "Cuzcatlán," the pre-Columbian indigenous name for El Salvador's territory. Upon doing so, he engages the trope of indigenous authenticity rooted in the land. He makes no racial distinctions, however, instead framing the heroes of his story as mythical animals from Salvadoran folklore: "On the volcanoes of El Salvador live magic dogs called cade-jos" (4). Through mythic folk discourse, he is able to incorporate nonindigenous revolutionaries (whom the *cadejos* clearly symbolize) as legitimate children of the land, who, like the indigenous, derive strength and resistance from their volcanic origins. A few pages on, he repeats this trope, situating the *cadejos* almost as tutelary spirits of the local population and landscape: "The people who live in the villages on the slopes of the volcanoes have always loved the cadejos. They say the cadejos are really the great-great-grandchildren of the volcanoes. They say the cadejos have always protected them from danger and misfortune" (6). Consistent with tropes developed by Claribel Alegría in *Ashes of Izalco* and her later poetry and by others such as Ernesto Cardenal in his *Canto nacional* (1973), Argueta frames revolutionary ideals and the revolutionaries themselves as natural, as derived from the landscape.

The *cadejos* are locked in a deadly struggle for control over the landscape with the fourteen mythical families of the Salvadoran oligarchy: "Don Tonio and his 13 brothers who owned the land on the volcanoes did not like the cadejos at all" (10). Don Tonio and his brothers call in lead soldiers to hunt down the volcano dogs. Trapped in desperate straights, the *cadejos* petition for help from their great-great-grandparents, volcanoes Tecapa and Chaparrastique, who heat the ground beneath the toy soldiers' feet, melting them partially. As is befitting in a children's story, the soldiers are not killed: this melting symbolizes a change of heart, in which they decide to dedicate themselves to professions other than soldiering. The story concludes with a moral: "From that day on there has been peace on the volcanoes of El Salvador. Don Tonio and his brothers ran away to other lands, while the cadejos and the people of the villages held a big party, which was later remembered as a national holiday" (30). The resolution in national holiday is highly indicative: published only shortly before the peace accord ending the civil war was reached in 1992, *Magic Dogs of the Volcanoes* foresees the peaceful triumph of revolutionary ideals as well as reinstitutionalizing the volcanic trope as a foundation for the national identity of future generations of Salvadoran children.

The domestication of the revolutionary volcanic trope would not be agreeable to all, however, as it situated what had formerly been a contestatory discourse as the status quo. In this perspective, the institutionalization of revolutionary symbolism amounted to renouncing the revolutionary subversion of authoritarian, official language, giving in to complacency and capitulation. In fact, fellow Salvadoran Roque Dalton had warned decades earlier of a dispersion in revolutionary ideals before the revolution's goals had been reached. In his collection *Poemas clandestinos*, he included a poem entitled "Parábola a partir de la vulcanología revisionista" (Parable Derived from Revisionist Volcanology) that referenced Izalco as a symbol of revolutionary struggle.[23] Like other poems in the "Historias y poemas contra el revisionismo salvadoreño" section of his book, this one attacks the pragmatic Left for abandoning its Marxist ideals and collaborating with the oligarchy.[24]

The poem opens with revolutionary vocabulary describing the Volcán de Izalco as having been "ultraleftist" in the past, spewing lava and stones in an "assault on peace and order" (atentando contra la paz y la tranquilidad). The volcano's association with the older generation of Salvadoran leftists leads to its downfall, however, as their "revisionism" contaminates the volcano, transforming it into a shadow of its former self. It renounces its rebellious nature, becoming a domesticated space, a "themed" ecological resort for the oligarchy, the revolutionary elite, and union leaders.[25] The phallic association of volcanic activity with revolutionary virility gives way to the impotence of old age, and the volcano, unable to discharge on its own, must have fireworks placed into its mouth to entertain the revisionist revolutionary tourists who pay hypocritical homage to its monumental status. In turn, the fireworks, as weak, revisionist simulacra of revolutionary fire, are compared to the populist speech of politicians, whose words no longer pack the force of action. As the poem concludes,

> Respectable and meek proletariat of the world,
> the Central Committee invites you
> to learn the lesson that the volcano of Izalco gives us:
> fire is no longer in style,
> why then would we want to carry it
> within our hearts?[26]

Of course, Dalton was himself a disastered subject, and social revolution symbolized for him a personal as much as a collective transformation.[27] Paradoxically, his disaster aesthetics translate into an appetite for destruction: he yearns for disaster, which he envisions as the only possibility for radical transformation.

In reality, there was already a long history of using satirical representations of volcanoes in Central America to delegitimize the social and political groups that used them as symbols. Roque Dalton's lampooning of the hollow leftist veneration of Izalco as a symbol of social revolution in El Salvador followed in the footsteps of Nicaraguan avant-garde poet José Coronel Urtecho's "Oda al Mombacho," an answer to Rubén Darío's "Momotombo" that he published in the "Rincón de la Vanguardia" supplement to *El Correo de Granada* newspaper in 1931. In contrast to Darío's epic Momotombo, Coronel Urtecho's Mombacho is a squat, passive volcano characterized by its bourgeois "*timba*," or belly: "Mombacho / Nappy hill / Eunuch volcano / Castrated ox / Big-bellied God / Get up! / Fat, lazy hill!" (Mombacho / Monte murruco / Volcán eunuco / Buey muco / Dios timbuco / ¡Arriba! / ¡Monte timba!). Coronel Urtecho uses avant-garde linguistic play, including alliteration and the rhythmic repetition of *b*, *m*, and *u* sounds, to construct a somewhat childish, disparaging representation of Mombacho as a doddering volcano in the last throes of senility. Impotent, castrated, Mombacho is incapable of protecting his native Granada from its internal rival León, never mind embodying the nation in a way akin to Darío's Momotombo. The poetic voice is unwilling to forgo completely emplacement in the geography of his childhood, however, rooting himself in the landscape of failure. After enumerating exhaustively Mombacho's abjection as a failed volcano, he nevertheless proclaims, "I love you / as one loves a toad" (Yo te amo / como se ama a un sapo). In Coronel Urtecho's avant-garde aesthetic, the landscape must be denigrated, demystified, and, above all, divested of patriotic symbolism to be loved. And, of course, the hope lingers that, with a little love, the toad may transform into a prince.

Although this poem was originally written in dialogue with Rubén Darío and published in 1931, it reappeared in a collection of poems entitled *Nicaragua: Un siglo en veinte y tres poemas* (Nicaragua: A Century in Twenty-Three Poems) that was anthologized by Sandinista founder Tomás Borge Martínez in 1986, seven years after the triumph of the revolution. As the book's title makes clear, this anthology was conceived of as a poetic history of Nicaragua, with all the transcendental connotations with which Marxism endows history, rather than being a simple historical retrospective of Nicaraguan poetry. Tellingly, the subtitle links the book directly to the Sandinista project: "1986: Twenty-five years later, every weapon against aggression" (1986: A veinticinco años, todas las armas contra la agresión). The date clearly alludes to the foundation of the Sandinista movement, while the second part of the subtitle situates poetry as a weapon in the battle against the US-backed Contra rebels.

Given the political orientation of Borge's anthology, the inclusion of a poem that so clearly subverts the force of volcanic imagery as a symbol for social revolution seems very strange, particularly when one considers the effectiveness of that imagery for constructing revolutionary iconography in El Salvador. It is tempting to suggest that the inclusion of this poem in Borge's collection is simply a nod to Coronel Urtecho's support for the Sandinista movement in the late 1970s, support that was celebrated particularly because of his importance as a paternal cultural figure and because he had held several positions in the Somoza regime in its early years. More is at work, however: the volcano was not available as a symbol for popular revolution in Nicaragua in the same way as in El Salvador because the Somoza regime had institutionalized it more effectively than had El Salvador's litany of military rulers. Anastasio Somoza García's regime conserved jealously the nineteenth-century national heritage as a way of combating criticism of its close ties to the United States. Part of this project involved exalting recently deceased Rubén Darío's poetry as a national cultural treasure. And Rubén Darío's "Momotombo" had set in stone the volcano as a trope of national identity; no patriot could contradict easily the founding father of Nicaraguan letters.

Coronel Urtecho's "Oda al Mombacho" was published in 1931, before the Somoza regime took power and instituted the Darían volcanic imaginary as national doctrine. Therefore, the poem did not directly threaten the national heritage in the moment of its publication. Furthermore, it was framed as an homage to Darío in the same quirky vein as his earlier "Oda a Rubén Darío" (1927), and it was self-disparaging rather than directly confrontational: Mombacho was the target, not Momotombo. The significance of Coronel Urtecho's poem changed drastically following the triumph of the Sandinista revolution in 1979, however, when everything Somoza became anathema.

Tellingly, Nicaraguan author and former Sandinista politician Sergio Ramírez satirizes the Somoza regime's appropriation of Rubén Darío and Darío's volcanic nationalism in his historical novel on Darío's Odyssean return to Nicaragua, *Margarita, está linda la mar* (Margarita, How Beautiful Is the Sea; 1998). Near the climax of the novel, a parade is organized to celebrate dictator Anastasio Somoza García's arrival in León, where he will eventually be assassinated by poet Rigoberto López Pérez, who, among other motives, resents Somoza's appropriation and misrepresentation of Rubén Darío's poetry. The centerpiece of this parade is a float featuring a huge papier-mâché replica of a stately smoking Momotombo. A nubile young woman dressed as Pallas Athena reclines against it, completing a ludicrous collage of Darían imagery that makes a mockery of the decontextualization of the Greek goddess as well as the representation of the volcano as a sort of Nicaraguan Parnassos, emblem of the national civilization. Evidently, the paradoxical elements provide commentary on Somoza himself, whose attempts to obscure his repressive acts with the trappings of Western civilization are no more congruous than draping a potentially catastrophic geological feature with the Greek goddess of wisdom.

In the context of Somoza's sublimation of Rubén Darío's cultural imaginary and the volcano as national icon, Coronel Urtecho's playful dismantling of Momotombo's symbolism in "Oda al Mombacho" confronts the dictator's regime *avant la lettre*. Therefore it falls perfectly in line with the Sandinista official ideology half a century later. In this sense, both the triumphant Sandinistas and the Salvadoran revolutionaries who entered into political pacts following the peace agreements reinstitutionalized volcanic imagery, even if the Nicaraguans did so only through negation: the volcano symbol was conspicuous in its absence following more than a century of national prominence.

Volcanic Aesthetics

All spaces are defined by the relationships that they mediate, whether individual or collective, and their conceptual landscapes reflect the scars of the struggle for control over their physical geography as well as cultural interpretation of them. Some landscapes heal rifts in national identities, creating shared space through consensus symbolism. Others, however, express the rifts, drawing attention to them. The latter seems to be the case with volcanic symbolism, in which the potential for eruption perennially negates semantic stability. This was certainly the case in Central America, where the conversion of the volcanic landscape into national emblem enshrined the conflict between the ruling classes that instituted volcanoes as key tropes in the national imaginary and the largely indigenous residents of the volcanoes themselves, who also identified with volcanoes as symbols, but of their struggle against oppression by those same ruling classes.

In the national imaginary, volcanoes became picturesque emblems of the nation, the backdrop for stamps and postcards featuring smiling peasants whose folkloric poverty beckoned to foreign tourists (Ramírez, *Balcanes y volcanes* 108). From the perspective of those who resisted this national caricature, however, volcanic eruption symbolized the restoration of a "natural" indigenous or popular order that had been disrupted by Spanish colonization, dictatorship, and modernity in the neoliberal, capitalist model. Furthermore, for revolutionaries with Marxist tendencies, volcanoes represented the potential for the cataclysmic disordering of a cycle of oppression in which time and progress had stagnated, thus ushering Central America into the international historical progression toward a socialist utopia. It is not in vain that literary critic Ramón Luis Acevedo speaks of a "volcanic irruption" of Central American literature into the international plane in the introduction to his collection of critical essays *Los senderos del volcán* (The Paths of the Volcano; 6). This bursting forth of narrative implies international recognition of the value of Central America's literary tradition, but also the eruption of local memory into historical agency achieved through the negotiation of international solidarity. As the case may be, the Central American volcanoes were enshrined from all angles, becoming monuments to internal social divisions that served to compartmentalize the trauma and to exteriorize the wounds incurred in the struggles between ethnic groups and social classes.

4 Fault Lines

Mexico's 1985 Earthquake
and the Politics of Narration

Absurd is the substance that collapses,
that which is penetrated by emptiness, the hollow.
No: substance cannot be destroyed,
the form we give it is pulverized,
our works are shattered.
> —José Emilio Pacheco, "Las ruinas de México"

The solidarity of the people was really a seizing of power.
> —Carlos Monsiváis, *Entrada libre*

THE EARTHQUAKE THAT CONVULSED MEXICO CITY at 7:19 in the morning on September 19, 1985, altered irrevocably a generation's view of life in Mexico. Despite a long and well-documented history of disasters in the area, appearing in texts as far back as pre-Columbian indigenous codices, no disaster in recent memory had affected the capital in such a drastic manner. Even prior earthquakes such as that of 1957, which caused notable damage to the capital and toppled the iconic Independence Angel from its perch on the Paseo de la Reforma, and the 1979 temblor that leveled the Universidad Iberoamericana did not compare to the violence with which the 1985 earthquake ruptured confidence in the Mexican government's century-long project to transform Mexico into a unified, modern nation.[1] Estimated at 8.1 on the Richter scale, with a 7.5 aftershock the following day, the sheer scope of the mortality and the physical destruction caused by the 1985 seismic movement seemed almost unimaginable to Mexico City's residents, but it also thrust into doubt the solidity of the governmental edifice, which appeared to have crumbled along with institutional buildings such as the Secretaría de la Marina (Ministry of the Navy), the Secretaría de Trabajo (Ministry of Labor), the Secretaría de Comercio (Ministry of Commerce), the Secretaría de Comunicaciones (Ministry of Communications), and the Procuraduría de Justicia del Distrito Federal (Attorney General's Office of the Federal District). Many of the structures that secured the government's clientelistic relationship with its citizens—the Centro Médico, the Hospital Juárez, and federal housing projects in the Cuauhtémoc neighborhood—also came crashing down, burying under their rubble the very people they were charged with aiding. On a symbolic plane, at least, the transformation of the iconic Parque de la Seguridad Social, monument to the achievements of the welfare state, into an immense morgue overflowing with the cadavers of earthquake victims represented the demise of an era of institutionalized social order that had already entered into crisis with the 1982 collapse of the peso and President Miguel de la Madrid's transition toward neoliberal economic policies.[2]

For many of the intellectuals who wrote about the disaster, the earthquake represented a political crisis more than a natural disaster. The seismic movement itself, although horribly frightening, was an unavoidable natural phenomenon. The disorganized response to the earthquake and generalized corruption in public works programs and the construction industry, which many observers believe led to the high mortality and material loss, however, fell squarely within the realm of human agency. These authors contended that the real problem was the state of the national body politic under the half-century rule of the Partido Revolucionario Institucional (PRI; Institutional Revolutionary Party), which had effectively disowned its citizens from any real political decision making. This discontent with the state of political agency under the PRI was further exacerbated by de la Madrid's shift to neoliberal economic policies, which limited many of the social benefits that the PRI had used to offset the lack of democracy. From this point of view, the natural disaster only revealed a preexisting social and political disaster that had been obscured by the PRI's politics of cooptation and the manipulation of the media.

This chapter discusses two forms of cultural production that Mexican intellectuals engaged to document and theorize the experience of the 1985 Mexico City earthquake. First, I examine the genre of the *crónica*, a kind of brief hybrid essay combining personal observation with social documentary that has been published in newspapers throughout Latin America since the nineteenth century. I argue that the Mexican earthquake *crónicas* were closely linked to the project of popular mobilization in the immediate response to the earthquake and the months after. Their function was to draw into the public eye issues of concern for the popular movements that arose from the experience of the earthquake, such as the lack of housing, corruption in the distribution of aid, and the threat of gentrification of the historic downtown district during the reconstruction process. Although the authors of the *crónicas* were not usually members of the popular movements themselves, they nevertheless served as mouthpieces and mediators for them in the public sphere, providing the public visibility of issues that Claudio Lomnitz and others have argued was required for collective groups to enter into dialogue and bargain for benefits with the corporatist state.[3]

In contrast to the immediacy of the *crónicas*, which were published in the heat of the moment, the majority of book-length literary and filmic representations of the earthquake appeared one to two years after the governmental response to the disaster had ended. Although not all of the popular movements' demands had been met by this point, the majority of the groups had signed the "Convenio de Concertación Democrática para la Reconstrucción de Vivienda" (Democratic Consensus Agreement for Housing Reconstruction) with the government in May 1986, thus making further negotiation moot and bringing to a close the *crónicas'* role in public debate over the earthquake response. I argue that the literary works and films that appeared after that date are involved in a distinct if related project: they construct a narrative of emerging democracy that locates the popular response to the earthquake, along with the Mexican revolution and the 1968 students' movement, as a key trope in the rise of civil society in Mexico. These works deploy earthquake imagery to depict the PRI as a regime on the verge of collapse.

Not coincidently, the majority of the more formal literary representations of the 1985 earthquake appeared shortly before the 1988 presidential elections, which were characterized by a rift within the PRI that led to the formation of an oppositional coalition called the Frente Democrático Nacional (FDN; National Democratic Front). I argue that these works' narrative of democracy supported the candidacy of Cuauhtémoc Cárdenas and the political platform proposed by the FDN, which promoted simultaneously a return to economic nationalism based on import-substitution industrialization and the democratization of political practice in Mexico. In the cultural sphere, a substantial facet of this project involved disrupting the PRI's control over the symbolic order linked to postrevolutionary Mexican nationalism, as well as creating new models for political discourse and practice centered on concepts of civil governance.

Corporatism and the State Response to the Disaster

In all fairness, the Mexican government's response to the enormity of the 1985 earthquake seems reasonably consistent, if by no means ideal, when compared with how other nations dealt with disasters of similar magnitude, such as Hurricane Katrina in 2005 in the United States, the 2008 Sichuan earthquake in China, and the 2010 earthquakes in Haiti and Chile, not to mention the 2011 triple disaster of earthquake, tsunami, and nuclear meltdown occurring in Japan as I write. Despite obvious contextual differences, many of the problems these nations faced were similar: a lack of emergency preparedness, social inequalities and construction practices that increased vulnerability, tardiness in initiating the rescue effort, challenges in providing adequate support for survivors, accusations of corruption in the handling of emergency funds and donations, and frustration with leadership. Given these parallels, it seems incongruous that Mexican cultural representations of the earthquake assume such a virulent stance toward the government, portraying its failings not as mere incompetence or corruption but as the systematic implosion of the state. Only careful analysis of the political and social context of the earthquake can reveal the logic behind these representations.

Although the earthquake's epicenter was actually located four hundred kilometers from Mexico City, off the coast of the state of Michoacán, its effects for the capital were intensified by geological and human factors. The downtown neighborhoods that were most damaged had been constructed over former lake beds that the Spaniards began draining in the seventeenth century to mitigate a succession of floods that had repeatedly inundated the city. In the twentieth century, rapid growth led to a massive increase in water needs; wells were drilled into the lake bed, which rapidly depleted the water table that supported the unstable ground above.[4] In fact, earthquakes were not requisite for damage to occur; the entire historic downtown has sunken considerably, and sinkholes that swallow streets and buildings have become increasingly common. On the other hand, geologists have theorized that the earthquake's seismic waves were amplified by an unfortunate complementation with the distances between rock outcroppings and unstable lake beds: the waves bounced back into the lake beds off rocky areas, and the refracted waves converged with oncoming waves to double the magnitude of the movement (Suárez and Jiménez 6). Others have postulated that the frequency of the seismic waves created by the earthquake resonated with buildings of a certain height, many of which were the product of a state-sponsored building boom in the 1950s and 1960s.[5] Furthermore, increased population density led to higher mortality.[6] The shortage of affordable housing, combined with the high cost of living in proportion to earnings and chronic underemployment, resulted in overoccupancy in many of the residential buildings that collapsed in the earthquake, a situation that Carlos Monsiváis describes in eloquent if abject detail in *Entrada libre*: "Here two disasters converge, the natural (nine dead) and that which these destroyed rooms evoke, the caging of beings and things, the almost-token washing basins, the reduced space in which a man barely fits standing, a woman lying down, four or five children in horizontal or vertical flight, an old woman who sews, a little dresser, and a television. The earthquake reveals the overcrowding, the over-crowding outlives the earthquake" (39). Due to these factors, the seismic movement was actually much more devastating in Mexico City than in areas closer to the epicenter.

Without prior experience with a disaster of such magnitude, there was no way that the government could anticipate such widespread dev-astation even if it had a more coherent disaster plan in place beforehand. Even Monsiváis, acerbic critic of all things governmental, found little fault with actions taken by lower-level state employees in the hours im-mediately following the disaster. His chronicles corroborate the myr-iad of testimonial texts emphasizing the selflessness of firemen, health workers, and the Red Cross in their efforts to rescue and treat victims. Likewise, the largely state-controlled media was employed initially in a highly efficient manner to provide essential information and instructions (*Entrada libre* 18).[7] In the first hours after the disaster there was no cen-sorship of the television images and radio descriptions of the destruc-tion: unfiltered information was given in order to highlight the serious-ness of the situation, while the exhortations to remain calm, not to go to work, to conserve water and electricity, and not to use the telephone except for emergencies all seem reasonable. Furthermore, the radio in particular was instrumental in establishing a forum for disaster victims to communicate with one another, since the telephone network was se-verely damaged. Radio broadcasters relayed messages from concerned family members and community organizations, thus playing a key role in mediating and coordinating the initial popular response to the disas-ter. However, the response of lower-level government workers and the media seems to have functioned autonomously from the highest eche-lons of governmental authority, which appeared to be suffering from a state of shock. The problems set in once the executive bureaucracy shook loose from its stupor and began to reassert its authority.

The fact that no information was withheld in the first moments of the earthquake response made it extremely unpalatable when censorship began to be exercised, and the hopes that the government would be forth-right and collaborative were shattered. As Monsiváis stated in his interview in Garza Toledo and company's *Esto pasó en México,*

> On television (with Televisa off the air Thursday morning), the initial reaction was timely and valuable. From Friday the 20th on, the media's traditional stance imposed itself. It cooperated enthusiastically with the minimization of the disaster, it lied prodigiously (Televisa affirmed repeatedly that the second earthquake caused no damage whatsoever), it praised the governmental officials (Imevisión insisted that the earthquake had occurred solely to showcase governmental efficiency), the Soccer World Cup was protected above all else. (12)[8]

The contradictory official positions ended up creating a lapse of credibility in which the government unwittingly situated itself as the earthquake victims' adversary. This antagonistic relationship was exacerbated by tardiness and incompetence in the immediate response to the earthquake as well as by the hierarchical formulism with which it responded to the victims' material demands in the months that followed. Despite appearances, the government doubtlessly did not set out to antagonize its citizens; I argue that it was constrained by its own organizational structure as well as by the ponderous mechanisms that it traditionally used for communicating and negotiating with the Mexican people.

Most political observers agree that the postrevolutionary Mexican government presided by the PRI and its earlier iterations (1929–2000) was characterized by a gap between constitutional ideals and political practice in which a legal democracy based on liberal citizenship was substituted for by what some observers have called a "corporatist" or "mass" democracy.[9] This is to say that the state preferred to negotiate not with individual voters but rather with social sectors based on labor and class divisions that were institutionalized hierarchically within what amounted to a single-party system. Opposition parties did in fact exist, but most elections were noncompetitive, as the PRI candidates always won, especially at the presidential level. The postrevolution Mexican state was not strictly an authoritarian regime, however; despite the prevalence of *caciquismo* and clientelism in a single-party system, the masses nevertheless had a large degree of agency in influencing governmental policy through corporate-interest bargaining. Furthermore, many of these internal organizations relied on democratic elections for the selection of leaders as well as to resolve competing political platforms.[10] As Jaime Tamayo summarizes exemplarily, the postrevolution

Mexican state was not detached from the masses despite the "flawed formal democratic representation in the Mexican political system," as the state created "sui generis mechanisms for expression and representations of the interests of subordinate classes" that allowed it to achieve consensus and legitimacy (123–24).[11] Nevertheless, others have pointed out that the clientelistic system of collective bargaining between the state and its component sectors often resulted in the weakest actors losing negotiating capacity as they sacrificed autonomy to corporate representatives, who may or may not have had their best interests at heart (Adler-Lomnitz et al. 32–37).

The corporatist structure of the modern Mexican state arose from necessity in the steps that President Álvaro Obregón (1920–1924) took to negotiate peace with the different sectors involved in the armed phase of the Mexican Revolution (1910–1920), but it was institutionalized during the presidencies of Plutarco Elías Calles (1924–1928) and Lázaro Cárdenas (1934–1940).[12] Calles, governing from the shadows once his term ended, formed the then Partido Nacional Revolucionario (PNR) in 1929 as an institutional framework within which the diverse national and regional political parties associated with the revolution could resolve their differences internally, without resorting to open violence. Similarly, Lázaro Cárdenas integrated oppositional labor and political organizations into the state as officially sanctioned institutions such as the Confederación de Trabajadores Mexicanos (CTM; Confederation of Mexican Workers) and the precursor to what is now the Confederación Nacional Campesina (CNC; National Peasant Confederation), often using techniques of collective bargaining pioneered by the same labor unions he wished to incorporate. Following Cárdenas's presidency, corporatism became the PRI's prime political strategy for negotiating political and social conflict, although bargaining was often accompanied by the threat or implementation of repression. At the national level, at least, popular political agency existed almost exclusively within this framework of corporate-interest bargaining with the national state; there were few other viable avenues for obtaining benefits or even the ear of the national state.[13] Furthermore, these corporate relationships had to be confirmed publicly at highly ritualized events, and they were reaffirmed ceremonially during each successive presidential campaign.[14]

I argue that one of the reasons the Mexican government appeared to be paralyzed in its initial response to the earthquake was due precisely to this highly codified corporatist structure. The national state's effectiveness in absorbing oppositional groups and in co-opting their political discourse, although highly efficient in stabilizing potentially volatile political situations, actually worked against it in emergency situations in which time was of the essence. After nearly sixty years of corporatist politics requiring extensive, ritualized negotiation of loyalty and benefits, the national state encountered difficulty when required to address the demands of individual citizens outside its corporate structure in a timely manner. The system was structured to provide stability by satisfying individual and sectoral interests in exchange for party loyalty, not to respond efficiently to contingencies. Likewise, the state's material distributive network was designed for use in planned political rituals such as land-redistribution ceremonies and handouts at festive political rallies, not for rapid disaster relief (Adler-Lomnitz et al. 256–57). This lack of flexibility outside of the government's corporate framework was a severe impediment to an effective response to a disaster of the magnitude of the 1985 earthquake.

Notably, the government's first impulse during the 1985 Mexico City earthquake was to mobilize its existing corporate ties, coordinating the disaster response within the bureaucratic framework that was already in place. It created two emergency commissions that cobbled together a host of agencies and organizations, one for Mexico City and one at the national level (Pan-American Health Organization 23–24). As critics such as Monsiváis have pointed out, the simple fact that this measure was necessary highlights the lack of a prior plan to coordinate disaster response among the various agencies, each of which had been created separately during a corporate bargaining process to respond to the demands of its corresponding social sector. Prior to this moment, much smaller disasters had been dealt with on a case-by-case, extemporaneous basis: the proper agency entered into action according to the "sector" to which the victims belonged. The scale of the 1985 earthquake made this impossible, however, as the disaster affected people from all social classes and labor sectors and on a massive scale.

Existing agencies had little experience working together, and due to overlapping duties, they had developed highly territorial organizational hierarchies (Monsiváis, *Entrada* 42). In fact, there were several overlapping disaster plans in place, but they were limited by the jurisdiction of the respective agencies that had developed them. Each individual agency adhered to its own procedures: the Cruz Roja Mexicana (Mexican Red Cross) acted according to its Plan 3000, while the military followed its DN-III plan, and so on. Furthermore, many of these plans were secretive and not widely distributed, which severely limited their effectiveness.

The details of the military DN-III plan in particular remained shadowy, and some people suspected that they called for the armed forces to assume roles in civil governance that were not strictly constitutional.[15] This plan was never fully implemented, perhaps because civil authorities were loathe to cede to military governance, even in disaster (Musacchio 83–88). These misgivings were far from baseless, given the history of military interference in politics in Mexico in the early years of the revolution and widespread military dictatorship throughout Latin America in the 1980s.

In any case, the government was as shocked by the earthquake as the rest of Mexico City's inhabitants were: many of its institutional buildings collapsed, including important centers of communications and hospitals, leaving in disarray institutions that would necessarily play key parts in the disaster response. Nonetheless, individual units reacted to the disaster as best they could, albeit in a chaotic fashion that resulted in an irregular distribution of resources, which were often apportioned by clientelistic routes and the existing corporate structure rather than according to the needs of the disaster victims. Tellingly, government medics and rescue crews rushed to help the tourists and business people trapped in the ruins of hotels in the city's business district, but they often took days to arrive at more marginalized neighborhoods inhabited by the urban poor and nonunion workers, who had few formal ties to the corporatist state.[16]

Many victims interpreted the government's sloth in the disaster response as unwillingness to interact with groups outside of its corporate structure, particularly when those groups formed an amorphous mass of victims with no clearly articulated demands or leaders with whom to negotiate and incorporate into its hierarchical structure. Furthermore, the neoliberal policies of fiscal austerity put in place by President de la Madrid following the 1982 collapse of the peso were designed to dismantle slowly the expensive obligations of the state with the corporations that it had absorbed; in this economic climate, the state certainly did not wish to contract new corporate obligations (Lomnitz 77–78). At the same time, neither did it wish to cede political or social authority over the public sphere, particularly to nongovernmental organizations that might challenge its political hegemony. I believe that these paradoxical impulses to limit state obligations while distrusting alternative routes of popular action and dialogue explain the contradictory signals in the state response, which many Mexican intellectuals construed as incoherence.

On the other hand, de la Madrid's technocratic approach to the disaster, which required gathering statistics and expert evaluation before taking action, failed to deploy at the critical moment the rituals associated with the PRI's corporatist politics to which Mexicans had grown accustomed. Although de la Madrid visited the disaster area daily, he did not cultivate a ceremonial presence with the masses: he interacted little with the victims, touring the rubble while surrounded by government officials and bodyguards, and he did not initially take even a symbolic hand in the rescue efforts or distribution of aid. Likewise, the administration's public speeches took the form of emotionless summaries more than reaffirmations of solidarity or populist distributive rituals. They were full of statistics that were useful for government planning but meant little to people who were in a state of emotional shock.[17] As Enrique Krauze wrote, "Their language was detestable: while the city lived one of the most intense dramas in its history, the authorities fell back on the typical technocratic rhetoric in which human life is merely functional" (13).

Nor was there initially a powerful state response that could be interpreted symbolically, as political ritual; in fact, the state took days or even weeks to appear at some disaster sites. The absence of ritual reaffirmation accentuated the rupture in the traditional relationship between the government and its citizens that had been opened by de la Madrid's eschewing of past economic nationalism for neoliberal policies. Needless to say, this did not lead to a positive perception of the president and his abilities as a leader in times of trouble. As one disaster victim wrote in a 2005 retrospective testimonial, "We saw our then President of the Republic for what he was: an insignificant little man who knew nothing, a man who had felt so much fear that he didn't even dare appear on TV to say: 'I am with you all, my heart is breaking alongside yours.' He revealed his pettiness."[18] Mexican intellectuals were left to interpret the lack of political ritual as absence, as the breakdown of political discourse, and, in some cases, as the collapse of the state itself.

The absence of the state was not the only concern, however; it actively opposed popular mobilization in the disaster response. Carlos Monsiváis notes that the first official message to the public following the disaster sought to limit collective action by emphasizing individual interests: at 10:00 a.m. the day of the earthquake, President de la Madrid made an individualist call for the Mexican people to "do what you have to do, to take care of your own interests, and help your fellow citizens. Everyone go home" (*Entrada* 33). This last phrase was repeated incessantly over the next several days by high-level government officials and the press, reinforcing discursively the political delimitation of spaces for state and private action. In practice, troops and police officers were dispatched to cordon off the disaster areas, restricting access to the public. As Monsiváis makes clear, however, this attempt to reinforce the traditional spheres of influence was fruitless. The earthquake itself had shattered that division along with the walls that sustained it. Furthermore, the government took three days or more to reach many disaster areas, during which time local volunteers and family members had already initiated rescue efforts. Impromptu rescuers who came to be known as "*topos*," or moles, sifted through the rubble, often working with little more than their bare hands to excavate tunnels to reach buried victims. Local people contributed medicines, foodstuffs, water, and clothing, and they created unofficial shelters for the victims. Thousands of local rescue "brigades" formed spontaneously throughout the city to support the rescue operations. These brigades incorporated people from every social class and walk of life. Local volunteers also assumed the control of several functions that normally fall specifically within the range of state jurisdiction, including directing traffic and policing their neighborhoods to control looting.

Rather than recognizing these concerned volunteers as an integral and necessary part of the rescue operation, however, the government situated itself as their antagonist: only two days after the earthquake, the Jefe de Gobierno del Distrito Federal (a position commonly known as "regent" due to its subordination to the president), Ramón Aguirre, attacked the volunteers for creating confusion and disorder (Monsiváis, *Entrada* 41). Likewise, the Secretario de Protección y Vialidad, General Ramón Mota Sánchez, stated that volunteers were impeding the work of "authentic" rescue corps (Monsiváis, *Entrada* 41). Objectively, there was some validity to the official position: the justification was that the presence of untrained rescuers and family members at highly unstable and dangerous disaster sites could lead to more injuries and deaths, as well as slowing the governmental rescue teams, as they would be forced to field questions and to deal with distraught relatives. Monsiváis devises more sinister intentions, however: for him, as for many of the disaster victims included in testimonial texts, the government feared losing face as its own ineptness was challenged by untrained but more effective grassroots rescue efforts, on the one hand, and on the other, it balked at ceding authority to local collective organization that could (and, in fact, did) blossom into political activism. Indeed, the government quickly recognized that it was treading on dangerous ground, and it made conciliatory gestures toward the volunteers, praising them publicly as examples of patriotic bravery and national solidarity, still without allowing them to infringe on what it viewed as a space for state, not private, action.

The disaster victims felt further alienated when the government began calling for a return to normalcy only four days after the disaster. Monsiváis ridicules the governmental disconnect with the reality of the disaster by juxtaposing the tenuous situation of the destitute disaster victims, many of whom remained buried under the rubble, with the president's promise on September 24, only five days after the earthquake, that "we will survive and we will reconstruct the nation with new models" (*Entrada* 38).[19] Monsiváis spares no sarcasm in labeling this untimely thrust for normalization and reconstruction as a call for a "return to the formulas of unconditional obedience," rather than any kind of interest in the material or psychological well-being of the disaster victims (*Entrada* 41). In fact, Humberto Musacchio cites a September 20 article in *La Jornada* stating that de la Madrid said, "We are ready to return to normality," as he flew over the disaster zone the day of the earthquake (16).

Not surprisingly, the government's push to normalize took the form of top-heavy bureaucracy. It had lost the opportunity to present a united front in the response to the disaster; it would attempt to recover its standing during the process of the "Reconstruction." On October 3, President de la Madrid decreed into existence the "National Reconstruction Program" (Programa Nacional de Reconstrucción), which he himself would head up (Presidencia 537). The reconstruction commission repeated the pattern of hastily assembling disperse bureaucratic entities into a task force, and without official corporate ties, the victims had no direct representation. Tens of thousands of disaster victims took umbrage at this measure, fearing that they would be written out of the reconstruction process and have no say over their futures. They were particularly worried about government plans to raze their damaged apartment buildings and to relocate them to commuter suburbs in the State of Mexico.

From Solidarity to Self-Organization: The Rise of the Popular Movements

The government's shifting attitude toward the volunteers is highly revealing: as individual citizens, they were out of place in the public sphere, but once they forced the government to recognize them as a collectivity, they became worth bargaining with. Tellingly, the presidency's report on the disaster describes the first negotiations with disaster victims as clouded by "discrepancies between individual and general demands"; the government clearly was looking for greater structure (Presidencia 545). Without formal organization, there were still no corporatist channels of communication or distribution. The indeterminacy in the government's position toward the volunteers would only be resolved when disaster victims mobilized as collective organizations with which the PRI could fall back into its traditional channels and methods of corporate negotiation.

Loathe to abandon the impetus arising from the popular disaster response and well aware that collective mobilization was necessary to engage the corporatist state, the disaster victims joined together initially as a series of neighborhood organizations throughout the disaster zone. In reality, many of these neighborhood organizations were already in existence before the earthquake; groups such as the Unión Popular de Inquilinos de la Colonia de Morelos (Popular Union of Tenants of the Morelos Neighborhood), Unión de Vecinos de la Colonia Guerrero (Union of Neighbors of Guerrero Borough), and Coordinadora de los Cuartos de Azotea de Tlatelolco (Coordinating Council of Rooftop Rooms of Tlatelolco) had formed during the economic crisis of the early 1980s to combat the rent increases that accompanied the high rates of inflation. As the testimonials of members of these groups in Leslíe Serna's *Aquí nos quedaremos* reveal, the fact that these groups were already well organized and located within the affected neighborhoods allowed them to mobilize very quickly in the minutes after the earthquake, accounting to a large degree for the efficiency of the popular response to the disaster. In any case, the neighborhood groups' membership and participation expanded enormously with the earthquake, and new organizations such as the Unión de Vecinos y Damnificados del Centro (Union of Neighbors and Disaster Victims of the City Center) and the Unión de Vecinos y Damnificados "19 de Septiembre" (Union of Neighbors and Disaster Victims "September 19th") as well as the Sindicato de Costureras "19 de Septiembre" (Seamstress's Labor Union "September 19th") emerged directly from the common experience of the disaster. The shared work and emotions in the volunteer rescue effort created extraordinary cohesion among these groups' members.[20] These relationships built on common experience became very important in the structuring and internal politics of the popular movements, creating the sense of shared destiny that allowed them to maintain cohesion when confronted with the threat of state repression or cooptation (Haber 28–30).

Popular mobilization was also catalyzed when Ramón Aguirre, Regente of Mexico City, announced two days after the disaster that the collapsed buildings would not be reconstructed; rather, they would be demolished and converted into green spaces.[21] While this concept appears sound from an urban-planning perspective, the thousands of people who had lived in those buildings were outraged at the prospect of displacement from the neighborhoods with which they had constructed lifelong relationships. Less than a week later, on September 27, the Comité Popular de Solidaridad para la Reconstrucción (Popular Committee for Solidarity in the Reconstruction) formed and carried out a silent march to the president's residence, Los Pinos, demanding that the government take into consideration their concerns and input in the reconstruction effort. Among the demands that they presented were many prior housing issues such as gentrification, rent freezes, and the expropriation of all condemned buildings. President de la Madrid met with their representatives on October 2 and agreed to study the possibility of expropriating the damaged buildings for public housing. The victims continued to apply pressure, carrying out a march in early October that drew together over fifteen thousand participants. On October 11, de la Madrid announced his plan to expropriate fifty-five hundred urban properties covering five hundred acres (Presidencia 550). Tellingly, the expropriation decree was announced in a ceremony that evoked the PRI's traditional distributive rituals, with the president surrounded by masses holding banners stating the popular movements' support for the expropriation.[22] De la Madrid seemed to have recovered his public standing, but it suffered anew two weeks later when the government, having been pressured by business groups, announced that twelve hundred of those properties would not be expropriated after all (Presidencia 552–55).

In any case, de la Madrid's gesture had unintended consequences, as he was met with a landslide of expropriation demands from neighborhoods and popular movement organizations not included in the earlier negotiations, as well as with what Paul Lawrence Haber describes as "enhanced self-confidence" in the popular movements' abilities to extract government concessions (180). On October 14, the government established the Programa de Renovación Habitacional Popular (Program of Popular Housing Renovation) to identify "*damnificados*" (victims) and to issue criteria for program participation. Haber notes, however, that many victims were obligated to become members of the PRI before they could receive benefits, which they considered an affront given what they viewed as the ineptitude of the state response to the disaster (181).

A powerful new earthquake victims' organization arose largely in response to this hegemonic definition of who constituted the collective category of "disaster victims" and, as such, were eligible for benefits, as well as to what those "benefits" entailed. On October 24, the Coordinadora Única de Damnificados (CUD; Common Disaster Victim Coordinating Council) formed with twenty-seven member organizations and twenty affiliates to present a united front in negotiations with the state (Haber 75). Two days later, the CUD held its first march, which attracted over thirty thousand participants. By mid-November, the CUD had forty-two member groups, incorporating together with the new neighborhood organizations preexisting housing associations such as the Coordinadora Inquilina del Valle de México (Coordinating Organization of Renters from Mexico's Central Valley; Haber 177).

Given the chronology of events, it seems clear that the CUD emerged from the process and initial successes of negotiation within the corporate structure of the PRI rather than in opposition to the government or from a governmental failure to engage its citizens, which is how many cultural works ended up portraying the relationship (largely to increase pressure on the government, as I argue later in this chapter). Furthermore, the earthquake became an opportunity to negotiate not only the demands of disaster victims but also the preexisting housing concerns of the urban poor involved with movements affiliated with the CUD. Indeed, Haber notes exponential growth of popular movements nationwide following the 1985 earthquake, even in places not directly affected by the disaster (74).

The Coordinadora Única de Damnificados and many of its member organizations had precedents in urban movements of the late 1970s as well as ideological roots in leftist political groups that grew out of the student movements of 1968. The urban popular movements of the late 1970s emerged from the rapid growth throughout Mexico of the urban poor, who by the 1980s had become the largest single social class (Haber 1).[23] The urban poor had very little representation in the PRI's corporate structure when compared with the rural *"campesino"* and workers' sectors (Haber 55). Umbrella organizations known as *"coordinadoras"* (coordinating councils), such as the Coordinadora Nacional del Movimiento Urbano Popular (CONAMUP; National Coordinator of the Urban Popular Movement), emerged to address this lack, consolidating popular-movement bargaining power and defending member organizations from state repression (Haber 63). In fact, CONAMUP was only one of several *coordinadoras* that formed in the late 1970s, each of which was designed specifically to counter one of the PRI's corporate sectors. As Ann L. Craig writes, "By establishing competing, relatively autonomous organizations, popular movements challenge one of the fundamental precepts of corporatism, that is, monopoly of representation through state-chartered institutions" (275).

Despite the *coordinadoras'* explicit challenge to the PRI's organizational hierarchy, their orientation was not specifically political—they defined themselves as popular rather than social movements.[24] Even though they often employed inflammatory, antigovernmental rhetoric, they sought primarily to increase their bargaining power with the state, on the basis of what Manuel Castells has called a "politics of consumption" or what Juan Manuel Ramírez Saiz calls "reproduction," rather than one of production, meaning that they focused on material concerns such as housing, food, medical care, education, and environmental safety rather than on class issues or regime change (Castells 328).[25] As Joe Foweraker pointed out in 1990, during the heyday of popular mobilization in Mexico, the goal of popular movements was to achieve institutional recognition, leading to linkages with the political system that would eventually be validated in law (11). Foweraker equated this strategy with a Gramscian "war of position," rather than a serious intent to overthrow the government (11). In this situation, maintaining a presence in the public sphere, through both nonviolent protest in public spaces and media representation, was a more effective strategy than armed struggle for attaining the movements' goals.

The earthquake movements followed similar patterns to preexisting popular movements in their organizational and representational strategies, initially eschewing political confrontation for concrete, material demands made in the public sphere. Indeed, the chronology of the interactions of the earthquake popular movements with the government revealed the state's willingness to negotiate early on, even before the formation of the Coordinadora Única de Damnificados. However, the state attempted to use its time-tested strategy of cooptation to resolve the negotiations: from the beginning, the head of the Secretaría de Desarrollo Urbano y Ecología (SEDUE; Ministry of Urban Development and Ecology), Guillermo Carrillo Arena, who was in charge of the reconstruction effort, directed spokespersons of the neighborhood organizations first to present their demands to their local congressperson and then to "merge themselves into the corporate channels" if they wanted their demands to be met (Presidencia 546; Musacchio 60–61).

Although corporate-interest bargaining was the ultimate goal of the CUD, its leaders also recognized that organizational autonomy was necessary to maximize its bargaining power. In fact, it was looking to engage in a process of linkage known as "*concertación*," rather than in traditional PRI corporatism, which would involve the subordination of the CUD within the PRI's rigid power hierarchy. In contrast, *concertación* was developed by the PRI following the 1968 student protests as a way of pacifying grassroots movements that refused formal integration or competed with already established corporate sectors of the state. This strategy functions similarly to the neoliberal publicly funded social-grant model, in which the state funds nongovernmental organizations to deal with specific social issues. Optimists praise this process as a democratic model that greatly increases popular political agency without compromising autonomy. Pessimists tend to view it as a kind of flexible neocorporatism more compatible with neoliberal economic principles, allowing the state to renegotiate clientelistic ties with a shifting demographic without lasting commitment while weakening the influence (and funding) of traditional corporate sectors.[26]

As the case may be, the aggregate structure of the Coordinadora Única de Damnificados made cooptation under the corporate model very difficult, as all member organizations would vote democratically on any *concertación* agreement. Such an agreement was indeed reached nearly a year after the earthquake, when the CUD's members approved the "Convenio de Concertación Democrática para la Reconstrucción de Vivienda" (Democratic Consensus Agreement for Housing Reconstruction) on May 13, 1986. The "Convenio" was touted as a triumph by both the popular organizations and the state. Indeed, the state ceded to many of the popular movements' demands during the bargaining process (including the dismissal of the head of SEDUE, Carrillo Arena, whom many people considered directly responsible for corruption in the construction industry) and in the final agreement, which resulted in an unprecedented urban public-housing program. As Haber explains, the popular movements' demand that expropriated property be held in collective ownership was not met, but between 1986 and 1987, forty-four thousand housing units were constructed, and many renters became property owners, a key CUD demand (183). The success of the negotiations transformed the political panorama in Mexico, leading to a situation in which popular movements no longer plead for benefits or favors from the corporatist state but rather demand their rights as citizens (Ramírez Saiz 235). As Foweraker pointed out, this augmented popular agency represented a direct challenge to the PRI's prerogative to rule arbitrarily (8).

Crónicas, Public Intellectuals, and Corporate Bargaining in the Earthquake Response

I am primarily interested here in the strategies that the Coordinadora Única de Damnificados and its affiliated organizations used to establish themselves as legitimate interlocutors of the state within the corporatist framework, as well as the steps that they took to improve their position during the nine-month negotiating process leading to the 1986 "Convenio." I argue that the popular movements united in the CUD used two prime strategies to maintain themselves in the public eye in their quest to achieve institutional recognition within the corporatist framework of the PRI, which was the initial step toward satisfying their material demands. The first strategy was the performative use of their bodies: the mass marches and impromptu camps in iconic public spaces reminded the viewing public of their continued status as disaster victims, but it also forced the government to recognize them as a collectivity that could not be negotiated with in an individual, extemporaneous, or behind-closed-doors fashion. The second strategy involved the use of the media to maintain visibility and to present the movement as a coherent collective body legitimized by shared suffering, public service, and political precedent.

Not all forms of mass media were equal for this endeavor. The visual mass media was controlled almost completely by the government, and radio was not, by and large, considered a forum for serious political discussion. In contrast, newspapers had long been considered the prime space for public debate on political issues. Indeed, Claudio Lomnitz has argued that newspapers were almost the sole space in which public debate on national political issues was permissible throughout much of Mexican history; hence, they played an indispensable role in the formation of the public sphere in Mexico.[27] Other observers display skepticism regarding the openness of debate in newspapers, which they consider available only to political insiders, but they nevertheless acknowledge the centrality of newsprint in negotiations and positioning in Mexican politics.[28]

I argue that the popular movements reached a tacit agreement with public intellectuals with access to the print media who became their spokespersons in the public sphere. This alliance between popular movements and public intellectuals was nothing new: Lomnitz has shown that throughout the long history of corporatism in Mexican politics, which he traces back to the colonial period, collectivities had to authorize representative intellectuals to speak on their behalf in negotiations with the state. This process of authorization involved the collective, which chose or at least accepted representatives assigned to it based on specific relations of communal respect, but also the state, which judged representatives' capacities for negotiation according to their knowledge of and connections within the political environment and their familiarity with political linguistic registers.[29] Tellingly, in the bureaucratic predominance of the "*ciudad letrada*," literacy was often a requirement for representation: only a "*letrado*" could participate in negotiations that were often carried out and formalized in writing, due both to the social prestige of writing and the large distances between political centers and rural populations.[30] If these public intellectuals had direct access to power, they were able to negotiate directly with the state; however, in many cases, the intellectuals had to draw the issue into the public sphere by converting it into a matter of public debate. Due to the distances involved and the difficulty of breaking into personalistic circles of power, this public debate was most often carried out in newspapers.[31]

In fact, the literary genre known as the *crónica* was developed precisely as a tool for negotiation between individuals or collectivities and the state: the earliest colonial chronicles were written in order to persuade the Spanish Crown to respond to legal demands.[32] Although the *crónica* transformed drastically with the rise of the newspaper and the accompanying creation of a "public sphere," as well as the remaking of the colonial "*letrado*" into the modern "*licenciado*," the genre's function in drawing social issues into the public (therefore political) limelight persists. A presence in print is still necessary to engage the state, whether one is a politician or a collective group seeking recognition (Adler-Lomnitz et al. 232–38). And respected public intellectuals already endowed with political or cultural authority clearly make much more effective representatives than those who might not be recognized by political circles.

Writers with an established presence in the public sphere, such as Fernando Benítez, Marco Antonio Campos, Carlos Monsiváis, Cristina Pacheco, Elena Poniatowska, and even more conservative intellectuals such as Enrique Krauze and Octavio Paz played a key role in bringing the popular movements' demands to the negotiating table in the months following the earthquake. This is not to say that the bargaining process was carried out exclusively by intellectuals writing in newspapers; ultimately, the negotiations were executed by the popular-movement leaders, who met with government officials in private meetings and brought the proposals to a vote before the Coordinadora Única de Damnificados.

Nevertheless, the writers were an important link in the chain of negotiations; their main duty was to position the popular movements favorably for their negotiations with the government.

Several journalistic genres were involved in the process, including news articles, testimonial interviews, editorials, and letters from readers, but I am most interested in the hybrid form of the *crónica*. The *crónica* is best known for its social focus, its concision, and its blending of literary tropes and symbolism with journalistic techniques and reporting. It is generally considered nonfiction, as it is based on observation, and it most often takes narrative form, creating chains of causality between current events and historical phenomena (Corona and Jörgensen, Introduction 4–5). *Crónicas* were particularly influential in postrevolution Mexican political culture due to their genealogy: early colonial chronicles such as Bernardino de Sahagún's *Historia general de las cosas de la Nueva España* (*General History of the Things of New Spain*; 1540–1585) and Bernal Díaz del Castillo's *Historia verdadera de la conquista de la Nueva España* (*True History of the Conquest of New Spain*; 1632) were instituted as foundational texts of Mexican nationality due to their negotiation of cultural identities, while the political projects associated with these early chronicles are often viewed as precursors of the popular struggle against hegemonic political domination, a key trope in postrevolution nationalism.[33] Likewise, the postindependence *crónicas* of authors such as Joaquín Fernández de Lizardi, Guillermo Prieto, Ignacio Altamirano, and Heriberto Frías, published by that point in newspapers, were used to position political projects in the public sphere throughout the nineteenth century.[34]

By the twentieth century, the *crónica* had become the genre of choice of the engaged intellectual in Mexico, embodying in writing that representative quality that Lomnitz views as absolutely necessary for collectives to engage the corporatist state in dialogue, what the writers themselves frequently describe as "giving a voice to the voiceless."[35] The *crónica*'s use of documentary and testimonial modes of discourse is highly effective in legitimizing political ideology with the objectivity of shared experience, while the inclusion of subjective observation and commentary provides a space for theorizing local political phenomena. Despite the ethnographic impulse that informs the *crónica*, the genre typically eschews scientific methodology for literary symbolism and a kind of practical social empiricism rooted in local consensus. As Ignacio Corona points out, "The totalizing gesture of the chronicle occurs outside of the 'comfort zone' of an explicitly defined methodology or a theoretical framework, and without a specific scientific or disciplinary goal" ("At the intersection" 138). I would add that more than data collection, the *crónica*'s ethnography is directed at making social groups visible to the public eye in order to promote concrete political projects. As Rossana Reguillo puts it, "The chronicle is a text that implicates itself in what it is explaining" (55). There are no pretensions of impartiality; objectivity becomes a strategy for persuading the reader of the irrefutability of the authors' arguments.

The *crónica*'s position as mediator in the public sphere between social collectivities and the state allows it to embed popular movements in historical precedent in a way that is accessible to a wide reading public beyond the specialized academic audiences where theorizing usually takes place. The *crónicas* do not claim definitive authority, and they typically eschew the kind of universalist theorizing that characterizes academic discourse for localized interpretations whose relevance is clear to a nonacademic readership. Their immediacy, generic openness, and location in a relatively public forum invite their readers to engage in the debate over the matter or event presented. In this way, *crónicas* representing popular movements endow them with meaning that transcends the movements' parameters, allowing them to engage the state with the backing of public opinion and political precedent.

Hundreds, even thousands of *crónicas* were published in the months following the earthquake, by well-known *cronistas* as well as relative newcomers, in nearly every newspaper and cultural magazine in Mexico City and many other parts of the country.[36] Most newspapers and cultural supplements dedicated entire numbers to coverage of the disaster, backing up the more interpretive bent of the *crónicas* with photographic and journalistic evidence. I devise four thematic phases in the writing of these *crónicas*, with a great deal of overlap due to authorial interests and affiliations as well as publishing lags, particularly in cultural magazines that appeared only weekly or monthly. The initial focus in the days after the disaster was generally on documenting the personal experiences of earthquake victims and the heroism of rescuers, whether local volunteers or those affiliated with the state. The majority of these texts employ testimonial modes of discourse, such as autobiography and the interview, to capture the immediacy of the experience of the disaster.

A second phase, which began only slightly later, involved the attempt to come to a psychological understanding of the experience as collective trauma. In these texts, the collective "we" predominates alongside tropes of loss such as silence, absence, ruins, and collapse. Indicative of this tendency are *crónicas* such as Antonio Saborit's "El estruendo que sofoca los gritos" (The Din That Drowns Out the Screams) which concludes with a fragment that laments, "silence is all," and speaks of the traumatic loss of collective identity: describing an old woman adrift in the ruins of her home, Saborit emphasizes that "no one knows her" except people buried under tons of cement (40). In the same vein, Lourdes Arizpe's "Mi ciudad, mis calles en tiempos de duelo" (My City, My Streets in Times of Mourning) speaks of "buildings emptied of life" (48), while Samuel Salinas Álvarez ends his "La ciudad y su destino" (The City and Its Fate) with, "Our homes are broken, and we have nowhere to go. Is this normality?" (18). Despite the tropes of loss, however, one notes the emergence of a specialized vocabulary of collective unity associated with the popular movements, first appearing in the chronicles of Miguel Aroche Parra, Fernando Benítez, Carlos Monsiváis, Raúl Trejo, and Gerardo Reyes Gómez.[37] In particular, Monsiváis's powerful *crónicas* in *El Proceso* were highly influential in popularizing collectivist language characterized by terms such as "solidarity" and "civil society" that served to empower individuals within a collective, offering a way to move beyond the psychological trauma through both speaking their experience and taking collective action to remedy it.

This collective was often constructed in opposition to the state, leading to a third thematic phase that documented the dire material situation of disaster victims and praised the popular response to the disaster while venting outrage at governmental negligence, corruption, and what some observers interpreted as the active antagonism of the armed forces and governmental officials. This phase, which took place primarily from early October through early November, was the one in which intellectuals pushed most strongly the popular movements' agendas, using attacks on the government to shame it into action. Tellingly, this period corresponds precisely to the initiation of negotiations with the state and the October 24 founding of the Coordinadora Única de Damnificados.

The language of Agustín Monsreal's *crónica* "Mi ciudad rota" (My Broken City), published in *El Excelsior* on October 8, was typical of *crónicas* published during this phase: "Much corruption [or rot] has come to the surface, and at the center of it the lack of foresight, the complete ineptitude, and the clumsiness of the authorities who don't know what to do or say; a power vacuum has been created in the city and the civil population, against all odds, has taken charge of the rough and unending fight to rescue its survivors and its dead" (1).[38] These *crónicas* imputed the dire consequences of the earthquake to governmental incompetence, while they described the popular action in the disaster response as the rise of a civil society characterized by horizontal camaraderie. In this way, they set up an opposition between the state and its citizens that the state, which had long represented itself as the revolutionary embodiment of the masses, would be forced to resolve in order to maintain its legitimacy. The *crónicas* covered all bases, engaging the state's prior corporatist framework as well as de la Madrid's neoliberal rhetoric: they staked a claim for special treatment for the victims as a collective social sector at the same time that they appealed to the liberal discourse of individual citizens' constitutional and universal human rights. When it became evident that the state would not respond adequately to many of the demands without prodding, they made a histrionic appeal for a new political order that would uphold its obligations with its citizens. Given that the popular movements were negotiating with the state the entire time, it is hard to take these calls overly seriously; they were a bargaining tool more than an actual call to arms for regime change.

The more recriminatory *crónicas* set the stage for others that presented concrete proposals for remedying the disaster victims' material situation, such as Margarita Nolasco, Jorge Legorreta, and María Luisa Acevedo's "Vivienda para los damnificados: Cuatro propuestas de acción" (Housing for the Victims: Four Proposals for Action) and Salvador Pinoncelly's "Expropriación minimosca," (Superlightweight Expropriation) both published in *México en la Cultura* on November 20, 1985.[39] Tellingly, these proposals for action cite explicitly as the foundation of their plans the expropriation that de la Madrid conceded to the popular movements on October 11 (Nolasco et al. 39). In any case, not only newspapers but also cultural and even high-art magazines became highly politicized in their criticisms of the PRI and support of the popular movements during this phase. Even Mexico's most prestigious literary journal at the time, *Vuelta*, which had become decidedly conservative, dedicated an issue to the earthquake in which editor Enrique Krauze and founder Octavio Paz voiced support for the popular movements' demands for inclusion in the reconstruction process and criticized the governmental response to the disaster, although they stopped short of attacking President de la Madrid or his neoliberal policies.[40]

Somewhat surprisingly, given the widely diverging ideological stances of the authors and publishers, the *crónicas* provide a relatively uniform presentation of the disaster, differing in tone more than content. Furthermore, the version of events provided by these more recognized public intellectuals was backed up by a legion of academic specialists who did not have such a direct link with the public sphere: anthropologists, geographers, geologists, psychologists, and sociologists who these writers cited or who published their own testimonies and assessments of the earthquake, also in newspapers. In this way, a concerted narrative of the earthquake emerged in the public sphere that supported the popular movements' demands. The homogeneous quality of these texts is not due entirely to documentary objectivity; rather, powerful discursive undercurrents hold the representations together. These undercurrents have to do with the disaster-relief effort as well as prior concerns with poverty alleviation, but there was also a more specific political project involved that spanned the political spectrum.

Although the intellectuals who wrote on the disaster were highly sympathetic to the popular movements' demands, they did not work for free. In return for representation in the public sphere, the popular movements allowed intellectuals to piggyback on their material demands a political project aimed at breaking the PRI's monopoly on power and implementing democratic political reforms. This project was dear both to left-leaning sympathizers of the 1968 student movements and to conservatives linked with the Partido de Acción Nacional (PAN), who yearned to imitate the economic and political structure of the United States. Indeed, contrary to the presentation of the earthquake as the spontaneous emergence of civil society, the theoretical complexity of early *crónicas* of authors such as Monsiváis and Poniatowska reveals that their reading (and writing) of the disaster as a democracy narrative was not informed exclusively by the disaster event; it was a political project well thought out beforehand. Although this political project took backseat initially to the material welfare of the disaster victims, by late November one notes a marked shift toward a more theoretical reading of the disaster, relating it to historical social and political circumstances in a narrative of the rise of civil society that would, ostensibly, lead to real democracy.

I do not mean by this to imply that the popular movements themselves had no prior interest in political change. On the contrary, many of their members and leaders had been involved in the 1968 student movements and espoused highly sophisticated political ideology; however, the immediate material needs of the disaster victims trumped political concerns, and those were the prime demands made in bargaining sessions with government agents. Topics such as regime change or transparency in elections did not come up in these negotiations. In the public sphere, however, intellectuals were successful in linking inextricably the popular movements with the rise of "civil society" and a push for effective democracy. Initially, this was mainly a tactic for pressuring the government to cede to the movements' demands; following the signing of the 1986 "Convenio," however, the demands for political reform overtook material concerns to become the key political issue in the elections of 1988.

Canonical *Crónicas*, the Crisis Paradigm, and the Literature of Democracy

I have argued that the *crónica* has played an important role in political debate in Mexico; one cannot say the same, however, of its position with respect to high culture. Literary critics have traditionally viewed the *crónica* as an ephemeral genre grounded in the immediacy of the present, which disallows it from achieving the ahistorical status of classic, while its focus on the local does not facilitate its integration into the "universal," Western cultural canon.[41] There are, of course, exceptions: those colonial *crónicas* that became useful as foundational narratives and anthologies of certain well-known authors' *crónicas* have achieved canonical status as Mexican classics. In the case of the canonization of colonial *crónicas*, however, there was little alternative: there were few traditional "literary" sources in Spanish from sixteenth-century Mexico that could provide a point of origin for national literature. More modern newspaper *crónicas*, on the other hand, can only achieve canonicity through compilation into a book-length anthology, and these anthologies are usually organized thematically in such a way that the segments conform a narrative orchestrated to transcend the historical moment for which the *crónicas* were originally written.

Those thematic narratives are what become useful in long-term political debates and projects, frequently leading to canonization as national literature. In Mexico, national narratives usually deal with what Mexican critics have called the canon of "national problems," which is what grants them renewed currency in cultural debates.[42] The authors of the earthquake *crónicas* postulated the disaster as a turning point in Mexican nationality, particularly with regard to two related themes or "national problems." The first was the rise of an enormous social class, the urban poor, that had not yet been institutionalized as such, in contrast to other social sectors such as the workers and the peasants who had their representative institutions within the state as well an established tradition of cultural representation within the national canon. The second was the issue of political representation and citizenship, a key national problem in the nineteenth century that the PRI claimed to have solved through corporatism, a resolution that these authors contested fiercely. The authors of earthquake narratives used literature's position within high culture to monumentalize the earthquake as a watershed historical moment in which these two "national problems" came to the forefront. Simultaneously, they used the popular earthquake response to canonize the "collective testimonial" as a hybrid, inclusive literary form that indicated a shift from authoritarian discursive positions to democratic processes, a project that had begun decades earlier with the rise of the testimonial as a distinct genre in Mexico.

Although a few book-length anthologies of earthquake testimonials and chronicles appeared in 1985, the majority were published from 1986 through 1988, most of them after the signing of the May 1986 "Convenio" that concluded the negotiations of the Coordinadora Única de Damnificados with the state. Clearly, those anthologies published after May 1986 could no longer play a role in the negotiation process, which had ended for all intents and purposes. When viewed casually, the timing may appear to be the product of a publishing lag, indicating simply the time that it took to compile, edit, and publish the anthologies. This was undoubtedly a factor, but this explanation does not seem entirely satisfactory when one considers that the earliest book-length works on the earthquake, Garza Toledo and company's *Esto pasó en México* (This Happened in Mexico), Musacchio's *Ciudad quebrada* (Broken City), and Gómez Coronel's *Terremoto en México* were all published in 1985, less than two months after the earthquake. Furthermore, even these early books have a distinct focus on weaving a historical narrative of the disaster that is present only in allusion in the newspaper *crónicas*.

The shift to the monographic format of texts dealing with the earthquake was by no means a "natural," accidental, or commercial evolution; rather, it indicated a conscious shift in thematic focus away from the material experience of the earthquake toward an ideological framework pushing political change. These works constituted a collective call to memory, but more than monumentalizing the losses sustained in the disaster, they evoked the memory of what was gained in the social response to the earthquake and its possibilities for future political change. In them, what had been a negotiating strategy in the chronicles, the rhetorical challenge to the PRI's hegemony, took on a life of its own, evolving into a powerful story about the rise of popular democracy in Mexico. These works canonized the earthquake as one of three key tropes in a narrative describing the decline of the autocratic PRI and the emergence of democracy and popular political agency in Mexico, the other two being the 1910 Mexican Revolution and the 1968 student movements. Basing themselves on these moments in which popular political agency figured prominently, the earthquake anthologies proposed a concept of citizenship that rejected the PRI's corporatism for individual participation in collective political projects.

Notably, nearly all the book-length works dealing with the 1985 earthquake draw parallels between it and the governmental massacre of students at Tlatelolco in 1968, despite enormous contextual differences.[43] Furthermore, they also evoke the Mexican Revolution as an unfinished popular project that was pushed off course by the PRI, particularly in the years since 1968. Consequently, the first book-length anthology of earthquake *crónicas* to appear, Garza Toledo and company's *Esto pasó en México*, opens by stating unequivocally in the introduction, "We don't consider it to be coincidence that such jarring devastation occurred precisely when the country is confronted (oh, imps from TV and the official PRIpaganda) with 75 years of governmental exploitation of the 1910 revolutionary movement."[44] The volume's cover drives home this point visually, incorporating five photos of the devastation, including one of the collapsed headquarters of the Sindicato del ISSSTE (Instituto de Seguridad y Servicios Sociales de los Trabajadores del Estado; Union of the Institute of Social Security and Services for State Workers), in which the PRI logo figures prominently, fractured down the middle. This photo reappears on page 11 with the caption, "As a premonitory warning, the mural advertising the Institutional Revolutionary Party at the Union of bureaucrats was destroyed."

Esto pasó en México goes to great lengths to establish parallels with the 1968 massacre of students, inscribing Tlatelolco as the representative topos of governmental repression. On page 16, a political cartoon appears depicting Tlatelolco as a heap of rubble from which protrude two grave-marking crosses, one labeled "October 2, '68," and the other "September 19, '85" (16). A few pages onward, a chapter entitled "Tlatelolco Murdered Once Again" (Tlatelolco otra vez asesinado) begins with an epigraph reading, "Just as in 1521, as in 1968, tragedy has descended once again on this little plot of martyred land. It seems that irrigating it with blood must be the price to pay so that the Mexican of the future may be born" (34).[45] The hopes for democratic change that were buried along with the victims of the 1968 massacre have seemingly resurrected with the popular movements that arose out of the 1985 earthquake. As Luis Hernández proclaims in a notably upbeat tone, "Not even the 1968 movement could compare with the extension and characteristics of this popular mobilization; the movement of '68 was anti-governmental, but it was formed primarily of the middle class; in contrast, that of September 19 drew together all social classes" (26). For Mexico's frustrated leftists, excluded from the political process due to the cooptation of political parties and labor unions as well as direct repression, the resurgence of civil engagement promised to bring to fruition the popular project that was truncated by the massacre in 1968.

Esto pasó en México and other hybrid anthologies and collections of *crónicas* published over the next year set the stage in the public sphere for a powerful political movement whose focus was no longer solely helping earthquake victims but rather the radical transformation of the Mexican state. Using collage techniques designed to replicate democratic political process within the text, they developed an inclusive narrative of the rise of civil society that would be put to work to support directly the political platform of the Frente Democrático Nacional and its candidate Cuauhtémoc Cárdenas, who challenged the PRI for the presidency in the 1988 elections. It can hardly be coincidental that the most visible and compelling works dealing with the disaster, Carlos Monsiváis's evocatively titled *Entrada libre: Crónica de una sociedad que se organiza* (Free Entrance: Chronicle of a Society in the Process of Self-Organization; 1987) and Elena Poniatowska's *Nada, nadie: Las voces del temblor* (*Nothing, Nobody: The Voices of the Mexico City Earthquake*; 1988), appeared two years after the disaster but mere months before the contentious 1988 presidential elections.

The switch in genres from the *crónica* to more formal literary production was part of this process. By 1987, when the presidential candidates began campaigning, too much time had passed since the earthquake for it to continue to be the focus of the journalistic *crónica*, which by definition deals with current events. Political *crónicas* published in newspapers continued to play an important part in the election process, but they did not have the weight of disaster behind them except in allusion, since the *crónica* typically concentrates on a single theme (here, the elections). In any case, the *crónicas* were too brief to uphold the extensive narrative that intellectuals across the political spectrum were developing to legitimize their push for democracy.

In fact, the shift from *crónica* to formal literary representations of the earthquake mirrored and complemented changes within the popular movements themselves. The 1986 "Convenio" represented a transformative moment for the popular movements united in the Coordinadora Única de Damnificados; under the old corporatist model they would have been institutionalized as subsidiaries of the PRI, but the neoliberal *concertación* model discouraged continued mobilization after negotiations concluded. Once the CUD entered into an agreement with the state, its reason for existence was called into question. This moment of crisis led to divisive internal tensions between factions who wanted the CUD to maintain its political autonomy as a popular movement and those who wished to transform it into a social movement that would work for the fundamental transformation of the political system (Haber 175). This latter faction split off from the CUD in 1987 to form the Asamblea de Barrios (AB; Assembly of Neighborhoods), whose name clearly announces the movement's intention to move beyond the earthquake response.[46] This new movement concentrated on political change, with the goal of promoting urban housing reform and poverty alleviation.

Meanwhile, tensions had surged within the PRI itself between those who supported de la Madrid's neoliberal economic reforms, which called for a dismantling of the corporatist state, and those who wished for a return to the era of economic nationalism in the import-substitution industrialization model.[47] The latter feared that de la Madrid would name the technocratic architect of his economic reforms, Carlos Salinas de Gortari, as the PRI's candidate for the upcoming 1988 elections, thus practically guaranteeing the demise of the power of the PRI's many entrenched corporate sectors. When it became evident that de la Madrid had no intention of reconciling with the PRI's old guard, Cuauhtémoc Cárdenas, then governor of the state of Michoacán and son of iconic General Lázaro Cárdenas, united with former PRI leaders Porfirio Múñoz Ledo, César Buenrostro, and Rodolfo González Guevara on September 30, 1986, to announce the formation of a "Corriente Democrática" (Democratic Current) within the PRI to push for democracy in the internal process of candidate selection. De la Madrid refused to acknowledge the fissures within the PRI or the existence of the Corriente Democrática, but he nevertheless threatened to excommunicate Cárdenas and his supporters from the party. In retaliation, Cárdenas accepted to run as the presidential candidate of the Partido Auténtico de la Revolución Mexicana (PARM; Authentic Party of the Mexican Revolution) on October 12, 1987, and he and his followers formed the Frente Democrático Nacional (FDN; National Democratic Front), a broad coalition including leftist opposition political parties, popular movements, and several political parties formerly affiliated with the PRI that were at odds with de la Madrid's neoliberal policies. The FDN with Cuauhtémoc Cárdenas as its figurehead claimed to be the true custodian of Mexico's revolutionary heritage, promising to bring to fruition effective electoral democracy within a framework of social justice (Adler-Lomnitz et al. 52).

The newly formed Asamblea de Barrios became one of the most vocal supporters of Cuauhtémoc Cárdenas and his Frente Democrático Nacional during the 1988 elections. As Haber writes, "Cárdenas's bid for the presidency provided the national project to which many movement organizations had aspired but which they had not been able to accomplish in the post-1968 era" (80). Likewise, leftist intellectuals jumped on the bandwagon, seeing in Cárdenas, if not a savior, at least a viable possibility for real political change. In private, many doubted his commitment to his political platform, fearing that he was more worried about preserving his father's legacy as the founder of the corporatist state than real democratic reform. In public, nonetheless, they threw their support behind him, attempting to exploit the political rifts within the PRI to their advantage.[48] This endorsement included publishing newspaper articles and *crónicas* on Cárdenas's campaign that linked him closely to the Mexican *pueblo* in a way that undermined the PRI's claims to corporate embodiment of the Mexican people. *La Jornada*, in particular, dedicated extensive coverage to Cárdenas's campaign, although many newspapers more closely affiliated with the government shied away from antagonizing the president by publicizing the challenge to his party's hegemony (Adler-Lomnitz et al. 232).

In any case, the presence in the media helped legitimize Cárdenas as a public candidate, but intellectuals did not simply want to create a personality cult to Cárdenas, particularly given the persistence of *caudillismo* in Mexican politics. Instead, they wove the thousands of earthquake texts into a democracy narrative whose protagonist was the people; in this way they were able to support the candidate's democratic platform without enshrining the candidate himself. In this sense, the formalization of the myriad earthquake chronicles and testimonials in anthologies represented a kind of canonization of popular political agency that worked in tandem with the institutionalization of popular movements such as the Asamblea de Barrios as political entities. As Marco Rascón, one of the AB's leaders, stated, the popular movements envisioned a "political earthquake" that would complement the popular mobilization that arose during the "natural earthquake" (Serna 147).

The intellectuals involved in this political project saw the possibilities for transforming the written experiences of disaster victims into a totalizing "narrative of the *pueblo*," what Krauze called in *Vuelta* a "collective saga" that was "higher and more noble than many falsely epic episodes in our history" (12). This "collective saga" was envisioned as a new, democratic foundational narrative that would displace the "falsely epic" official history constructed by the PRI, with its focus on the "great men" of the Mexican Revolution. There were several interrelated facets to this project, including the construction of the earthquake as a historical event subject to political and social causality (rather than an ahistorical "freak accident"), the reframing of the earthquake within precedents of popular political action, the representation of the popular response as the rise of the liberal citizen capable of participation in civil society, and the rewriting of political language and symbolism for democratic political participation.

The first step was to integrate the earthquake response within a historical framework. This was achieved both by explicit commentary linking the earthquake to the two other canonical moments of popular political agency in modern Mexican history, the 1910 Mexican Revolution and the 1968 student movements, and by creating a causal chronology of the earthquake within the works that brought out key moments when the government failed and the popular response succeeded. Marco Antonio Campos's *Hemos perdido el reino* (We Have Lost the Kingdom; 1986), Cristina Pacheco's *Zona de desastre* (1986), Carlos Monsiváis's *Entrada libre* (1987), and Elena Poniatowska's *Nada, nadie* (1987) all present their material in roughly chronological order, beginning with the sensations felt during the earthquake itself and moving through key moments such as initial news reports, the popular mobilization, the president's first speech, the aftershock, the appearance of government troops at the disaster sites, the arrival of international aid, the discovery of tortured bodies in the ruins of the Procuraduría General (Attorney General's Offices), the organization of the CUD, and so on. This chronological approach may seem intuitive given the historical narrative that these works elaborate, but the historicity of the narrative itself has political ends, as it creates chains of causality that place the state in a very poor light while extolling the popular response.

In fact, the historical narrative of the earthquake, with its allusions to the Mexican Revolution and the 1968 student movements, has a double function in divesting the state of authority by prying loose its hold on historical symbolism linked to the Mexican Revolution, while undertaking what David Snow and his colleagues have called "frame alignment," that is, linking a social movement's concerns to preexisting symbolism that serves to legitimize it within a historical framework.[49] In rural Mexican popular movements, this was often done through association with

Zapatismo, but this imagery did not function well within urban spaces due to its primary emphasis on agricultural issues. Instead, urban popular movements gravitated toward the 1968 student movements and earlier urban labor movements such as the 1959 railroad workers' strike to position themselves within a legitimizing historical precedent. For this reason as well as for practical concerns (many intellectuals and popular-movement leaders had been involved with the 1968 student movements), 1968 became a key reference within these works, orienting the earthquake response within a historical trajectory of popular mobilization against the state.

Nevertheless, 1968 was only one seminal trope in a much larger historical frame. Paradoxically, this frame was originally developed by the state to justify its corporatist politics, but after 1968 it was gradually turned against it by its detractors. I refer to what might be called the crisis paradigm, an interpretation of Mexican history brought to the forefront in the first half of the twentieth century by intellectuals such as Antonio Caso, Samuel Ramos, and Octavio Paz.[50] Although there are many facets to this discursive construction of Mexico as a state in permanent crisis, they all have in common the trope of failure: they present Mexican history as a series of failed projects to achieve political and territorial sovereignty, cultural autonomy, democratic self-governance, economic independence, and social equality.[51] As Roger Bartra has argued in *La jaula de la melancolía* (1987), these negative projections of Mexican history and identity coalesced in a series of projects to re-create the Mexican subject as a kind of *"hombre nuevo mexicano"* (Mexican New Man, playing off Che Guevara's concept) based on revolutionary transformation, an objective that he views as inextricable from the political consolidation of the PRI.[52] As the putative embodiment of the popular revolt against the nineteenth-century Mexican social and political order, the PRI based its legitimacy on transformation: rhetorically, at least, its aim was to convert the downtrodden Mexican subaltern into a modern citizen, and the nation with it, leaving behind the disastrous legacy of colonialism and foreign intervention. Only through its leadership could Mexico free itself of its history of crisis.

As Bartra argues so convincingly, the postrevolution Mexican state promoted the artistic and literary construction of a contradictory image of the ideal Mexican citizen simultaneously as traumatized, subaltern subject and revolutionary hero. According to this perspective, the subaltern subject, though laudable for throwing off its history of oppression during the Mexican Revolution, was too debased for effective self-governance and too traumatized for the rational demands of modernity. Therefore, real democracy had to be deferred until the revolutionary party (the PRI), which embodies the revolutionary-hero essence of national identity, channeled the revolution's collective energy toward goals of modernization and social justice, thus transforming the subaltern subject into a modern citizen fit for self-governance at some point in the distant future. The crisis paradigm justified the state's corporatist politics despite their blatant unconstitutionality: crisis denoted a state of political emergency in which the constitutional guarantee of democracy was perennially postponed until such time as its citizens were fit for citizenship. This argument was highly effective initially for justifying the lack of real democracy to Mexico's middle and upper classes, who retained the lion's share of political and economic agency and who were historically highly distrustful of the lower classes, especially after the revolution.

The PRI's basing of its legitimacy on the crisis paradigm turned out to be a risky maneuver in the long run, however. Its detractors soon turned the discourse to their own uses. By the early 1940s, the shift to capitalist economic policies following the socially oriented or populist (depending whom one consults) presidency of Lázaro Cárdenas led intellectuals such as Jesús Silva Herzog and Daniel Cosío Villegas to speak of a "crisis" in the Mexican Revolution, a diagnosis that became generalized with the massacre of students at the Plaza de las Tres Culturas in Tlatelolco in 1968.[53] Tellingly, these intellectuals did not question the interpretation of Mexican history as a permanent crisis but rather included the PRI in this assessment. They charged that the Mexican Revolution under the PRI's leadership had failed to remedy the "subterranean conditions of crisis" that underpinned Mexican society, a position that Paz echoed in his iconic *Laberinto de la soledad* (1950) and more directly in *Posdata* (1970).

In any case, the symbolic order that the revolutionary government had created, linking itself to the *pueblo* through embodiment, began to unravel. In the glitter and glitz of the 1968 Olympics and following an intense campaign of misinformation that preyed on fears of foreign intervention in Mexico (the social unrest was attributed to the influence of "foreign agitators"), the crisis was again swept under the rug, only to reappear with the 1985 earthquake, which more than a "natural" disaster was viewed by many people as a political crisis occasioned by the failures and corruption of the PRI. In its literary representations, at least, the earthquake exposed the unbridgeable depths of the fault line that divided the government from its citizens.

The chronology of guilt was not the democracy narrative's only concern, however: the collapse of the state's political contract with its citizenry was only half the story. The other half was a tale of redemption about the rise of a responsible citizen embedded in civil society. This narrative was clearly designed to counter the PRI's corporatism, which viewed the Mexican masses as unfit for civic responsibilities. The crisis paradigm of Mexican history, which was used to justify the PRI's corporatism, relied on the premise that the Mexican individual had been forced into subalternity due to the evolution of a psychology of dependence during the experience of colonization and foreign intervention. In this view, disasters were precisely the moments when Mexicans would be least able to react in a viable manner, as the subservient passivity of the colonized identity would impede decisive action. Imprisoned in a fatalist mentality produced by years of oppression, the Mexican people would necessarily defer to the authority of illuminated heroes who would lead them to salvation in times of trouble.

Clearly, the local volunteers who participated in the rescue effort during the 1985 earthquake did not buy into the crisis paradigm or its postulation of deferred citizenship. Their actions in moments of extreme duress constituted a decisive refutation of the fatalism that the crisis paradigm situated at the heart of the "national essence" as the indigenous contribution to the "mestizo character." Likewise, they rejected explicitly Samuel Ramos's and Octavio Paz's diagnoses of schizophrenic resentment, the product of feelings of inadequacy when confronted by unattainable foreign models, as the core of the Mexican subject. As one interviewee in Poniatowska's *Nada, nadie* asserted vigorously, "I would think that the old inferiority complex that we have should be questioned. We are not incompetent. What is incompetent is the system that we live in" (172). The popular response to the earthquake, with its emphasis on collectivism and equality, turned the crisis paradigm on its head: it was the state that was in crisis, not its citizens.

The tales of heroic popular mobilization and individual self-sacrifice conformed a powerful unifying discourse supporting assertions of the emergence of civil society during the earthquake response; however, the democracy narrative depended on form as much as content. The collage-like structures of works such as Garza Toledo's *Esto pasó en México*, Campos's *Hemos perdido el reino*, and Poniatowska's *Nada, nadie* cobble together sources from journalistic *crónicas*, interviews, and testimonial fragments from every representative social sector, re-creating textually the democratic plurality of civil society. These works continue the earthquake *crónicas'* project of bringing a pluralistic range of individuals' voices into the public sphere, challenging the corporatist tradition in which only authorized intellectuals were allowed to represent collectivities: here everyone's story was valid. Of course, these collective testimonials were still edited and published under the authority of representative intellectuals, a technical issue that they never addressed satisfactorily, preferring instead to defer to the lofty democratic ideals of their political project.

In any case, the anthologies' structures attack the PRI's politics at a formal as well as a thematic level. It is no coincidence that these works are structured within the generic conventions of the collective testimonial that Elena Poniatowska first pioneered in *La noche de Tlatelolco* (*Massacre in Mexico*; 1971) as a contestatory discourse disputing the government's version of the 1968 massacre of students with an overwhelming accumulation of accusatory evidence. Following Poniatowska's lead, these works are characterized by the trademark orchestration of personal observation in the style of the journalistic *crónica* with an overwhelming chorus of supporting voices excerpted from hundreds of interviews with people from all spheres of social and political life, as well as intertextuality with multiple genres from high, mass, and popular culture.[54] Dialoguing transparently with official sources, which are often cited in ironic juxtaposition with an accusatory counterdiscourse, these testimonials create an inclusive, totalizing overview of the disaster that is nevertheless concerted to provide a direct refutation of the symbolic order instituted by the state.[55]

The final aspect of the democracy narrative that I wish to examine here is its handling of language. I have already discussed how the authors of earthquake *crónicas* developed and promoted a vocabulary of popular collectivism centered on the concepts of "solidarity" and "civil society" in the days after the response. The *crónicas* could not carry this project to full term, however, for they appeared only briefly, dispersed in time and space. Literary mediation would be necessary to consolidate the new grammar of Mexican nationalism and citizenship that these authors desired to implement. This grammar would be based not on the corporatist formulas and outdated revolutionary rhetoric that abounded in the public sphere but rather on interactions in domestic spaces, the spaces that had been most affected by the disaster and in which its most effective response took place.

Although nearly all the works dealing with the earthquake emphasize the importance of reinventing political language to catalyze new relationships between citizens and the state, Poniatowska's *Nada, nadie: Las voces el temblor* takes the most sophisticated approach to this project. Written in collaboration with eighteen students from a writing workshop that Poniatowska led, as well as hundreds of interviewees, *Nada, nadie* provides the most totalizing and democratic narrative of the earthquake. It is nonetheless emblematic that Poniatowska returns to Octavio Paz's trope of absence (nobody, nothing) to entitle her work. From the title, she inscribes her work within the crisis paradigm of Mexican history as characterized by lack and failure. Unlike Paz's disembodied masks, however, Poniatowska's use of the trope of absence has concrete as well as philosophical implications; she relocates it within the specific context of the disaster, rather than postulating a generalized metaphysical condition. The title words reappear in sentences extracted from interviews throughout the text, punctuating testimonial fragments. As the extracts featuring these words reveal, *nada* refers to material losses as well as the psychological trauma caused by the earthquake, while *nadie* denotes the absence of loved ones as well as political subalternity and the social invisibility of the marginalized. These words clearly evoke the sense of unreconciled loss associated with psychological trauma, a loss that is incommunicable as it has not yet been processed fully into the individual's self-narrative. Nevertheless, this trauma is not exclusively a product of the earthquake; playing off the disaster paradigm, many of the quotations associate it with the long-term loss of political and historical agency under the PRI, in which the Mexican citizen has literally become a *"don Nadie"* (Mr. Nobody).

The tropes of loss and absence, despite their force, nevertheless cede to presence in the second part of the title: those *"voces del temblor"* (voices of the earthquake). The voices fill the void, assuming the therapeutic function of narrating trauma in order to come to grips with loss, but they also elicit the vocal solidarity of slogans chanted in collective marches and political meetings. The chorus of voices and collective action seal the gaping wound inflicted by the loss of loved ones as well as the lack of political participation. Furthermore, those voices simultaneously dismantle and reconfigure the symbolic order of which the PRI saw itself as the sole custodian, often using informal channels of communication such as invective and rumor.

The testimonials included in Poniatowska's text divorce the PRI's hackneyed political lexicon, rooted in the discursive appropriation of "revolution," from the language of the people, replacing it with popular signifiers that emerged from the streets during the literary chronicling of the earthquake. On the one hand, the invention of a new, experiential vocabulary counteracted the PRI's technocratic assessment of the earthquake and its social implications. Words born or refashioned in the popular response to the disaster, such as *topos* (moles), *cuadrillas de salvamento* (rescue squads), and *túneles* (tunnels), were incorporated into a new lexicon to describe and coordinate the local experience of the disaster. Specialized terminology from the construction industry entered general usage, while household objects acquired new symbolism in light of their function for the rescue effort. Medicine, food, clothing, water, and even plastic buckets to haul rubble all became representative of the government's failure to provide basic services to the disaster victims and to distribute equitably the thousands of tons of donations that arrived from throughout Mexico and abroad. On the other hand, terms originating in Marxist discourse, especially those associated with the student movements of the 1960s, such as *solidarity*, *civil society*, and *brigades*, were denatured and inscribed by popular use in a social context beyond the reach of political pandering. As Monsiváis and others have argued, for those who were not politically active, the militant Left had become nearly as anathematized as the government due to its equally hierarchical structure in the closed framework of political parties. For collective engagement in politics to emerge as a real possibility, both politics and the symbolic order that defined them had to be stripped from the hands of politicians and reformulated for popular action.

Attacks on governmental language—what Campos called the bureaucratic idiom of the "authorized" (125)—were used to open a rift between sign and signifier, allowing a process of resemantization to take root. The first step was to disrupt the symbolic order through direct refutation. Antiauthoritarian language associated with marginalized groups with a long history of resistance to governmental control became widespread. In particular, antagonistic argot for describing the police and the military, which had its origins in poor neighborhoods such as Tepito with a history of subsisting on the margins of the law, reappear throughout the testimonies. Expressions such as *"cuicos," "sardos,"* and *"la tira"* (all negative terms for describing the police or soldiers) predominate these descriptions, highlighting the degree to which the state had inscribed itself as the citizens' other. As one victim notes bitterly, "The only ones that in my judgment deserve the name of 'public servants' are the firemen, the Honorable Corps of Firefighters, who instead of exercising power through their uniforms feel compelled to do a disinterested job" (*Nothing, Nobody* 195).[56] The linguistic dividing line was reinforced visually by the cordons that the authorities put in place to demarcate the public and private spheres of action. A section title summarizes the interviewees' readings of this act: "To cordon off is to impede, to oppress, to intimidate" (*Nothing, Nobody* 75). Victim after victim queries why the soldiers appeared with machine guns rather than shovels. An opposition newspaper headline echoed popular opinion: "The government demonstrated that it is better prepared to squelch the people's popular movements than to meet natural disasters" (*Nothing, Nobody* 107).

Faced with the governmental push to retake control of the disaster response both physically and discursively, the disaster victims undertook a resemantization of the state's own technical discourse, turning it to highly politicized ends that frustrated the government's attempts to present the disaster as an apolitical event. Apparently neutral words became charged with accusatory meaning: the "*damnificados*" (disaster victims) became "*damnificados desde siempre*" (the usual victims), the "*derrumbes*" (collapses) of buildings such as the Nuevo León symbolized "*el derrumbe de las ilusiones de la clase media*" (the collapse of the middle class's dreams) (*Nada, nadie* 63), the mere mention of the word "*rescate*" (rescue) represented an indictment of the government's push to "*echar tierra al terremoto*" (bury the entire situation; *Nada, nadie* 129). Tellingly, the government's postearthquake project to "decentralize" its bureaucracy, spreading its power among several cities in order to control the risk posed by future catastrophes, became highly symbolic: the people did not want a decentralization of bureaucracy but rather a decentering of institutional power itself. In these popular rescriptions of governmental bywords, all of Mexico, not just the area affected by the earthquake, was inscribed as a disaster zone, and the politicians were the disaster.

Beyond the testimonials' role in informing the reading public and attacking the discursive order instituted by the government, they elaborate an open formula for constructing a new symbolic order that endows each individual voice with agency, providing a step-by-step manual for dealing with the psychological trauma of the earthquake as well as the political trauma inflicted by the PRI. As *Nada, nadie*'s title underscored, the initial moment of rupture caused by the experience of disaster is represented as silence and loss, that verbal absence that must be filled in order for recovery to occur. This trope of absence acquires powerful embodiment in the figures of children sundered violently from the social and linguistic order—orphans and children who have lost the ability to speak due to the impression caused by the disaster (*Nothing,*

Nobody 311). Following this moment of violent rupture, a new vocabulary for dealing with the disaster emerges slowly, constructed initially of the same tropes of absence and loss: "The small heads of dolls, children's strollers, sheet music, calendars, the remains of mattresses, empty clothes, the keyboard of a piano that looks like it might have fainted from exhaustion on the ground, all this constitutes the language of the rubble" (*Nothing, Nobody* 191). This "language of the rubble" configures a kind of interlanguage, a way of expressing trauma based on the enumeration of objects that have been lost or rendered useless, objects whose symbolic value has come into question. Snatched violently from their context, their meaning can only be provisional, connoting indeterminacy between the roles that they occupied in their owners' lives in the past and their present as emblems of loss that drive home the collapse of the symbolic order of which they formed part.

The testimonials develop an emotive language of pain and suffering that leads the victims to take that first step toward processing the trauma, which is to acknowledge the loss that has occurred within a linguistic framework, but they also develop a grammar of support and mechanisms for recovery that go far beyond the governmental plan for reconstruction. Speaking, eliciting those "voices of the earthquake," is a key step in this process. As one interviewer insists, "You've got to make them talk. It's the only way to go forward" (*Nothing, Nobody* 186). Indeed, Poniatowska inscribes this mutual recounting of the experience of the earthquake as the first step for reinitiating dialogue, that is, collective social interaction: "In Mexico, everybody recounted to me his or her earthquake. Moreover, no friend I reencountered would give me the chance to say good morning. The earthquake came first. It became the indispensable condition to resume dialogue" (*Nothing, Nobody* 317).

In turn, this dialogue becomes the source of popular solidarity. Following this recounting of the personal experience of the earthquake, the individual could begin to relate his or her own experience to that of other individuals, thus creating a collective or communal notion of the disaster. The testimonial format configures this sense of community textually, allowing people with no direct relationship or interaction to come into contact symbolically. The incipient feelings of shared experience and trauma are reinforced through a vocabulary of emotional support and affectivity that counteracts directly the governmental language of detachment and distance: terms of endearment such as *m'hijo* (my son) and the use of the affectionate diminutive (e.g., *Mora, Morita*) draw individuals into a shared linguistic register with its roots in the domestic space rather than in the public or political sphere.[57] Nevertheless, this grammar of solidarity is drawn into the public sphere through literary mediation, thus converting the collective healing process into a project of political transformation.

Tellingly, the democracy narrative obscures the corporatist organization of the popular movements within the Coordinadora Única de Damnificados, which was designed for effective negotiation with the clientelistic state, presenting it instead as spontaneous, organic, democratic self-organization. I have argued that the popular movements were well aware of the national state's preference for dealing with collectivities through corporate bargaining and that they structured themselves accordingly; the democracy narrative, however, disavows this version of events in favor of a story of the emergence of the engaged citizen in the midst of the rubble of the corporatist state. In this rendering, the affective community that formed during the earthquake response becomes politicized primarily as an extension of the domestic space rather than as social sector or political party. This story downplays the prior existence of many of the organizations in the CUD; here, neighborhoods band together spontaneously in horizontal camaraderie during the rescue effort, and this solidarity later converts into political activism when the government fails to live up to its obligations.

In contrast to the model of corporate citizenship developed by the PRI, in which citizens had to renounce their political agency as a condition for induction into the political order, the democracy narrative posits that the earthquake popular organizations based their legitimacy solely on inclusion in a geosocial space: a neighborhood, an apartment building, a refugee camp. Furthermore, the solidarity in the disaster response exemplified the "deep, horizontal camaraderie" going beyond individual circumstances that Benedict Anderson ascribes to inclusive nationalism. In short, the democracy narrative depicts these organizations as the seeds for Mexico's future democracy: despite their imperfections, they nevertheless provide the unconditional democratic inclusion and horizontal camaraderie based on geosocial space (ultimately, the nation) that the government refused to grant. Hopes were high; as Poniatowska beseeches in *Nada, nadie*'s parting words, "Let the enthusiasm of all the *señoras* who distributed thousands of meals not be lost. Let the bags of food and clothing be accompanied by a will to know each other, the will to build a strong civil society that will know how to overcome the inept and corrupt government, a society that can say with Carlos Monsiváis, 'Democracy is also the sudden importance of each individual'" (*Nothing, Nobody* 314).

For Mexico's intellectuals, the popular response to the earthquake in conjunction with the theoretical framework provided by the *crónica* and the collective testimonial provided a long-awaited opportunity to redefine the relationship of the individual to the political collective outside the rigid parameters imposed by Mexico's political history. The possibilities for political action based on class consciousness had been effectively proscribed by the PRI's corporatism and cooptation of revolutionary discourse, on the one hand, and the closed political hierarchy of both the PRI and its oppositional parties, on the other. The testimonials devise new mechanisms for popular integration into a politically active collective based not on class distinctions but rather on common geosocial space, shared experience, thematic concerns, and language.

From Solidarity to the National Program of Solidarity (PRONASOL) and Back

The 1985 Mexico City earthquake, in its literary representations at least, denoted the collapse of the symbolic order that had dominated Mexico's political scene for half a century, as well as the opportunity to rewrite a much more inclusive script. The widespread wrath incurred by the governmental tardiness and callousness in responding to the needs of the earthquake survivors, as well as the history of corruption and fraud, led to a rejection of the government's political discourse and, with it, its conceptual legitimacy as the embodiment of the people. The crisis paradigm that it had used to justify its corporatist political tactics, postulating itself as the sole institution capable of resolving Mexico's history of political and economic crises, came crashing to the ground when it revealed itself ineffectual in dealing with real disaster. In contrast, the popular mobilization restored faith in civic engagement, and the deeds performed in the earthquake response by local volunteers translated into the emergence of a new symbolic order that rooted its legitimacy in democratic consensus rather than in corporate encompassment.

Perhaps nowhere was the ongoing struggle for control over the symbolic order more clear than in the 1988 presidential campaign. Both the PRI and Cuauhtémoc Cárdenas's Frente Democrático Nacional claimed legitimacy as the embodiment of popular sentiment and political agency. Mere days after the term "solidarity" entered popular usage in the earthquake response, the PRI's politicians attempted to turn the word to their own uses. Notably, "solidarity" became a key buzzword in President de la Madrid's "Programa Nacional de Reconstrucción," without any concrete policies associated with it. Leftist journalists who had popularized the term confronted the contradictions in its use by the government, however, leading to a verbal showdown in which the government came out worse for the wear.

Cárdenas also consciously engaged the grammar of "solidarity" and "civil society" in his campaign speeches. In contrast to the PRI's rather empty use of the terms, however, Cárdenas had the explicit support of the Asamblea de Barrios and many of the other popular movements themselves to legitimize his use of the vocabulary. Furthermore, the democracy narrative written by sympathetic intellectuals rooted his political platform in the historical precedent of popular mobilization during the 1910 Mexican Revolution and the 1968 student movements at the same time that they disarticulated the PRI's use of revolutionary symbolism through satire and parody.

Meanwhile, the PRI's candidate, Carlos Salinas de Gortari, attempted to campaign on a tepid platform of modernization and neoliberal economic reform, a surprisingly ingenuous move given the still fresh scars of the earthquake and the rifts within the PRI between the old corporatist guard and neoliberal technocrats. Faced with delegitimization, Salinas was forced to rebrand his campaign, changing his slogan from "Modern Politics" to "Let Mexico Speak" (Adler-Lomnitz et al. 135–36). Clearly, the new slogan was designed to compete with the democracy narrative elaborated by Poniatowska and others, whose main strategy was to create democratic dialogue by using the testimonial mode to bring marginalized voices into the public sphere. Ironically, in Salinas's question-and-answer sessions at political rallies, the public was only allowed to ask scripted questions (Adler-Lomnitz et al. 236).

Given the PRI's missteps in the earthquake response and Salinas's inability to engage successfully the symbolism that would allow him to claim popular embodiment, all indicators pointed to Cárdenas winning the elections. Suspiciously, the new electronic voting system "crashed" just before the polls closed on July 6, 1988, and Salinas was subsequently declared the victor by the then PRI-run Federal Electoral Commission. Exit polls indicated that Cárdenas had won the urban vote but that the PRI had carried rural areas. Many observers considered the rural vote results to be highly suspect, since those areas were largely controlled by local political *caciques* affiliated with the PRI. On the other hand, scholars have pointed out that the corporatist system that channeled votes to the PRI was still very powerful in rural areas, meaning that those wins may not have been fraudulent. In any case, allegations of fraud surfaced immediately, and millions took to the streets in protest. A powerful civic movement challenged the election results and the legitimacy of Salinas's government, a movement that coalesced shortly after in a political party, the Partido de la Revolución Democrática (PRD; Democratic Revolutionary Party). In any case, the perspective of the PRI's rule as a political catastrophe became generalized, spreading far beyond the victims of the 1985 earthquake.[58]

With victory in hand, but on the brink of a political abyss and confronted with the specter of an invalidated political discourse that could sway neither markets nor the masses, Salinas mounted a desperate attempt to reestablish the PRI as a viable political brand. Salinas's first official act upon taking office was to decree on December 2, 1988, the creation of a massive, nationwide social program aimed at alleviating the effects of the economic crisis and the discontent caused by his neoliberal reforms, especially those designed to terminate the state's obligations with its incorporated social sectors. Extraofficially, of course, it is widely recognized that the program was intended to recover the votes lost to Cárdenas in the 1988 elections. In any case, Salinas's program spent a total of nearly eighteen billion dollars (up to 1.2 percent of the GDP annually) paving streets, bringing electricity to rural areas, providing microloans to small businesses and farmers, and constructing roads, schools, and hospitals. Tellingly, this program was conceived as a direct continuation of de la Madrid's Programa Nacional de Reconstrucción, with only one key change in its title: it was now called the "Programa Nacional de Solidaridad" (PRONASOL; National Solidarity Program).

Salinas's appropriation of the "solidarity" trope that had arisen during the popular response to the 1985 earthquake clearly adheres to the PRI's time-tested strategy of coupling the cooptation of language that threatens its political legitimacy with the incorporation of oppositional figures into its ranks. PRONASOL's language could not be more unambiguous on this point, as one official report makes blindingly clear: "Therefore, from a social point of view, Solidarity's methodology converts the management of public works into processes of mobilization, organization, and coresponsibility. Through Solidarity, the existence of mobilized social subjects is recognized, and at the same time, a procedure of concerting and rationalizing is stimulated in the management of social policies" (Consejo Consultivo 68).[59] Furthermore, Salinas named a well-known leftist intellectual and popular-movement organizer, Carlos Rojas, as director of PRONASOL.

Salinas's administration further attempted to tame the urban popular movements that many researchers associate with Cárdenas's success by creating a unit within its Confederación Nacional de Organizaciones Populares (CNOP; National Confederation of Popular Organizations) called UNE: Ciudadanos en Movimientos (UNITE: Citizens in Movement). Furthermore, Salinas chose leaders of existing popular movements, many of whom had formerly opposed him in the elections, to head up UNE (Haber 113–15). These leaders were charged with channeling low-income urban residents toward PRONASOL resources. As Haber points out, UNE largely became a way to endow elected officials with credibility; in the post-1988 electoral environment, candidates needed to demonstrate their commitment to work with popular movements (118).

Needless to say, opposition intellectuals such as Carlos Monsiváis took a dark view of this "cooptation." In *No sin nosotros* (Not without Us), Monsiváis declared starkly that "the purpose is simple: to turn civil society into an appendix of the government, without giving up anything" (33). Nothing if not pragmatic, however, Salinas actively courted artists and intellectuals, who already felt a certain affinity with a president who held a PhD in political economy and government from Harvard. The new president met personally with many of them, and he founded and funded institutions such as the Consejo Nacional para la Cultura y las Artes (CONACULTA; National Counsel for Culture and the Arts) for which they had long been pleading.[60] Furthermore, he championed (in word, at least) electoral reforms such as the 1990 Federal Code of Electoral Institutions that removed the Federal Electoral Commission from the hands of the PRI, establishing it as a nonpartisan institution under the leadership of respected leftist intellectual José Woldenberg.[61] Finally, PRONASOL created local committees charged with proposing projects and managing their funds, effectively creating the impression of the decentralization of institutional power. Democracy seemed to be a real possibility in the near future. With these gestures, Salinas appeared to offer a renewed partnership with both the Mexican people and the powerful intellectual class, revalidating the legitimacy of the PRI's political discourse as a shared code of communication. By taking these steps toward reestablishing dialogue between the state and its citizens, Salinas was able to mitigate criticisms of his discursive appropriation of solidarity. In this sense, PRONASOL represented a mechanism for patching the ruptured symbolic order as much as for rebuilding the nation.[62]

Salinas's cooptive strategies placed his opponents in disarray. Many of the popular movements and intellectuals accepted incorporation; lured in by formerly undreamed-of funding, they chose to see PRONA-

SOL as a concession that they had won from the PRI. On the other hand, the Asamblea de Barrios refused to negotiate with the state, declaring an end to the era of concessions. Instead, it played a key role in the formation of the opposition Partido de la Revolución Democrática, in which many of AB's leaders held important party positions. Nonetheless, Salinas's strategies were highly successful in the political arena, and the PRI experienced a substantial electoral recovery in the 1991 midterm elections.

Salinas seemed to have rescued the PRI from the brink: his politics of *concertación* had neutralized many of his opponents, and his linguistic appropriation of the vocabulary of solidarity, which he backed up with PRONASOL's acts in the social sphere, seemed to have restored the PRI's legitimacy within the national symbolic order. The scandals that plagued the end of Salinas's presidency and the transfer of power to Ernesto Zedillo in 1994 did not bode well for the PRI, however. In particular, the murder of the PRI's candidate, Luis Donaldo Colosio, which many people suspected to be the result of internal rifts within the PRI, shook confidence in Salinas's remaking of the party's image. The economy was also on highly uncertain footing, due in part to the huge expenses incurred by PRONASOL, many of which were financed by selling off state interests to private investors, often at scandalous prices (Haber 188). Indeed, upon entering into the presidency, Ernesto Zedillo was forced to devaluate the peso, leading to an even greater economic crisis than in 1982. Likewise, the 1994 Zapatista rebellion in Chiapas placed Salinas's economic policies into question, particularly regarding the benefits for poor, rural Mexicans of the North American Free Trade Agreement, which Salinas brokered. These fresh problems tarnished the PRI's reputation to such a degree that in 1997 it lost its majority in Congress for the first time, to a coalition of opposition parties. This downward slide finally culminated in the loss of the presidency in the 2000 elections, to conservative Partido de Acción Nacional (PAN) candidate Vicente Fox Quesada. In appearance, at least, the democracy narrative had finally come to fruition, twenty-five years after it was elaborated.

Conclusion

On Writing and the Nationalization of Catastrophe

THIS BOOK SPRANG FROM MY INTEREST in how disasters catalyze lasting political and cultural changes and in the roles that writing has played in promoting and consolidating those changes throughout Latin America. I have argued that disasters force the renegotiation and modification of the individual, collective local, and national narratives that endow social and political life with meaning. Every disaster compels those who are affected to generate new, localized narratives, whether written or not, to come to terms with their experience of the catastrophe. These disaster narratives have multiple, overlapping uses, from helping individuals to resolve traumatic experience to upholding explicit political platforms or challenging established political and social orders. In the heat of the moment, at least, newly formulated disaster narratives take precedence over the preexisting, broad life narratives associated with political and social order, forcing their revision.

Nevertheless, disaster narratives cannot stand alone; they only function by arriving at a working consensus with preexisting discourse. For people to move beyond catastrophic experience, disaster stories must be reconciled with prior narratives. This process of arriving at a consensus between narratives allows for the renegotiation of political power, as the narratives that sustain power relations are modified to incorporate the experience of disaster. And these narratives reauthorize or deauthorize political figures and ideologies. Indeed, scholars have long known that disaster precipitates political crises, particularly in political orders characterized by unequal power relations (Aldana 189). The experience of disaster frequently catalyzes political action as individuals and collectivities engage in the assignment of blame as well as the construction of greater security.

Political movements arising from disaster require as a basis for action the weaving of individual disaster narratives into a collective framework, a process of negotiation of meaning in which distinct parties position themselves through rhetoric as well as performative action. The principal strategy of these collectivized disaster narratives is to frame the catastrophes as political, not natural, events. In these narratives, disaster is neither subject nor object—it is the point of intersection of natural geological or climactic phenomena with social, political, and cultural factors that have placed people in a state of vulnerability. The politicization of disaster hinges on this posterior assessment of vulnerability and the unequal distribution of risk, as well as the assignment of blame, which are all posited within the sphere of human, not natural, agency. Indeed, the primary function of disaster narratives is to determine causality, a process that cannot fail to have political implications when collectivities are involved and implicated.

At the same time, the political focus of disaster narratives restores faith in the collective project of human dominance over nature. By inscribing vulnerability as a question of social or political marginalization rather than of natural spite or chance, we are able to sidestep the traumatic feeling that we live at the mercy of nature. Individual and collective human agency can be reinstated if disasters are due to our political failures, not to impartial or even antagonistic natural forces. On the other hand, established political orders often take the opposite tack: well aware that political interpretations of disaster are inevitably bound up with the assignment of blame, they hope to minimize political ramifications by framing disasters as exclusively natural events.

Despite recent trends in economic globalization and international political cooperation, politics continue to be negotiated primarily at local and national levels. This is particularly the case in disaster; the localized aftermath of catastrophe has a centripetal effect in retracting the political gaze from globalized policy to local issues. From the viewpoint of those who are affected, disaster cannot be addressed adequately from without, even when international aid and solidarity are involved in the disaster response. In this setting, academic narratives of disaster arising from broad, international scientific frameworks often have little weight in the political decision making surrounding disasters unless local narratives engage them to their own ends. Indeed, intellectual abstraction often becomes offensive for those who have suffered a disaster in the flesh. For this reason, local disaster narratives, more than generalized theoretical perspectives, hold the key to understanding the political ramifications of particular disasters.

I have analyzed two distinct kinds of localized disaster narratives from Latin America: those dealing with single disaster events (Cyclone San Zenón of 1930 and the 1985 Mexico City earthquake) and those that mediate natural disasters that recur over long periods of time (drought in northeastern Brazil and volcanic imagery in Central America). As my study has made evident, both powerful one-time events and long-term, recurring natural disasters spawn disaster narratives that advance and legitimize cultural and political change. Nevertheless, there are some key differences in the narratives that arise from these events. Long-term, recurring disasters tend to be textualized as legitimizing narratives themselves; the frequency and repetition of the disasters give rise to canonical interpretations of events that uphold particular political orders. Even in cases in which a particular disaster event provides an opening for criticizing or revising preexisting orders, with time and repetition, those initially subversive versions of disaster are institutionalized as foundational narratives for new orders, which may be challenged in turn when disaster precipitates the questioning of order once again. Such was the case with the Great Drought of 1877–1879 in northeastern Brazil, which served as fodder for republican criticisms of the Brazilian Empire and rapidly became a sustaining narrative for the Brazilian Republic following the publication of Euclides da Cunha's *Os sertões* (1902), only to be attacked in turn by the northeastern authors of the Romance de 30 following the drought of 1915. Likewise, the volcanic imagery that underpinned independence in Central America rested on a foundational narrative of potential eruption that revolutionary movements turned against the repressive political orders it sustained from the 1960s on.

Single catastrophic events, on the other hand, are usually incorporated as supporting tropes into preexisting or emerging narratives not based exclusively on disaster that attempt to disrupt or renegotiate established orders. In these cases, the opponents of particular political orders represent a disaster as a trope of rupture with the past or, alternatively, as the embodiment or culmination of a history characterized by a series of social, economic, and political disasters for which the existing political order is directly responsible. Dominican dictator Rafael Leonidas Trujillo's regime engaged both these uses of disaster in its representations of Cyclone San Zenón of 1930, portraying the hurricane as the endpoint in a disastrous history of abjection, corruption, and servility. According to this version of events, the Dominican Republic could only be saved from perpetual catastrophe by rebirth as the "New Patria" under Trujillo's oversight. Proponents of democratic political reform in Mexico put the 1985 Mexico City earthquake to similar uses, postulating it as the culmination of a rupture between the Mexican people and the ruling Partido Revolucionario Institucional (PRI) that had been decades in the making. In contrast to this history of institutional failings, these authors represented the popular response to the earthquake as the rebirth of a civil society that heralded the capacity for democratic self-governance.

Tellingly, both Trujillo's regime and the proponents of democracy in Mexico inscribed single disaster events within a historical framework of protracted disaster. This strategy was highly effective in politicizing the events, as they were represented as tropes in political history rather than as singular interruptions of history by uncontrollable natural forces. On the other hand, this strategy reveals that there is not a definitive separation between the modes of narrative associated with single and recurring natural disasters. Both kinds of narratives require the insertion of disaster events within a historical framework in order for them to acquire political heft.

I have argued that in Latin America, at least, literary texts play an important role in instituting the political changes that emerge from disaster through canonization. Clearly, literary mediation is not always necessary for a disaster to have political consequences; direct mobilization and mass-media representations may play equally or even more important roles in the politicization of disaster. Literary mediation has been central throughout Latin American history, however, due to a variety of factors, including the historical prominence of writing as a tool of power; the centrality of the written page as a space for theorizing political, social, and environmental relationships; the use of newspapers as a forum for the negotiation of power relations; and the role of literature in developing and canonizing national foundational narratives.

The canonizing function of literature is almost indispensable for a disaster to be endowed with lasting national significance in Latin America. Widespread sympathy for victims perceived as fellow citizens does much to structure horizontal feelings of solidarity throughout a nation during disaster, but the mere presence of those feelings is not sufficient for a particular disaster narrative to acquire political heft at the national level. The inscription of disasters as political events and, therefore, markers in political history is a first step, but they must also be inserted into national foundational narratives for them to acquire national primacy. This is most often done through literary mediation, due to the historical power of writing and its role in the construction of foundational narratives.

There are certainly cases in which disasters came to be considered "national catastrophes" without extensive, protracted literary mediation (the 1972 Managua earthquake comes immediately to mind), but even then writing almost inevitably played a role, even if through inscription in historical narrative rather than strictly "literary" texts, as nebulous as that distinction may be. In any case, the influence of single disaster events rapidly fades from public view without a written presence in genres that have traditionally sustained foundational narratives—national histories but also poetry and prose fiction. In this sense, writing continues to serve that ancient function in sacralizing interpretation with the transcendental quality of abstract or symbolic history that is necessary to generate national imaginaries. Through this process of incorporation into national narratives, disaster symbolism becomes a powerful tool within the national imaginary, which is put to work by political actors at specific moments to uphold their political platforms.

Notes

All translations are my own, unless otherwise noted.

Introduction

1. As Virginia García Acosta puts it, disasters "detonate" preexisting social, economic, or political crises (Introduction 18).

2. I defer on this point to the long genealogy of thinkers from Gramsci to Foucault who study the interweaving of culture and politics in the configuration of power relationships.

3. Regarding the process by which cultural change results from the experience of disaster, consult Jon Anderson's "Cultural Adaptation," Greg Bankoff's *Cultures of Disasters,* and Susanna Hoffman and Anthony Oliver-Smith's edited volume, *Catastrophe and Culture.* As Oliver-Smith and Hoffman summarize in their introduction to *Catastrophe and Culture,* "hazards and disasters, and how societies fare with them over long periods of time, are potential indices of not only appropriate environmental adaptations, but ideological ones as well. These cultural adaptations include innovation and persistence in memory, cultural history, worldview, symbolism, social structural flexibility, religion, and the cautionary nature of folklore and folktales" (9).

4. See, for instance, Lévi-Strauss's *The Savage Mind* and *The Raw and the Cooked.*

5. See chapter 2 of Callicot's *Earth's Insights* and Taliaferro's "Early Modern Philosophy," respectively.

6. For instance, Virginia García Acosta suggests that the Iberian conquest and colonization of Latin America, together with the implementation of Western models of development not designed for Latin America's very distinct geographic and social environments, led to sharp increases in the vulnerability of its population to natural disasters (Introduction 32–34).

7. As Jon Anderson suggests, "in acute crises where disaster-culture patterns are absent or lack development, interpretations tend to be extemporaneous,

unstable, and individualized, and definitions of the situation remain private," which often leads to psychological trauma (299).

8. I follow García Acosta's lead here in emphasizing that electing to narrate a history in which disaster becomes the unifying thread of social and economic processes represents a highly charged ideological position (Introduction 20). Indeed, as García Acosta underscores, many national histories gloss over disasters or fail to mention them altogether, which can only be viewed as an ideological decision.

9. Regarding the history of man-made alterations of the environment leading to desertification, consult Shawn William Miller's *Environmental History of Latin America*, Alfred Crosby's *Ecological Imperialism*, and Elinor G. K. Melville's *Plague of Sheep*.

10. See, for example, the discussion of natural hazards and vulnerability in Andrew Maskrey's *Disaster Mitigation* or Ben Wisner's "Disaster Vulnerability."

11. Linda Manzanilla and Anthony Oliver-Smith detail several preventative techniques developed by indigenous groups in their "Indicadores arquelógicos de desastres" and "Peru's Five Hundred Year Earthquake," respectively. Regarding indigenous engineering of the environment in Latin America, consult also Whitmore and Turner's *Cultivated Landscapes in Middle America* and Denevan's *Cultivated Landscapes of Native Amazonia and the Andes*.

12. See, for instance, Manzanilla's "Indicadores arqueológicos de desastres"; Gerald Haug et al.'s "Climate and the Collapse of Maya Civilization"; Richardson Gil's *Great Maya Droughts*; and Harvey Weiss and Raymond S. Bradley's "What Drives Societal Collapse?"

13. These beliefs were documented in the texts of Spanish and postconquest indigenous historians and chroniclers such as Fernando de Alva Ixtilxóchitl, Francisco López de Gomara, Fray Bernardino de Sahagún, Guaman Poma, the Inca Garcilaso de la Vega, and Pedro Cieza de León. Many of them are summarized in María Eugenia Petit-Breuilh Sepúlveda's *Naturaleza y desastres en Hispanoamérica*.

14. Regarding this conceptualization of a genealogical link between humans and nonhuman nature, see Whitt et al., "Indigenous Perspectives" 4–8.

15. See chapters 2 and 3 of Petit-Breuilh's book.

16. The 1755 Lisbon quake shook things up considerably, however: Mike Davis describes it as the "Hiroshima of the age of reason," a cataclysm so powerful that it challenged Enlightenment philosophical optimism and gave rise to a new genre of European disaster literature (282–83).

17. Regarding this hurricane, see Peter Martyr d'Anghiera's *De Orbe Novo: Decades of the New World* (Dec. 1, Book IV, p. 113) and Christopher Columbus's letter to the Spanish monarchs dated October 14, 1495.

18. Rossano C. Calvo gives a historical background of these two deities in his "Del folklore a la antropología del terremoto."

19. See Emanuel 18–19.

20. See, for instance, Jesuit priest Fernão Cardim's report on his travels throughout the *sertões* of northeastern Brazil, in which drought is represented not as an exceptional circumstance but rather as a minor part of a general panorama of hardship. Likewise, Bernal Díaz del Castillo undoubtedly experienced volcanic eruption and earthquakes during his sixty-odd years in Mexico and Guatemala, but he barely mentions disaster in his *Historia verdadera*.

21. I am thinking particularly of works such as Pedro de Oña's poem on the 1609 Lima earthquake and Archbishop don Melchor de Liñán y Cisneros's report on the 1687 earthquake in Lima and Callao (cited in Pérez-Mallaína 70).

22. Perhaps not surprisingly, this trope reappeared in the twentieth century in revolutionary writing on volcanoes in Central America, in which volcanic eruptions became associated with popular uprisings against local oppression and foreign intervention, a topic that I deal with in chapter 3.

23. An important exception to this would be the escaped slaves who formed villages in the wilds, far from Spanish settlement. Two of the most famous of these are Palenque, Colombia, and Palmares, Brazil. Freed from the colonial strictures imposed by their masters, escaped slaves would have developed their own ways of relating to their environment, and, as they often lived in close contact with indigenous people, transculturation undoubtedly occurred.

24. Luhmann proposes this thesis in *Risk: A Sociological Theory*. This does not mean, however, that religious interpretations exclude entirely human agency. Susanna Hoffman points out that framing disasters in religious terms establishes at least a degree of mastery over them: if God controls disasters, they are not entirely outside the sphere of human influence (134).

25. See the introduction to Freedgood's *Victorian Writing about Risk*.

26. For an overview of the discursive construction of paradise in Brazil, see the first half of my "National Nature and Ecologies of Abjection in Brazilian Literature."

27. Ángel Rama coined the term *ciudad letrada* to describe the unprecedented influence on political decisions that the educated or intellectual "lettered" class exercised during the Spanish colonial period. He describes this bureaucratic class as a literal city within a city, capable of withstanding changes in administrations and policies without relinquishing its power. Furthermore, Rama asserts that this model of social and political organization was not only maintained but often strengthened following independence in the Spanish American nations.

28. Consult the first two chapters of Carlos Alonso's *Spanish American Regional Novel*, as well as the introductions to Jennifer L. French's *Nature, Neocolonialism, and the Spanish American Regional Writers* and Durval Muniz de Albuquerque, Jr.'s *A invenção do Nordeste*.

29. As García Acosta points out, "dominant schools of thought from sociology have preached an ahistorical and even antihistorical vision of disasters" ("Historical Disaster Research" 49).

30. See Hoffman 139.

31. I deal at length with this political construction of views of national histories as sustained disasters in my chapters on the Dominican Republic and Mexico. Even seminal Mexican disaster-historian Virginia García Acosta, somewhat surprisingly given her focus on contextualization, cannot resist referring to "five centuries of disastrous Latin American history" in the final lines of her introduction to *Historia y desastres* (34). As I argue in my chapters, this kind of assertion does not represent a critical view of Latin American history but rather corresponds to generalized ideologies of national and continental histories as a series of failed projects that were developed for very specific uses in particular contexts, such as justifying or attacking violent political change.

32. In fact, Anthony Oliver-Smith asserts that "some scholars in disaster research suggest that disasters are entirely sociocultural constructions—that is, the presence or activation and impact of a hazard are not necessary for a disaster to take place. All that is necessary for a disaster to have occurred is the public perception that either a hazard threat exists or an impact has taken place" ("Theorizing" 37).

1. Disaster and the "New Patria"

1. For an exhaustive listing of the changes in Dominican place names implemented by the Trujillo regime, consult Jesús de Galíndez's *Era of Trujillo* and Luis Alemar's *Santo Domingo/Ciudad Trujillo*.

2. Bosch's *Trujillo: Causas de una tiranía sin ejemplo* (Trujillo: Causes of an Unprecedented Tyranny), which he published from exile in Caracas in 1959, describes the dictator as the sole capitalist of the development of Santo Domingo due to his single-handed dominion over the country's economy, politics, and military (115). As the title makes clear, Bosch's book was written as a direct offensive against Trujillo's regime; in spite of its programmatic orientation, it offers many valid observations.

3. For an in-depth analysis of the role of urban spaces in collective memory and agency, see Dolores Hayden's *Power of Place: Urban Landscapes in Public History*.

4. "Una serie de vicisitudes, guerras, matanzas, prosperidades, asaltos de la naturaleza, determinan su historia, convulsionada y agitada, como la de ningún otro pueblo de América" (42). Trujillo sponsored the publication of translations of many of his defenders' works, including several of Osorio Lizarazo's books, into English and occasionally French as part of his international relations campaigns. There are also a large number of other books by his supporters that were never translated or reprinted due to the international rejection of Trujillo's regime toward the end of his rule, their questionable aesthetic quality, and/or untenable ideological positions. This does not preclude their interest for this study, however. Among this latter group, I have myself translated passages pertinent to the argument; since many subtleties are lost in translation, I also

include the original Spanish quotations in notes when wording is paramount. Furthermore, some of the works that the regime had translated into English edit drastically, transform, or alter almost entirely the tone of the Spanish original. Such is the case with James I. Nolan's translation of Osorio Lizarazo's *La isla iluminada*. While speculation as to the why of these omissions, compressions, and alterations is entertaining and perhaps even revealing (are they due to haste or distaste? or perhaps the translator remained faithful to the text's propagandistic mission, realizing that some passages were so outrageous that they would undermine the cause), such amusements add little to my argumentation. I have therefore chosen to retranslate these particular quotations myself.

5. "El pasado siniestro de nuestra nacionalidad, hoy floreciente, está ahí, en escombros, como un estigma" (22).

6. "Un concepto propio de la democracia"; "la prosperidad y el bienestar colectivos, la plenitud de la libertad espiritual, la felicidad auténtica del pueblo" (13).

7. "Una perfecta compenetración entre el mandante y el mandatario" (20–21).

8. See Benedict Anderson, *Imagined Communities*.

9. While the *Listín Diario*, Santo Domingo's oldest surviving newspaper, was apparently supportive of Trujillo's relief efforts in the early days of the Trujillato, it was fiercely critical of Trujillo's regime and supported his opponents, the Alianza Nacional-Progresista (Galíndez 12–13). After 1933, however, it became Trujillo's mouthpiece, and the son of the *Listín Diario*'s owner, Arturo Pellerano, held important political positions under the dictator. Eventually the newspaper fell into disfavor once again and suffered financially when Trujillo removed his protection and founded his own news source, *La Nación* (Galíndez 24, 121).

10. "Nuestra habitación corre hacia nosotros. El cerebro lo reconstruye tal cual era y uno por uno pensamos en todos sus detalles. Recordamos tal cuadro que nos regalaron. El retrato de un amigo con flamante dedicatoria. Nuestra mullida cama que abandonamos para siempre la noche anterior" (52).

11. "Sobre la ciudad de Santo Domingo 50 mil Jeremías se lamentan sobre las ruinas de sus hogares" (52).

12. "Santo Domingo está en ruinas. Santo Domingo es todo un solo escombro. Santo Domingo es todo un solo lamento" (52).

13. "Aquí, en estas páginas, el personaje de la narración, el personaje principal, es el pueblo entero de Santo Domingo. Se necesita hablar de todos. Se necesita hablar del banquero, del escritor, del profesional, del oficinista y del obrero en general. Se necesita hablar del pobre y del rico, del que tiene salud y del enfermo. Necesitamos entrar tanto en el hogar del débil como el del poderoso. Aquí lo que hay realmente es el hogar dominicano, el hogar de todos en ruina" (54).

14. "Las fogatas iluminan espantosamente hacia el Sur, junto al Mar Antillano. Esto, le hace a uno pensar que no vive en Santo Domingo; que se ha trasla-

dado de un salto al África del Sur, al Congo, por ejemplo, y allí cumple, cruel y largo destierro. El pueblo dominicano de la Capital, sufre una deportación terrible sin salir de su Ciudad. 'Aunque Ud. no lo crea,' de Ripley" (115).

15. "El hombre llega a sumergirse en la idea de que la vida es realmente amarga. Piensa que no vale la pena preocuparse y que debe mantener el descuido hasta un grado en que siempre esté colindando con la sinvergüencería" (78).

16. "El desastre hace ser normal, ante nuestros ojos, lo que anteayer teníamos en el grado superlativo de la anormalidad" (79).

17. "Necesitamos una fábrica artificial de alientos. Necesitamos maquinarias para hacer voluntades. Necesitamos un mecanismo para fabricar alegrías. Necesitamos un engranaje especial que produzca como cosa única, nuevos optimismos" (83).

18. "Los escombradores, los que ejercen la acción de escombrar, limpiar, aclarar, llevan bastante adelantada dentro de una terrible lentitud su labor en nuestra vieja Ciudad Primada. Se escombra también en los corazones entumecidos y en las almas con moho; se escombra en el hogar y en la vía pública, dondequiera que unas ruinas materiales o espirituales contribuyen a seguir manteniendo la voluntad y el cielo gris" (165).

19. "La hecatombe ciclónica constituyó un golpe de Estado de la naturaleza; fue para la República, lo que un brusco despertar para el profundo sueño de un dormido por siglos. Ciertamente dormíamos a pierna suelta, con la hereditaria haraganería que produce un violento cruce de razas antagónicas" (13).

20. "Pero, toda tragedia, es a la vez, sepulcro y cuna, meta y partida, descanso y sendero. Se presentaba un momento propicio para que surgiera un hombre, y en efecto surgió, con toda la predestinación de quien trae en su cerebro y su alma poderes singulares" (13).

21. "No somos nosotros los que mañana recibiremos los resultados de esta gran catástrofe. Serán nuestros hijos y nietos, los que recogerán los frutos. Veinte, treinta, cincuenta años, y el árbol del huracán de hoy, florecerá en las almas de las nuevas generaciones, con flores blancas, flores portadoras de un nuevo perfume como símbolo de una nueva vida" (124).

22. "Santo Domingo florecerá como una urbe moderna, en amplitud y en progreso, sobre lo que ahora riega con lágrimas y desconsuelo" (125).

23. "Ven, extranjero. Toma mi mano que yo te llevaré a una sola esquina de la Ciudad para que contemples las víctimas. Ven, camina tras de mí. Anda con cuidado para que no te hieras con un clavo o te maltrates con alguna plancha de zinc. Ve mirando los destrozos. Ve examinándolo todo que por mucho tiempo no contemplarás tragedia igual" (65).

24. Regarding strategies for dealing with psychological trauma through literary creation, consult Geoffrey Hartman's "On Traumatic Knowledge and Literary Studies."

25. "Por todas partes se ven frases en el que el pueblo expresa sus sentimientos, en los jardines, en las paredes de los edificios, y aún en el interior de las casas

privadas. Los choferes rebautizan sus vehículos con nombres laudatorios. La fotografía del presidente decora los hogares y todas las cosas se denominan con palabras que tengan relación con él" (26).

26. In a nod to the union of politics and masculine sexuality during Trujillo's rule, this phallic-shaped monument was nicknamed the "Obelisco Macho," while the monument constructed in 1941 to commemorate the signing of the Trujillo-Hull Treaty became known as the "Obelisco Hembra," for obvious reasons.

27. "Impulsada por su voluntad dinámica [la de Trujillo], la ciudad surgió de entre sus propias ruinas, mucho más hermosa, reconstruida en cemento, con una arquitectura audaz y joven. Es hoy, por su aspecto, por su confort, por sus seducciones, por sus servicios, por su higiene, una de las más modernas ciudades de las Antillas" (26).

28. "En una fuente pública, una mano tosca, con letras casi indescifrables, ha escrito: 'Bendigamos a Trujillo que nos da el agua.' La policía ha borrado esta inscripción hiperbólica. Pero se trata de una región que era estéril e infecunda y que ahora es fértil y prodigiosamente cultivada a consecuencia de una colosal obra de ingeniería hidráulica ordenada y dirigida personalmente por Trujillo" (26).

29. Turits's analysis of Trujillo's rural politics lays bare the partiality of the conventional view that his regime had almost no popular support and depended strictly on the use of state violence to maintain itself in power. As he demonstrates, "Despotism, in the sense of absolute personalistic power or an autonomous state, did not exist even under Trujillo in the Dominican Republic" (5). The consent of the people is a requirement in any political system, even in the case of a despotic "predatory state" (Turits 4–5). Since Trujillo's regime, in contrast to the majority of Latin American right-wing dictatorships, did not enjoy the support of the island's relatively limited economic elite, it turned to the rural lower classes. By portraying itself as a "friend of the worker" and frequently taking the side of the workers and small-time farmers against the oligarchy, the regime was simultaneously able to create a lower-class power base and to co-opt any possible social mobilization that could threaten its power (Turits 21–22).

30. See the third chapter of Turits's book, entitled "Peasant-State Compromise and Rural Transformation under the Trujillo Dictatorship."

31. "Cerca de la frontera con Haití, sobre una colina puede verse la frase que ha dado margen a críticas mordaces: 'Dios y Trujillo.' También la policía la destruyó una vez y otra, la prohibió con sanciones, vigiló el lugar. Pero en la frontera se vivía una tremenda existencia insegura, los pueblos eran asaltados periódicamente por haitianos, que se llevaban a las mujeres, las cosechas, los ganados. Trujillo organizó la seguridad en la frontera y transformó, con una sabia mezcla de diplomacia y energía, aquel peligroso lugar en una serie de centros de progreso donde la vida es fácil y seguro. Y el letrero vuelve a aparecer" (26).

32. As Ignacio López-Calvo notes, Trujillan discourse "racializes black Do-

minicans and tries to obliterate the African ethnic and cultural component of the national 'family,'" which it displaces to Haiti (xvii).

33. Fischler, anchoring himself in Foucault and Rabinow, among others, links the socially violent abstraction of urban planning with the concrete practice of political, economical, and moral power in "Strategy and History in Professional Practice: Planning as World Making."

34. Emilio José Brea García remarks that the first Dominican licensed in architecture was Juan Bautista del Toro Andújar, who did not receive his degree from the Polytechnical School in Paris until 1930 ("Algunas fechas").

35. See chapter 2 of Escobar's *Encountering Development*.

36. See Alemar (25–26) and Osorio (42). Alemar attributes his information to Gonzalo Fernández de Oviedo's *Historia General*, quoting directly a considerable section (37).

37. See the letters of Fray Domingo Fernández Navarrete and Fray Fernando Carvajal y Rivera that are included in the third volume of Emilio Rodríguez Demorizi's *Relaciones históricas de Santo Domingo* (11–12, 170, and 184).

38. See Hurricane City's online data for Santo Domingo, Oviedo, and El Macao.

39. See the storm data on Santo Domingo provided online by StormCarib: The Caribbean Hurricane Network.

40. See Hurricane City's list of hurricanes that have struck El Macao, on the island's northeastern shore (http://www.hurricanecity.com/city/elmacao.htm).

41. Frank Moya Pons suggests as much when he attributes a pessimistic outlook to Dominicans affected by the convergence of the psychology of dependence that was created during the Trujillo regime and the political instability that followed its collapse (228).

42. Fornerín writes, "When they tell me that reconstruction has begun and that the government will not forget the disaster victims, I think about the fictions that surround us and about the need that people have to believe in these myths" (48).

43. Tellingly, this disaster imagery works within a broader negative paradigm of Dominican history that Pedro L. San Miguel labels the "tragic narrative" of Dominican history in the introductory chapter to *The Imagined Island*. Likewise, Teresita Martínez-Vergne and Alba Josefina Záiter-Mejía both describe a "great Dominican pessimist" (*gran pesimismo dominicano*) tradition of historical thought in the first chapter of *Nation and Citizen in the Dominican Republic* and on page 94 of *La identidad social y nacional en Dominicana*, respectively. Martínez-Vergne traces this pessimism to fears of political illegitimacy due to a legacy of *caudillismo*.

44. See Vargas Llosa's interview with Mexican writer and historian Héctor Aguilar Camín, in which he states that he lived in the Dominican Republic for eight months in 1975 (Vargas Llosa, "Nos mató la ideología").

45. See pages 106, 109, 265, 282, and 289, among other examples.

46. In one moment in the novel, in fact, Trujillo actually refers to his own family as a "calamity" (161). And, of course, the greatest "cataclysm" imaginable for all concerned is the looming possibility of another US intervention and a subsequent loss of sovereignty (289).

2. Drought and the Literary Construction of Risk in Northeastern Brazil

1. As Nísia Trindade Lima points out, Brazilian intellectuals at the turn of the twentieth century often read the *sertão*'s isolation from modernizing projects as its constitutive quality as well as its saving grace: its inaccessibility preserved its essential Brazilianness from the onslaught of European immigration that these intellectuals viewed as somehow denaturalizing Brazilian culture (60, 117–20).

2. Chapter 6 of Alfredo Macedo Gomes's *Imaginário social da seca*, entitled "Aspects of *Sertanejo* Self-Image," delineates the fluidity between literary tropes of *sertanejo* identity—particularly Euclides da Cunha's iconic description of the *sertanejo* as *"um forte"*—and the self-image held by people that he interviewed in the *sertão*. Of course, one must retain a certain healthy skepticism regarding the survey's methodology, since the questions asked of interviewees may well have determined their answers (i.e., "Would you consider yourself *um forte?*"), while Macedo Gomes's own literary interests may also have influenced how he frames the responses. Nevertheless, there are several mechanisms through which literary tropes could engage the "popular imagination" despite the high index of illiteracy in the region, whether through traditional media such as political speeches or religious sermons by educated speakers or through more modern innovations such as film, radio, and television.

3. *Literatura de cordel*, literally "clothesline poetry" or "poetry on a string," as Candace Slater calls it, constitutes a complex and engaging phenomenon in localized literary production. They are typically poems written by local poets in traditional meters and rhyme schemes, published locally at rustic presses on sheets of letter paper that are usually folded into eight or sixteen pages, and sold hanging from strings or wires at village markets and fairs (and more recently, official cultural centers). Replete with moral advice and humor, they cover topics ranging from the deeds of saints and bandits to national and even global political happenings, providing local, often contestatory readings of events.

4. The *Invunche* or *Imbunche* is a monstrous Chilean folk figure who, like Frankenstein, consists of a dismembered human body pieced awkwardly together. It was formed by a witch using a child stolen from its parents, and it could not speak; therefore, it became a useful cultural metaphor for alluding to the silencing and mutilation of the body politic during the dictatorship of Augusto Pinochet (1973–1990) without arousing censorship. I invoke the figure here in its association with the disjointed unification of disparate components

into a single identity as well as its evocations of subaltern silence and elite fears of a monstrous body politic.

5. See the first chapter of Macedo Gomes's *Imaginário social das secas*, entitled "A seca como campo representacional," and the introduction to Muniz de Albuquerque, Jr.'s *Invenção do nordeste*.

6. See Fernão Cardim's *Tratados*, 292. Regarding the effects of cattle on arid ecosystems, see Melville's *Plague of Sheep*.

7. For an extensive summary of the history of drought in northeastern Brazil, consult Marco Antonio Villa's *Vida e morte no sertão*.

8. In fact, Carlos Alonso postulates in *The Spanish American Regional Novel* that regionalism's postulation of an autochthonous cultural essentialism was, in fact, a reaffirmation of national legitimacy and unity in the face of modernity's relegation of Latin American nations to positions of cultural and economic dependence. Highlighting this nationalistic function of regionalism, literary historians such as John Brushwood and Raymond L. Williams often give preference to the term *criollismo* and its tense juxtaposition of transplanted European heritage with a nationalist essentialism rooted in the land rather than indigenous cultures (see *The Spanish-American Novel* and *The Twentieth-Century Spanish American Novel*, respectively). Alonso's thesis would seem to be upheld in Brazil by Durval Muniz de Albuquerque, Jr.'s study of the "invention" of the Northeast, which reveals how regionalists headed by Gilberto Freyre rewrote the national geography in an effort to regain political centrality and cultural legitimacy that it had lost with the rise of the "República do Café" (Coffee Republic) in the South.

9. Trindade Lima notes a similar intermeshing of literature and sociological studies on the *sertão* (53).

10. This assertion is backed up by the exhaustive study of the literary drought tropes that Teoberto Landim undertakes in *Seca: A estação do inferno*. As his study reveals, these tropes varied only slightly once a consensus was reached among more divergent early representations, a consensus that I argue was configured by Euclides da Cunha's encyclopedic *Os sertões* (1902).

11. Tellingly, a mere year after the conclusion of the 1897 War of Canudos, Arinos published a novel on the conflict entitled *Os jagunços* (1898), which places the Canudos rebels in a much more positive light than Euclides da Cunha's *Os sertões* (1902) did four years later. In Arinos's novel, the rebels are simple peasants swayed to religious fanaticism by ignorance, superstition, and government persecution. Neither drought nor race plays a determining role in his assessment of the conflict, in stark contrast to Cunha's representation. In fact, drought is mentioned only in passing.

12. Refer to Vidal e Souza's *A pátria geográfica* for a more in-depth recounting of the history of the formation of the conceptual geography of Brazil as sundered between *sertão* and *litoral*.

13. According to Fernando de Azevedo, isolation became not only a national

preoccupation but also the definitive experience of Brazilian nationality due to the prevalence in the national geography of enormous expanses of sparsely populated lands (75).

14. See Renato Braga's *História da comissão científica de exploração* regarding the most interesting of these expeditions, in which famed Romantic poet Antonio Gonçalves Dias participated as "chief ethnographer."

15. See the first and second chapters of Vidal e Souza's *A pátria geográfica*.

16. I do not mean to imply that the earlier, more open connotations of *sertão* have disappeared completely from usage; nevertheless, the first image that comes to Brazilians' minds when one mentions o *sertão* is almost certainly that of the arid interior of the Northeast, unless contextualization indicates otherwise.

17. See chapters 2 and 3 of Luhmann's *Risk*.

18. The tradition of locating Brazil's essence in the *sertões* was already well established by 1922, when literary critic Tristão de Ataíde (the pseudonym of Alceu Amoroso Lima) published a study of Afonso Arinos in which he documents meticulously the genealogy of this line of thought, which he denominates *"sertanismo"* (93–97). Tellingly, he finds the apogee of this tendency in the rise of *"a literatura da seca"* (drought literature), recognizing implicitly the ties between the construction of Brazilian nationality and negative representations of the *sertão* as a disaster zone, although he opines that the works' nationalistic preoccupations hindered their "universality" (110–18).

19. Brazilian historian Sérgio Buarque de Holanda postulates in *Caminhos e fronteiras* that the *sertanejos* as a people lived on not only a geographical but also an ethnic frontier (viii). Paradoxically, the *sertão*'s historical isolation and position on the fringes of the nation transformed it into what many intellectuals (including Cunha in his better moments) viewed as a potential laboratory for the concoction of a homogeneous, national ethnic identity rooted in the fusion of the European and indigenous phenotypes.

20. I refer here to the tense allegories of national integration that Doris Sommer analyzes in Alencar's *O guaraní* and *Iracema* in chapter 5 of *Foundational Fictions*.

21. "A seca, com um tremendo golpe, destruiu as fortunas e aniquilou os preconceitos, e, desaparecidas as posições, a todos nivelou" (183).

22. "A maioria dos negociantes da Fortaleza entregavam-se ao comércio de cativos, que faziam embarcar para o sul do império, como faziam outrora com o algodão, café e açucar para o estrangeiro" (96).

23. These statistics appear in *Os retirantes*, 2:105, and *A fome*, 159. Due to the impossibility of obtaining a printed edition of *Os retirantes* even in Brazil, I was forced to use the electronic version hosted at the Biblioteca Virtual de Literatura. Unfortunately, the original pagination of the paper edition was lost online, so here and throughout the chapter the page numbers I cite are those that correspond to the print-out of the electronic version.

24. "O ar beatífico do semblante, que mais acentuava a funda melancolia do

olhar, de reprente se transformava em tão feroz catadura, que horrorizava vê-lo. Estes eclipses, toldando por instantes a placidez da fisionomia, se anunciavam por uma série de crispações dos músculos do rosto" (33).

25. "A terra da seca, que é toda essa região, é tambem a terra do crime, da violência e do morticínio, não do crime como ele aparece em toda parte, mas do crime tomando uma feição especial de luta de raça, de casta, e produzindo criminosos que fazem lembrar os *outlaws*, os *bandidos* primitivos, ora prestigiados pelo terror que inspiram e vivendo na sociedade, ora verdadeiramente fora das suas leis, dela banidos e por ela acossados e perseguidos" (262).

26. Walnice Nogueira Galvão summarizes the etymology of the two words in *Gatos de outro saco*, noting that *jagunço*, which originally meant "a hired gun," was an expression more commonly used in Minas Gerais and Bahia, while *cangaceiro* was employed in the rest of the Northeast, but she emphasizes that both were synonymous with banditry (74–75).

27. Louis Anthony Cox lists several nonprobabilistic (nonstatistical) methods for reasoning under uncertainty, including analogy and similarity, conditional logics, default logics, and fuzzy logic (338). The naturalist works that I have analyzed all use these strategies. Fuzzy logic, in which the argument is as strong as its weakest links, is particularly important in Teófilo's work, while conditional logic prevails in Patrocínio's *Os retirantes*: the causes for the disaster are conditioned by the moral climate in the village.

28. One of Teófilo's most vehement complaints was the continued presence in Fortaleza of "beggar suburbs" composed of women, children, "good-for-nothings," and invalids living a "parasitic" existence, abandoned to their own devices after "the good people" returned to the *sertão*: "Each drought has left in our capital a new population of three or four thousand souls—the dregs of the *sertanejo* people" (Cada secca nos tem deixado a nossa capital como população adventicia de tres a quatro mil almas—a escoria da gente sertaneja; *Seccas* 169).

29. For a more extensive history of the Canudos conflict, see Robert M. Levine's *Vale of Tears*.

30. See my article "From Natural to National Disasters: Drought and the Brazilian Subject in Euclides da Cunha's *Os sertões*." Roberto Ventura also discusses the influence of Taine's thought on Cunha in "Visões do deserto."

31. As Luiz Fernando Valente's article "Brazilian Literature and Citizenship: From Euclides da Cunha to Marcos Dias" makes clear, *Os sertões* is widely regarded as having played a key role in the construction of Brazilian nationality due to its attempt to reconcile the margins with the center. Maria Zilda Ferreira Cury notes that the work has become "almost a foundational frame for the nation" due to its epic qualities (72), while other critics have gone to more hyperbolic extremes: Herbert Parentes Fortes calls Cunha "the stylizer of our history" and writes of a "Euclidean moment in our cultural evolution" (13), while Paulo Dantas dubs him the "proto-thinker," the "designer of the master plan of our nationality" (10).

32. "O deserto invoca o deserto. Cada aparecimento de uma seca parece atrair outra, maior e menos remorada, dando à terra crescente receptibilidade para o flagelo" (82).

33. See SUDENE, "Levantamiento" 65–70; Rufino and Albuquerque 4; and Villa 87–248.

34. See chapter 3 of Villa's *Vida e morte no sertão* for a detailed recounting of the horrors of the drought of 1915 as well as the inadequacy of the political response.

35. Many northeastern authors discounted the aesthetics championed by São Paulo's 1922 Semana de Arte Moderna, viewing them as glaring examples of the southern disconnect with the national reality. This did not mean, however, that they rejected completely avant-garde or "modernist" aesthetics: authors as varied as Joaquim Inojosa, Ascenso Ferreira, and even Gilberto Freyre himself claimed them for the Northeast.

36. See Araújo Lima's *Amazônia: A terra e o homem* (1932).

37. "O recruzamento arbitrário, as escórias da mestiçagem, como uma balbúrdia de pigmentos" (57).

38. "Párias da bagaceira, vítimas de uma emperrada organização do trabalho e de uma dependência que os deshumanizava, eram os mais insensíveis ao martírio das retiradas" (8).

39. "A história das secas era uma história de passividades" (9).

40. "Para eles o governo era, apenas, essa noção de violência: o espaldeiramento, a prisão ilegal, o despique partidário. . . . Não o conheciam por nenhuma manifestação tutelar" (51).

41. "Quem é mais criminoso—o réu que matou um homem ou a sociedade que deixou por culpa sua morrerem milhares de homens?" (134).

42. As Cunha's writings on the Amazon show, his views on the *sertanejo* transformed radically during the war with Bolivia over the province of Acre (1899–1903), in which *sertanejo* migrants to the Amazon defeated the Bolivian military with almost no government support, leading to Brazilian annexation in the Treaty of Petrópolis.

43. As Hewitt underscores, "Disasters themselves are treated as places or archipelagos of extreme and more or less random events. They tend to be cordoned off as areas of spacial disorganization or national security crisis. Thus, the geography of disaster is also constructed in stark contrast to the *patterns* of 'land utilization,' the space economy, urban systems, and development issues" ("Sustainable Disasters?" 122). The emphasis is Hewitt's.

44. See point "C" of the manifesto's "Plano de reconstrução educacional" (Educational Restructuring Plan).

45. For a summary of the shift toward academic specialization and European models of higher education in Brazil, see the introduction to Simon Schwartzman's "Brazil's Leading University: Between Intelligentsia, World Standards, and Social Inclusion."

46. These reports, originally published in O *correio da manhã* in 1958, were compiled a year later in Os *industriais da seca e os "Galileus" de Pernambuco*.

47. Chapter 5 of Beverley's *Against Literature*, entitled "Second Thoughts on *Testimonio*," analyzes this problem in depth. As he points out, "The possibilities of distortion and/or co-optation in the production and reception of *testimonio* are many" (88).

48. Magalhães relies on extensive interviews with popular practitioners as well as what is considered common knowledge in the region.

49. Although the fifth chapter of Macedo Gomes's *Imaginário social da seca* deals primarily with religious beliefs associated with the *experiências*, he also postulates several alternative scientific explanations for the phenomena. Likewise, Galeno, Magalhães, and César all proffer more "rational" explanations for the *experiências*, even if the latter does so primarily to criticize *sertanejo* superstitiousness.

50. Macedo Gomes details some of the factors leading to the decline in these traditional practices at the end of his fifth chapter. Without studying the *experiências* in particular, Allen Johnson frames decision making by subsistence farmers in Ceará within concepts of risk assessment in "Security and Risk-Taking among Poor Peasants: A Brazilian Case."

51. Tellingly, many of these strategies are captured in the ethnographic impulse of literary drought narratives, but they typically portray them as ineffective at best and, at worst, as the product of superstition and desperation.

52. Villa's *Vida e morte no sertão* documents carefully these fluctuations in governmental aid, showing how funding varied wildly depending on the political climate.

53. See Anthony Smith's *The Newspaper: An International History*. Regarding the process by which journalistic modes of discourse developed in accordance with commercial viability, see chapter 2 of Jean Chalaby's *Invention of Journalism*. Although Chalaby focuses on the context of the United Kingdom in the nineteenth century, his study sheds light on the field as a whole.

3. Volcanic Identities

1. In this chapter, I make use of the distinction between physical geography (avoiding the use of *natural*, as that term negates human influence in shaping it) and landscape, which Denis Cosgrove and Stephen Daniels define as "a cultural image, a pictorial way of representing, structuring, or symbolizing surroundings" (Introduction 1). However, I acknowledge that the term *geography* itself implies culturally constructed knowledge about the land and its inhabitants; therefore I also refer to the *cultural geography* to draw attention to competing modes of viewing and experiencing surroundings. For further elaboration, refer to Cosgrove and Daniels's introduction to *The Iconography of Landscape* and Cerwonka's and Zimmer's studies on the political uses of landscape in *Native to the Nation* and "In Search of Natural Identity," respectively.

2. I use the term *heritage* in the sense that Brian Graham and Peter Howard define it, as a compendium of "ways in which very selective past material artifacts, natural landscapes, mythologies, memories, and traditions become cultural, political and economic resources for the present" (Introduction 2).

3. Darío says of Roosevelt, "You believe that life is fire, / that progress is eruption" (Crees que la vida es incendio, / que el progreso es erupción).

4. I base my discussion of how Western concepts of nationalism resulted in changes in notions of territoriality on Benedict Anderson's *Imagined Communities* and Partha Chatterjee's *Nation and Its Fragments*.

5. The heartland is conceived of as an internal, inland space, shielded from direct contact with the threatening exterior, as Halford J. MacKinder's 1904 "heartland" theory of geopolitics reveals. He proposed that the land-bound "heartland" territories of central Eurasia held strategic advantages in the imperialist struggle for world dominance over the "rimlands," or nations such as his native England that were open to naval attack and interrupted supply lines. For a more in-depth discussion of MacKinder's "heartland" theory, see Gerald Kearns's *Geopolitics and Empire*.

6. Indeed, it is hardly coincidental that Nicaraguan writer and politician Sergio Ramírez entitled his 1983 meditation on Central American cultural identity *Balcanes y volcanes*, juxtaposing in a dialectical relationship the fragmentation evoked by the reference to the Balkans with the centripetal visual draw of the volcano. Of course, for Ramírez, the volcano unites primarily through tragedy: it symbolizes solidarity through the common trauma of a disastrous history (112).

7. See Francisco Espinosa's *Símbolos patrios*, 16.

8. See Legislative Decree No. 29 of the Provincias Unidas del Centro de América.

9. For a history and discussion of the varied symbolism of the Phrygian cap in revolutionary France, see Richard Wrigley, "Transformations of a Revolutionary Emblem."

10. Hugo clearly took great liberties with Squier's text, confusing the book's title as *Voyage dans l'Amerique du Sud*, and he apparently made up the supposed quotation that he includes in the epigraph, although Squire does mention a bishop blessing an unnamed volcanic vent.

11. Lipari is the largest of the Aeolian Islands, famed for its volcanic composition and activity. It lies just to the north of the island Vulcano. Mongibelo is the Sicilian name for celebrity volcano Mt. Etna.

12. "¡Triste fama la de todos mis paisanos de Centroamérica: no poder pasar unos cuantos años sin que corra sangre de hermanos!" (2).

13. "Padre de fuego y piedra, yo te pedí ese día / tu secreto de llamas, tu arcano de armonía, / la iniciación que podías dar; / por ti pensé en lo inmenso de Osas y Peliones, / en que arriba hay titanes en las constelaciones y / abajo dentro la tierra y el mar."

14. "Y llegué y vi en las nubes la prodigiosa testa / de aquel cono de siglos, de aquel volcán de gesta, / que era ante mí de revelación. / Señor de las alturas, emperador del agua, / a sus pies el divino lago de Managua, / con islas todas luz y canción. / ¡Momotombo!—exclamé—¡Oh nombre de epopeya!"

15. "Ya estaba yo nutrido de Oviedo y de Gomara / y mi alma florida soñaba historia rara, / fábula, cuento, romance, amor / de conquistas, victorias de caballos bravos, / incas y sacerdotes, prisioneros y esclavos, / plumas y oro, audacia, esplendor."

16. "Cuando las babilonias del Poniente / en púrpureas catástrofes hacia la inmensidad / rodaban tras la augusta soberbia de tu frente, / eras tú como el símbolo de la Serenidad. / En tu incesante hornalla vi la perpetua guerra, / en tu roca unidades que nunca acabarán. / Sentí en tus terremotos la brama de la tierra / y la inmortalidad de Pan."

17. "¡Con un alma volcánica entré en la dura vida, Aquilón y huracán sufrió mi corazón / y de mi mente mueven la cimera encendida / huracán y Aquilón!"

18. Luis de Lión is the pen name of José Luis de León Díaz, who many critics consider Guatemala's first indigenous writer to publish in Spanish. He won the Premio Centroamericano de Novela in 1972 for *El tiempo principia en Xibalbá* (Time Begins in Xibalbá), which was only published posthumously in 1985. He authored three short-story compilations as well as two volumes of poetry before he was kidnapped and executed by the Guatemalan military in 1984.

19. Following Spivak, I use here a broad Gramscian definition of *subaltern* as any person or group forced into a subservient position in a hierarchy of linguistic as well as political power relations.

20. Julio Valle-Castillo associates *Cenizas de Izalco* with the Boom because Alegría was in contact with several of the writers of the Boom in Paris in the 1960s and because her novel was published by Seix-Barral (8).

21. Sergio Ramírez argues in *Balcanes y volcanes* that this trope of a disastered nation unified only by trauma is not limited to El Salvador but is generalized throughout Central America. He speaks of the growth of national and regional culture "not despite, but precisely because it arises from a mutilated, disperse culture, constantly under threat, a large part of whose possibilities are cut short halfway or in the womb" (112).

22. Citing several authors, Sarah McDowell uses the concept of "postmemory" to describe the phenomenon by which "memories are passed down through generations to be represented by people who have no personal attachment to that memory. Subsequently, they seek to re-use, re-enact, and re-represent those memories in order to feel closer to their ancestors" (41). As one who assiduously avoids the apocalyptic denomination *post-*, I prefer more mundane terminology such as *inherited memory*.

23. This collection was published posthumously in 1981. The majority of the poems included in it were written in the year before Dalton's death at the

hands of his fellow revolutionary fighters in the Ejército Popular del Pueblo in 1975. Its original title was "Historia y poemas de una lucha de clases."

24. Notably, the poems in this section are attributed to "Juan Zapata," who, according to the footnote biography, was born April 2, 1944, the date of the "revolution" in which a group of civilians took control of several state installations, setting in motion the events that forced General Hernández Martínez, who had ordered the Matanza of 1932, to renounce his dictatorship.

25. I refer to the role of "themed spaces" in collapsing fantasy with historical reality in order to immerse the spectator in an ahistorical experience that nevertheless feels "authentic." For a more in-depth discussion of themed spaces, see the introduction to Scott Lukas's *Themed Space*.

26. "Proletarios respetables y mansos del mundo / el Comité Central os invita / a aprender la lección que da el volcán de Izalco: / el fuego ha pasado de moda, ¿por qué habremos entonces de querer llevarlo nosotros / dentro del corazón?"

27. Indeed, Dalton uses a vocabulary of disaster to describe himself in poems such as "Huelo mal" (I Reek), in which he states, "I reek of the (hi)story of a minor catastrophe" (Huelo a historia de pequeña catástrofe), or the furious pathos of "El humillado" (The Humiliated One): "Everything, remorse, hate is reduced to ash / to singed tears / everything is come to nothing, desolation / the horizon weighs on me / because of its fury / its distant invitation to dead footsteps / to the insanity / of the bird of prey" (Todo a ceniza el remordimiento el odio reducido / a lágrima quemada / todo a desolación / venido a menos / pésame el horizonte / por su furia / su lejana invitación al paso muerto / a la locura / del pájaro de presa).

4. Fault Lines

1. For a listing of the earthquakes that have struck Mexico City since 1475 CE, see the appendix entitled "Grandes sismos sentidos en la ciudad de México a través de su historia," in Gerardo Suárez R. and Zenón Jiménez J.'s *Sismos en la ciudad de México y el terremoto del 19 de septiembre de 1985*.

2. No one is entirely sure how many people died in the earthquake, but reasonable estimates range from ten to twenty thousand, with tens of thousands more injured and hundreds of thousands displaced from their homes.

3. See the introductory chapter of Lomnitz's *Deep Mexico, Silent Mexico* and that of Adler-Lomnitz, Salazar Elena, and Adler's *Symbolism and Ritual in a One-Party Regime*.

4. Ezcurra, Mazari-Hiriart, Pisanty, and Aguilar note that by 1995, Mexico City pumped 50 percent more water out of its aquifers than was recharged by rainfall, leading to a deficit of more than eight hundred million square meters per year (84). The subsequent consolidation of deep subterranean layers has caused the ground to subside six centimeters per year on average, totaling up to ten meters in some areas (85).

5. See Heberto Castillo's interview in Garza Toledo et al.'s *Esto pasó en México*, 16; and Robinson et al., 87.

6. Between 1960 and 1980, the Distrito Federal's population increased from 5,186,000 inhabitants occupying 36,000 hectares (139 square miles) to 14,500,000 inhabitants occupying 100,000 hectares (386 square miles) (Pan-American Health Organization 8).

7. All sources back up this view, including Campos's *Hemos perdido el reino*, which includes fragments of radio-broadcast transcripts gleaned from archives. See also Poy Solano's "Y la radio salió a la calle."

8. "En la televisión [con Televisa fuera del aire la mañana del jueves], la reacción inicial fue oportuna y valiosa. A partir del viernes 20, la tradición de los medios se impuso. Se cooperó con entusiasmo a la minimización del desastre, se mintió pródigamente [Televisa aseguró reiteradamente que el segundo temblor no había causado daño alguno], se aduló a los funcionarios [Imevisión se empeño en probar que el temblor ocurrió para realzar la eficacia gubernamental] y se protegió el Mundial de Fútbol sobre todas las cosas" (12).

9. See, for instance, Aziz Nassif's "Electoral Practices and Democracy in Chihuahua, 1985."

10. Of course, Sergio Zermeño takes a darker view, evoking the tradition of *charrismo* as the "bureau-politicization of Mexican social action," an exchange in which "the leader offered to deliver his social bases, which were then disorganized and disarticulated, in return for his ascent within the state bureaucracy" (178).

11. See also Roderic Camp's chapter 2, Lomnitz's chapters 3 and 4, and the introduction to Beatriz Magaloni's *Voting for Autocracy*.

12. In fact, Lomnitz traces corporatism even further back to the colonial period, when collective groups were assigned representatives with whom the Spanish Crown communicated exclusively. Following independence, only citizens could dialogue with the state, and the definition of citizenship was restricted by property ownership, gender, and race; these citizens ended up representing "nationals" who could not claim citizenship (11, 62–80).

13. Jeffrey Rubin challenges this characterization of Mexican politics, arguing that considerable political agency was negotiated and wielded at the local and regional levels outside the corporatist framework. Nevertheless, the intersections of local with national politics were typically negotiated using the clientelistic mechanisms of corporatist politics.

14. See Adler-Lomnitz et al., 8 and 47; and Lomnitz, 158.

15. See the vignette entitled "No sabría decirle" in Garza Toledo et al.'s *Esto pasó en México* (74) and Elena Poniatowska's *Nada, nadie*, 286.

16. The testimonials emphasize this point over and over again, particularly those of the seamstresses who worked in clandestine sweatshops. One of them claims that the government "aid" took two weeks to arrive, and even then only to create obstacles for the self-organized rescue operations, which by then had

dedicated themselves to searching for the remains of co-workers (Poniatowska, *Nada, nadie* 154–55). See also Campos 55.

17. Rafael Pérez Gay, in his *crónica* "Piedra sobre piedra," speaks of a "macabre dance of the numbers," a "statistics of horror" that "says very little about the pain, the panic, the sadness, and the crushing atmosphere of the tragedy" (41).

18. "Vimos a nuestro entonces presidente de la república tal como era: un tipo gris que no sabía nada, un hombre que había sentido tanto miedo que ni siquiera se atrevió a salir en la televisión para decir: 'estoy con ustedes, me voy a partir el alma con ustedes.' Mostró su pequeñez" (Loaeza et al. 21).

19. "Viviremos y reconstruiremos el país con nueva pautas" (*Entrada* 38).

20. See, for example, disaster victim Alejandro Villamar Calderón's discussion of the transition from solidarity in the rescue effort to unification in a popular movement in his testimonial interview entitled "20 años después: No aprendimos," in Loaeza et al.'s *Terremoto*, 17–21.

21. See the chronology in Serna's *Aquí nos quedaremos*, pages 161–66.

22. See the photo on page 551 of the presidency's official chronicle of the disaster (Presidencia).

23. As Sergio Zermeño points out, poverty in 1985 had risen 25 percent from its 1980 levels, while 44 percent of the labor force was unemployed or underemployed (165).

24. See Manuel Castell's discussion of the differences and overlap between urban popular movements and social movements in chapter 33 of *The City and the Grassroots*, entitled "The Social Significance of Urban Movements."

25. See Juan Manuel Ramírez Saiz's "Urban Struggles and Their Political Consequences," 234–35.

26. Zermeño proffers this perspective in "Crisis, Neoliberalism, and Disorder."

27. See the introduction to *Deep Mexico, Silent Mexico* as well as chapters 7 and 12.

28. See Adler-Lomnitz, Salazar Elena, and Adler's study of the 1988 presidential elections, in which they found that newspapers and media presence played central roles in the jostling among PRI insiders for the presidential candidacy. This jostling was more about positioning within the political community than in public opinion, however, as the language and style used by the press to discuss governmental topics could often only be decoded by political insiders (26).

29. See chapter 12 of Lomnitz's *Deep Mexico, Silent Mexico*.

30. See the first three chapters of Ángel Rama's *La ciudad letrada*.

31. See Benedict Anderson 44–46 and Lomnitz 147–50.

32. See chapter 1 of González Echevarría's *Myth and Archive*.

33. Corona studies the role of the *crónica* in negotiating cultural identities in "At the Intersection."

34. See Monsiváis's comments on the history of the genre and its role in Mexican nationalism in "On the Chronicle in Mexico."

35. See chapters 9 and 12 of Lomnitz's *Deep Mexico, Silent Mexico.*

36. Consult Camarillo's 610-page bibliography in *Memoria periodística del terremoto* for a near exhaustive listing of journalistic pieces published in the month following the earthquake.

37. Regarding the emergence of this discourse of popular solidarity arising from "civil society," see Bernardo Avalos's "El vaivén de la palabra."

38. "Ha salido a flote mucha podredumbre, y en medio de ella toda la imprevisión, toda la incapacidad, toda la torpeza de las autoridades que no saben qué hacer ni qué decir, se ha creado un vacío de poder en la ciudad y la población civil, sobreponiéndose a todo, se ha hecho cargo de la lucha áspera e infatigable por rescatar a sus vivos y sus muertos" (1).

39. See also Fernando Benítez's "Lo que se llevó y lo que trajo el temblor."

40. See Krauze's "Revelación entre ruinas" and Paz's "Escombros y semillas," both published in *Vuelta*'s November 1985 edition.

41. See Corona and Jörgensen, Introduction 9–13.

42. See Adler-Lomnitz et al. 114–25 and chapter 11 of Claudio Lomnitz's *Deep Mexico, Silent Mexico*

43. Of course, there were similarities as well, such as the government's drive to normalize at any cost in order to maintain appearances for athletic events in which it was to figure prominently on the world stage: the 1968 Olympic Games and the 1986 Soccer World Cup.

44. "No consideramos casual que tan devastador sacudimiento se produzca precisamente cuando el país es enfrentado [oh manes de la televisión y de la PRI-paganda oficial] con los 75 años de gobiernos usufructuarios del movimiento de 1910" (5).

45. "Como en 1521, como en 1968, nuevamente sobre ese pedazo de tierra mártir, se cierne la tragedia. Tal parece que regarla con sangre tiene que ser el precio para que nazca el mexicano del futuro" (34).

46. Regarding the internal tensions within the CUD, see chapter 4 of Serna's *Aquí nos quedaremos.*

47. According to Serrano, de la Madrid cut total spending by 6.8 percent between 1983 and 1988, while social programs were reduced by 33.1 percent (28).

48. As Cook has written, "For dissident movements in authoritarian political systems the most likely facilitator of political space short of systemic crisis is elite conflict or disunity" (11).

49. See Snow, Rochford, Worden, and Benford's "Frame Alignment Processes."

50. I refer to the line of thought that dominates works such as Caso's *El problema de México y la ideología nacional* (The Problem of Mexico and Its National Ideology; 1924), Ramos's *El perfil del hombre y la cultura en México*

(Profile of Man and Culture in Mexico; 1934), and Paz's *El laberinto de la soledad* (*The Labyrinth of Solitude*; 1950).

51. John Ochoa traces this fixation with failure all the way back to the colonial time period in his *Uses of Failure in Mexican Literature and Identity*. Together with Bartra, I would contend, however, that the framing of Mexican history as a failure was primarily a turn-of-the-twentieth-century project with concrete political uses in upholding first Porfirio Díaz's dictatorship and then the PRI's legitimacy.

52. See the introduction to Bartra's *La jaula de la melancolía* (*The Cage of Melancholy*), entitled "Penetración" in parody of Paz's thesis in *El laberinto de la soledad* tracing the foundations of all Mexican social interaction to the originary sexual violence of the conquest.

53. I refer here to Silva Herzog's *La revolución mexicana en crisis* (1944) and Cosío Villegas's "La crisis en México" (1947). From 1968 onward, a slew of works were published in Mexico and abroad portraying the PRI's economic, political, and social policies within a framework of extended or permanent crisis.

54. As Beth Jörgensen notes, dialogism lies at the heart of Poniatowska's literary technique; she uses the interview to gather materials not only for her testimonial texts but also for her novels and short stories (xix). Regarding the incorporation of journalistic techniques, particularly those of New Journalism, into Poniatowska's testimonial writing, see also Judy Maloof's "Construction of a Collective Voice."

55. Kay García points out that much of the governmental discourse in *Nada, nadie* is left in the shadows, in a pretextual space to which it is assumed that the reader has access (49). This does not preclude dialogue, however; I argue that the antigovernmental crisis paradigm through which Poniatowska and the other authors studied here read the earthquake arose precisely through this interaction in the shadowy margins of the government's own textualization of Mexican history. Furthermore, Ignacio Corona demonstrates that the generic indeterminacy of this dialogue opens political symbols and meanings to a process of constant renegotiation ("Representación" 13).

56. Most quotations in this section come from Aurora Camacho de Schmidt and Arthur Schmidt's translation of *Nada, nadie*; however, when I feel that it is necessary to conserve the original Spanish, I indicate the Spanish edition by including its title in the parenthetical reference and the text in a note.

57. This localized, affective language is common throughout the testimonials in López Jiménez's *Un lugar para vivir*, for example.

58. Following the experience with the 1988 elections, less than one-third of Mexicans expected fair results in the upcoming 1994 elections, according to opinion polls cited by the Carter Center in its report (6–7).

59. "Así, desde el punto de vista social, el método de trabajo de Solidaridad convierte la gestión de las obras públicas en procesos de movilización, organización y corresponsabilidad. A través de Solidaridad se promueve el reconoci-

miento de la existencia de sujetos de la sociedad movilizada, y a la vez, se induce un procedimiento de concertación y racionalización en la gestión de la política social" (68).

60. For an in-depth analysis of Salinas's relationship with intellectuals, see chapter 5 of Claire Brewster's *Responding to Crisis in Contemporary Mexico*.

61. Regarding political reforms that Salinas undertook and the tenuous position he and the PRI found themselves in, see Stephen D. Morris's "Political Reformism in Mexico: Salinas at the Brink."

62. For an in-depth analysis of the discourse used by PRONASOL to restore the PRI's position in the symbolic order, refer to Luis Miguel Bascones Serrano's exhaustive doctoral thesis, "La exclusión participativa: Pobreza, potenciamiento y orden simbólico en el Programa Nacional de Solidaridad (México: 1989–1995)."

Works Cited

Acevedo, Ramón Luis. *Los senderos del volcán: Narrativa centroamericana contemporánea*. Guatemala: Editorial Universitaria, 1991.

Adler-Lomnitz, Larissa, Rodrigo Salazar Elena, and Ilya Adler. *Symbolism and Ritual in a One-Party Regime*. Translated by Susanne A. Wagner. Tucson: University of Arizona Press, 2010.

Alcântara, Lúcio. Introduction to *Vida e morte no sertão: História das secas no Nordeste nos séculos XIX e XX*, by Marco Antonio Villa, 7–9. São Paulo: Ática, 2000.

Aldana Rivera, Susana. "¿Ocurrencias del tiempo? Fenómenos naturales y sociedad en el Perú colonial." In García Acosta, *Historia y desastres* 1:167–94.

Alegría, Claribel, and Darwin J. Flakoll. *Cenizas de Izalco*. 1966. Edited by Julio Valle-Castillo. San Salvador: Consejo Nacional para la Cultura y el Arte, 1997.

———. *Ashes of Izalco*. Translated by Darwin J. Flakoll. New York: Curbstone, 1989.

Alemar, Luis E. *Santo Domingo/Ciudad Trujillo: Apuntaciones históricas de la muy noble y muy leal ciudad de Santo Domingo, primada de América y la predilecta de los Colones; Historia de sus calles, plazas y paseos, origen de sus nombres antiguos y modernos y sus tradiciones, así como de sus principales edificios públicos y privados*. Santiago: El Diario, 1943.

Alencar, José de. *O gaúcho: Romance brasileiro*. 1870. Edited by Manoel Cavalcanti Proença. Rio de Janeiro: Edições de Ouro, 1966.

———. *O guaraní: Romance brasileiro*. 1857. São Paulo: Melhoramentos, 1967.

———. *Iracema: Lenda do Ceará*. 1865. Rio de Janeiro: José de Olímpio, 1965.

———. *O sertanejo*. 1875. São Paulo: Martin Claret, 2005.

Almeida, José Américo de. *A bagaceira*. 1928. Edited by Manoel Cavalcanti Proença. Rio de Janeiro: José Olympio, 1980.

———. *O boqueirão*. 1935. Rio de Janeiro: Leitura, 1971.

———. *O ciclo revolucionário do Ministério da Viação*. Bahia: Livraria Duas Americas, 1934.

——. *Coiteiros.* 1935. Rio de Janeiro: Leitura, 1971.

——. *A Paraiba e seus problemas.* 1923. João Pessoa: Estado da Paraíba, Secretaria da Educação e Cultura, Diretoria Geral de Cultura, 1980.

——. *Reflexões de uma cabra.* 1922. Rio de Janeiro: Leitura, 1971.

Alonso, Carlos. *The Spanish American Regional Novel: Modernity and Autochthony.* Cambridge: Cambridge University Press, 1990.

Amado, Jorge. *Seara vermelha.* São Paulo: Livraria Martins, 1946.

Anderson, Benedict. *Imagined Communities: Reflections on the Origin and Spread of Nationalism.* London: Verso, 1991.

Anderson, Jon. "Cultural Adaptation to Threatened Disaster." *Human Organization* 27, no. 4 (1968): 298–307.

Anderson, Mark D. "From Natural to National Disasters: Drought and the Brazilian Subject in Euclides da Cunha's *Os sertões.*" *Hispania* 91, no. 3 (2008): 547–57.

——. "National Nature and Ecologies of Abjection in Brazilian Literature at the Turn of the Twentieth Century." In *The Natural World in Latin American Literatures: Ecocritical Essays on Twentieth-Century Writings,* edited by Adrian Kane, 208–32. Jefferson, NC: McFarland, 2010.

Araújo Lima, José Francisco de. *Amazônia: A terra e o homem.* São Paulo: Editora Nacional, 1937.

Argueta, Manlío. *Magic Dogs of the Volcanoes/Perros mágicos de los volcanes.* San Francisco: Children's Book Press, 1990.

Arinos, Afonso. *Os jagunços.* 1898. Rio de Janeiro: Philobiblion Livros de Arte, 1985.

Arizpe, Lourdes. "Mi ciudad, mis calles en tiempos de duelo." *México en la Cultura* 1235 (20 Nov. 1985): 48–49.

Asturias, Miguel Ángel. "¡Salve, Guatemala!" In *Torotumbo/La audiencia de los confines/Mensajes indios.* Barcelona: Plaza y Janés, 1967.

Ataide, Tristão de [Alceu Amoroso Lima]. *Afonso Arinos.* São Paulo: Livros Irradiantes, 1981.

Avalos, Bernardo. "El vaivén de la palabra." In *Y aún tiembla: Sociedad política y cambio social, el terremoto del 19 de septiembre de 1985,* edited by Adolfo Aguilar Zinzer, Cesáreo Morales, and Rodolfo Peña, 209–30. Mexico City: Grijalbo, 1986.

Azevedo, Aluísio. *O mulato.* 1881. Edited by Fernando Góes. São Paulo: Martins, 1969.

Azevedo, Fernando de. *A cultura brasileira: Introdução ao estudo da cultura no Brasil.* São Paulo: Melhoramentos, 1958.

Aziz Nassif, Alberto. "Electoral Practices and Democracy in Chihuahua, 1985." In *Electoral Patterns and Perspectives in Mexico,* edited by Arturo Alvarado, 181–205. La Jolla: University of California, San Diego, Center for US-Mexican Studies, 1987.

Báez López-Penha, José Ramón. *Porque Santo Domingo es así.* Santo Domingo: Banco Nacional de la Vivienda, 1992.

Balaguer, Joaquín. "El azar en la historia dominicana." In *Discursos*. Santo Domingo: n.p., n.d.

Bankoff, Greg. *Cultures of Disasters: Society and Natural Hazard in the Philippines*. New York: Routledge, 2003.

Barthes, Roland. *Camera Lucida: Reflections on Photography*. Translated by Richard Howard. New York: Hill and Wang, 1981.

Bartra, Roger. *La jaula de la melancolía: Identidad y metamorfosis del mexicano*. Mexico: Grijalva, 1987.

Bascones Serrano, Luis Miguel. "La exclusión participativa: Pobreza, potenciamiento y orden simbólico en el Programa Nacional de Solidaridad (México: 1989–1995)." PhD diss., Universidad Complutense de Madrid, 2002.

Beaverstock, Jonathan V., Peter J. Taylor, and Richard G. Smith. "A Roster of World Cities." *Cities* 16, no. 6 (1999): 445–58.

Bello, Andrés. "Silva a la agricultura de la zona tórrida." 1826–1827. In *Silvas americanas y otros poemas*, edited by Luis Iñigo Madrigal. Madrid: Biblioteca Nueva, 2001.

Benítez, Fernando. "Lo que se llevó y lo que trajo el temblor." In *19 de septiembre: 7:19 horas*, edited by Manuel Becerra Acosta, 69–77. Mexico City: Unomásuno, 1985.

Bernucci, Leopoldo. "Além do real, aquém do imaginário: Domingo Faustino Sarmiento e Euclides da Cuna." *Brasil* 3, no. 4 (1990): 51–68.

Beverley, John. *Against Literature*. Minneapolis: University of Minnesota Press, 1993.

Borge Martínez, Tomás. *Nicaragua: Un siglo en viente y tres poemas*. Santo Domingo: Alfa y Omega, 1986.

Bosch, Juan. *Trujillo: Causas de una tiranía sin ejemplo*. Caracas: Librería Las Novedades, 1959.

Braga, Renato. *História da comissão científica de exploração*. Fortaleza: Imprensa Universitária do Ceará, 1969.

Brea García, Emilio José. "Algunas fechas de importancia para la arquitectura dominicana." *Arquiteca: Arquitectura Dominicana*, edited by Tommy Rodríguez. Web. Last modified 10 July 2007. Accessed 25 May 2010.

———. "Vicisitudes de un monumento: Cuento lineal para intencionales." *Arquiteca: Arquitectura Dominicana*, edited by Tommy Rodríguez. Web. Last modified 10 July 2007. Accessed 25 May 2010.

Brewster, Claire. *Responding to Crisis in Contemporary Mexico: The Political Writings of Paz, Fuentes, Monsiváis, and Poniatowska*. Tucson: University of Arizona Press, 2005.

Brushwood, John S. *The Spanish American Novel: A Twentieth-Century Survey*. Austin: University of Texas Press, 1975.

Buarque de Holanda, Sérgio. *Caminhos e fronteiras*. São Paulo: Companhia de Letras, 1994.

Cabral de Melo Neto, João. *Morte e vida severina.* 1955. Rio de Janeiro: Nova Fronteira, 2006.

Callado, Antonio. *Os industriais da seca e os "Galileus" de Pernambuco: Aspectos da luta pela reforma agrária no Brasil.* Rio de Janeiro: Civilização Brasileira, 1960.

Callicot, J. Baird. *Earth's Insights: A Multicultural Survey of Ecological Ethics from the Mediterranean to the Australian Outback.* Berkeley: University of California Press, 1994.

Calvo, Rossano C. "Del folklore a la antropología del terremoto: El Señor de los Milagros (Lima) y el Señor de los Temblores (Qosqo)." *Folklore Americano* 57 (1994): 99–113.

Camarillo, María Teresa, ed. *Memoria periodística del terremoto (19 de septiembre–10 de octubre, 1985).* Mexico City: Universidad Nacional Autónoma de México, 1987.

Camp, Roderic. *Intellectuals and the State in Twentieth-Century Mexico.* Austin: University of Texas Press, 1985.

Campos, Julieta. *La imagen en el espejo.* Mexico City: Universidad Nacional Autónoma de México, 1965.

Campos, Marco Antonio. *Hemos perdido el reino.* Mexico City: Joaquín Mortiz, 1987.

Candido, Antonio. *On Literature and Society.* Edited and translated by Howard S. Becker. Princeton: Princeton University Press, 1995. Originally published as *Literatura e sociedade,* 1965.

Cardenal, Ernesto. *Canto nacional.* Buenos Aires: Carlos Lohlé, 1973.

Cardim, Fernão. *Tratados da terra e a gente do Brasil.* São Paulo: Editora Nacional, 1939.

Carter Center. "Elections in Mexico: Third Report." Web. Last modified Aug. 1994. Accessed 25 May 2010.

Caso, Antonio. *El problema de México y la ideología nacional.* 1924. In *Obras completas,* vol. 9. Mexico City: Universidad Nacional Autónoma de México, Dirección de Publicaciones, 1971.

Castells, Manuel. *The City and the Grassroots: A Cross-Cultural Theory of Urban Movements.* Berkeley: University of California Press, 1983.

Castelo Branco, Francisco Gil. *Ataliba, o vaqueiro.* 1878. Teresina: Universidade Federal do Piauí, 1994.

Castillo, Bernal Díaz de. *Historia verdadera de la conquista de la Nueva España.* Mexico City: Editores Mexicanos Unidos, 2005.

Castro-Klarén, Sara. "Santos and Cangaceiros: Inscription without Discourse in *Os sertões* and *La guerra del fin del mundo.*" *Modern Language Notes* 101, no. 2 (1986): 366–88.

Cavalcanti Proença, Manoel. Introduction to *A bagaceira,* by José Américo de Almeida, xx–lxiii. Rio de Janeiro: José Olympio, 1980.

Cerwonka, Allaine. *Native to the Nation: Disciplining Landscapes and Bodies in Australia*. Minneapolis: University of Minnesota Press, 2004.

César, Getúlio. *Crendices do Nordeste*. Rio de Janeiro: Pongetti, 1941.

Céstero Burgos, Túlio. *Filosofía de un regimen* . . . Ciudad Trujillo: Montalvo, 1951.

Chalaby, Jean K. *The Invention of Journalism*. New York: St. Martin's, 1998.

Chatterjee, Partha. *The Nation and Its Fragments: Colonial and Postcolonial Histories*. Princeton: Princeton University Press, 1993.

Columbus, Christopher. "Carta de Colón a los Reyes Católicos: Vega de la Maguana, La Española, 14 de octubre 1495." In *Biblioteca Garay: 500 años de México en documentos*, edited by Paco Garay. Web. Accessed 25 May 2010.

Consejo Consultivo del Programa Nacional de Solidaridad. *El Programa Nacional de Solidaridad*. Mexico City: Fondo de Cultura Económica, 1994.

Cook, María Lorena. *Organizing Dissent: Unions, the State, and the Democratic Teachers' Movement in Mexico*. University Park: Pennsylvania State University Press, 1996.

Corona, Ignacio. "At the Intersection: Chronicle and Ethnography." In Corona and Jörgensen, *Contemporary Mexican Chronicle* 123–55.

———. "Representación y estrategias retóricas en *Nada, nadie* de Elena Poniatowska." *Journal of Interdisciplinary Studies* 8, no. 1 (1996): 12–26.

Corona, Ignacio, and Beth Jörgensen, eds. *The Contemporary Mexican Chronicle: Theoretical Perspectives on the Liminal Genre*. Albany: State University of New York Press, 2002.

———. Introduction to Corona and Jörgensen, *Contemporary Mexican Chronicle*.

Coronel Urtecho, José. "Oda al Mombacho." 1931. In *Nicaragua: Un siglo en veinte y tres poemas*, edited by Tomás Borge Martínez. Santo Domingo: Alfa y Omega, 1986.

Cosgrove, Denis, and Stephen Daniels, eds. *The Iconography of Landscape: Essays on the Symbolic Representation, Design, and Use of Past Environments*. Cambridge: Cambridge University Press, 1988.

———. Introduction to Cosgrove and Daniels, *Iconography of Landscape*.

Cosío Villegas, Daniel. "La crisis en México." *Cuadernos Americanos* 32 (1947): 29–51.

Cox, Louis Anthony. *Risk Analysis: Foundations, Models, and Methods*. Norwell, MA: Kluwer, 2002.

Craft, Linda J. *Novels of Testimony and Resistance from Central America*. Gainesville: University Press of Florida, 1997.

Craig, Ann L. "Institutional Context and Popular Strategies." In Foweraker and Craig 271–84.

Crassweller, Robert D. *Trujillo: The Life and Times of a Caribbean Dictator*. New York: Macmillan, 1966.

Crosby, Alfred W. *Ecological Imperialism: The Biological Expansion of Europe, 900–1900*. New York: Cambridge University Press, 1986.

Cunha, Euclides da. *Contrastes e confrontos*. 1907. São Paulo: Cultrix, 1975.

———. *Um paraíso perdido: Reunião dos ensaios amazônicos*. Edited by Hildon Rocha. Petrópolis: Editora Vozes, 1976.

———. *Os sertões (campanha de Canudos)*. 1902. Edited by Adelino Brandão. São Paulo: Martin Claret, 2005.

Dalton, Roque. *Poemas clandestinos*. 1981. San Salvador: Universidad Centroamericana José Simeón Cañas, 1999.

Daniels, Stephen. "The Political Iconography of Woodland in Later Georgian England." In Cosgrove and Daniels, *Iconography of Landscape* 43–82.

Dantas, Paulo. *Os sertões de Euclides e outros sertões*. São Paulo: Conselho Estadual de Cultura, Comissão de Literatura, 1969.

Darío, Rubén. "A Roosevelt." In *Cantos de vida y esperanza*. 1905. Madrid: Espasa-Calpe, 1965.

———. "La erupción del Momotombo." *El Mercurio*, 16 Jul. 1886, 2.

———. "Momotombo." In *El canto errante*. 1907. Madrid: Espasa-Calpe, 1965.

———. *El viaje a Nicaragua e Intermezzo tropical*. 1909. Buenos Aires: Corregidor, 2003.

Davis, Mike. *Ecology of Fear: Los Angeles and the Imagination of Disaster*. New York: Metropolitan, 1998.

Debord, Guy. *The Society of the Spectacle*. New York: Zone, 1994.

Denevan, William. *Cultivated Landscapes of Native Amazonia and the Andes*. Oxford: Oxford University Press, 2003.

Douglas, Mary. *Risk and Blame: Essays in Cultural Theory*. London: Routledge, 1992.

Eça de Queiroz, José Maria. *A cidade e as serras*. 1901. Edited by Helena Cidade Moura. Lisbon: Livros do Brasil, 1950.

Emanuel, Kerry. *Divine Wind: The History and Science of Hurricanes*. Oxford: Oxford University Press, 2005.

Escobar, Arturo. *Encountering Development: The Making and the Unmaking of the Third World*. Princeton: Princeton University Press, 1995.

Espinosa, Francisco. *Los símbolos patrios*. San Salvador: Ministerio de Educación, Dirección de Publicaciones, 1982.

Ezcurra, Exequiel, Marisa Mazari-Hiriart, Irene Pisanty, and Adrían Guillermo Aguilar. *The Basin of Mexico: Critical Environmental Issues and Sustainability*. Tokyo: United Nations University Press, 1999.

Farrel, Kirby. *Post-traumatic Culture: Injury and Interpretation in the Nineties*. Baltimore: John Hopkins University Press, 1998.

Ferreira Curry, Maria Zilda. "*Os sertões*, de Euclides da Cunha: Espaços." *Luso-Brazilian Review* 41, no. 1 (2004): 71–79.

Ferreira Tolentino, Célia Aparecida. *O rural no cinema brasileiro*. São Paulo: Editora Universidade Estadual Paulista, 2000.

Fischler, Raphael. "Strategy and History in Professional Practice: Planning as World Making." In *Spatial Practices: Critical Explorations in Social/Spatial Theory*, edited by Helen Liggett and David C. Perry, 13–58. Thousand Oaks, CA: Sage, 1995.

Fondeur, Nerva. "Los primeros reglamentos antillanos para la gestión de las ciudades." In *Arquiteca: Arquitectura Dominicana*, edited by Tommy Rodríguez. Web. Last modified 10 July 2007. Accessed 25 May 2010.

Fontes, Amando. *Os Corumbas.* 1933. Rio de Janeiro: José Olímpio, 1946.

Fornerín, Miguel Ángel. *La dominicanidad viajera: Ensayos sobre diáspora, cultura, sociedad, política y literatura en el Santo Domingo de fin de siglo.* San Juan: Universidad de Puerto Rico en Cayey; Imago Mundi; Librería La Trinitaria, 2001.

Foucault, Michel. *Order of Things: An Archeology of the Human Sciences.* New York: Pantheon, 1970.

Foweraker, Joe. "Popular Movements and Political Change in Mexico." In Foweraker and Craig 3–22.

Foweraker, Joe, and Ann L. Craig, eds. *Popular Movements and Political Change in Mexico.* Boulder, CO: Lynne Rienner; San Diego: University of California, San Diego, the Center for US-Mexican Studies, 1990.

Freedgood, Elaine. *Victorian Writing about Risk.* Cambridge: Cambridge University Press, 2000.

French, Jennifer L. *Nature, Neocolonialism, and the Spanish American Regionalist Writers.* Lebanon, NH: University Press of New England, 2005.

Freyre, Gilberto de Melo. *O Nordeste: Aspectos da influência da cana sobre a vida e a paisagem do Nordeste do Brasil.* Rio de Janeiro: José Olympio; Recife: Fundarpe, 1985.

Galeno, Alberto. *Seca e inverno nas "experiências" dos matutos cearenses.* Fortaleza: Sindicato dos Bancários, 1998.

Galíndez, Jesús de. *The Era of Trujillo: Dominican Dictator.* Edited by Russell H. Fitzgibbon. Tucson: University of Arizona Press, 1973.

Gallegos, Rómulo. *Doña Bárbara.* 1929. Edited by Domingo Miliani. Madrid: Cátedra, 1997.

García, Kay. *Broken Bars: New Perspectives from Mexican Women Writers.* Albuquerque: University of New Mexico Press, 1994.

García Acosta, Virginia, ed. *Historia y desastres en América Latina.* 2 vols. Bogotá: Tercer Mundo, Red de Estudios Sociales en Prevención de Desastres en América Latina, Centro de Investigaciones y Estudios Superiores, 1996.

———. "Historical Disaster Research." In Hoffman and Oliver-Smith 49–66.

———. Introduction to García Acosta, *Historia y desastres* 1:15–37.

Garza Toledo, Enrique M. de la, Liliana de la Garza, Janette Góngora, Andrés Hernández, Enrique Laviada, Miguel Ángel Mendoza, Humberto Nicolás, Armando Rodríguez Suárez, Héctor Rodríguez de la Vega, Mario A. Trujillo, Carlos Vargas, and Horacio Vásquez, eds. *Esto pasó en México.* Mexico City: Extemporáneos, 1985.

Gazón Bona, Henry. *La arquitectura dominicana en la Era de Trujillo.* Vol. 1. Ciudad Trujillo: Impresora Dominicana, 1949.

Gil, Richardson. *The Great Maya Droughts: Water, Life, and Death.* Albuquerque: University of New Mexico Press, 2000.

Gómez Coronel, Xavier. *Terremoto en México.* Mexico City: Porrúa, 1985.

González Echevarría, Roberto. *Myth and Archive: A Theory of Latin American Narrative.* Cambridge: Cambridge University Press, 1990.

Graça Aranha, José Pereira de. *Canaã.* 1902. Edited by Dirce Cortês Riedel. Rio de Janeiro: Edições de Ouro, 1979.

Graham, Brian, and Peter Howard, eds. *The Ashgate Research Companion to Heritage and Identity.* Aldershot, UK: Ashgate, 2008.

————. Introduction to Graham and Howard, *Ashgate Research Companion.*

Gramsci, Antonio. *Selections from the Prison Notebooks of Antonio Gramsci.* Edited and translated by Quintin Hoare and Geoffrey Nowell Smith. London: Lawrence and Wishart, 1971.

Greenfield, Gerald Michael. *The Realities of Images: Imperial Brazil and the Great Drought.* Philadelphia: American Philosophical Society, 2001.

Guimarães Rosa, João. *Grande sertão: Veredas.* Rio de Janeiro: Nova Fronteira, 1984.

Güiraldes, Ricardo. *Don Segundo Sombra.* 1926. Edited by Angela B. Dellapiane. Madrid: Castalia, 1990.

Haber, Paul Lawrence. *Power from Experience: Urban Popular Movements in Late Twentieth-Century Mexico.* University Park: Pennsylvania State University Press, 2006.

Hansson, Sven Ove. "Risk." In *Stanford Encyclopedia of Philosophy,* edited by Edward N. Zalta. Metaphysics Research Lab, Center for the Study of Language and Information, Stanford University. Web. Last modified 13 Mar. 2007. Accessed 25 May 2010.

Harley, J. B. "Deconstructing the Map." *Cartographica* 26, no. 2 (1989): 1–20.

————. "Maps, Knowledge, and Power." In Cosgrove and Daniels, *Iconography of Landscape* 277–312.

Hartman, Geoffrey. "On Traumatic Knowledge and Literary Studies." *New Literary History* 26, no. 3 (1995): 537–63.

Haug, Gerald, Detlef Günther, Larry C. Peterson, Daniel M. Sigman, Konrad A. Hughen, and Beat Aeschlimann. "Climate and the Collapse of Maya Civilization." *Science* 299, no. 5613 (2003): 1731–35.

Hayden, Dolores. *The Power of Place: Urban Landscapes as Public History.* Cambridge: MIT Press, 1995.

Henríquez Gratereaux, Federico. *Un ciclón en una botella: Notas para una teoría de la sociedad dominicana.* Santo Domingo: Alfa y Omega, 1996.

Heredia, José María. "A Emilia." 1824. In *Antología herediana,* edited by Emilio Valdés y de Latorre. Havana: Siglo XX, 1939.

Hernández, Luis. "La credibilidad se gana junto al pueblo con acciones concretas, no con agitación." In Garza Toledo et al. 26–29.

Hewitt, Kenneth. "The Idea of Calamity in a Technocratic Age." In *Interpretations of Calamity from the Viewpoint of Human Ecology*, edited by Kenneth Hewitt, 4–32. Boston: Allen & Unwin, 1983.

———. "Sustainable Disasters? Perspectives and Powers in the Discourse of Calamity." In *Power of Development*, edited by Jonathan Crush, 115–28. London: Routledge, 1995.

Hodgkinson, Peter E., and Michael Stewart. *Coping with Catastrophe: A Handbook of Post-disaster Psychological Aftercare*. London: Routledge, 1991.

Hoffman, Susanna M. "The Monster and the Mother: The Symbolism of Catastrophe." In Hoffman and Oliver-Smith 113–42.

Hoffman, Susanna M., and Anthony Oliver-Smith, eds. *Catastrophe and Culture: The Anthropology of Disaster*. Santa Fe, NM: School of American Research Press, 2002.

Huezo Mixco, Miguel, ed. *Pájaro y volcán*. San Salvador: Universidad Centroamericana Editores, 1989.

Hugo, Victor. "Les raisons du Momotombo." In *La légende des siècles*. 1895. Edited and translated by G. F. Bridge. Project Gutenberg. Web. Accessed 25 May 2010.

Hurricane City. "El Macao, Dominican Republic's History with Tropical Systems." Edited by Jim Williams. Web. Accessed 25 May 2010.

Jimenes Grullón, Juan Isidro. *La República Dominicana: Una ficción; análisis de la evolución histórica y de la presencia actual del coloniaje y el colonialismo en Santo Domingo*. Mérida: Talleres Gráficos Universitarios, 1965.

Johnson, Allen W. "Security and Risk-Taking among Poor Peasants: A Brazilian Case." In *Studies in Economic Anthropology*, edited by George Dalton, 143–78. Washington, DC: American Anthropological Association, 1972.

Jörgensen, Beth. *The Writing of Elena Poniatowska: Engaging Dialogues*. Austin: University of Texas Press, 1994.

Kastenbaum, Robert. "Disaster, Death, and Human Ecology." *Omega* 5, no. 1 (1974): 65–72.

Kearns, Gerald. *Geopolitics and Empire: The Legacy of Halford MacKinder*. Oxford: Oxford University Press, 2009.

Krauze, Enrique. "Revelación entre ruinas." *Vuelta* 9, no. 108 (1985): 11–14.

Landim, Teoberto. *Seca: A estação do inferno*. Fortaleza: Casa de José Alencar, 1992.

LeFebvre, Henri. *The Production of Space*. Translated by Donald Nicholson-Smith. Oxford: Blackwell, 1991.

Levine, Robert M. *Vale of Tears: Revisiting the Canudos Massacre in Northeastern Brazil, 1893–1897*. Berkeley: University of California Press, 1992.

Lévi-Strauss, Claude. *The Raw and the Cooked: Introduction to a Science of*

Mythology. Translated by John and Doreen Weightman. New York: Harper and Row, 1969.

———. *The Savage Mind*. Chicago: University of Chicago Press, 1966.

Lins do Rego, José. *Cangaceiros*. Rio de Janeiro: José Olympio, 1953.

———. *Pedra Bonita: Romance*. 1938. Rio de Janeiro: José Olympio, 1956.

Lión, Luis de. *Poemas del Volcán de Agua: Los poemas míos*. 1980. Guatemala: Serviprensa, 1994.

Loaeza, Guadalupe, Daniel Carbajal, Gonzalo R. Cerillo, Stephanie Kurian Fastlicht, and Martha Merodio. *Terremoto: Ausentes/presentes, 20 años después*. Mexico City: Planeta, 2005.

Lomnitz, Claudio. *Deep Mexico, Silent Mexico: An Anthropology of Nationalism*. Minneapolis: University of Minnesota Press, 2001.

López-Calvo, Ignacio. *God and Trujillo: Literary and Cultural Representations of the Dominican Dictator*. Gainesville: University Press of Florida, 2005.

López Jiménez, Rafael. *Un lugar para vivir: Historias de la reconstrucción*. Mexico City: Océano, 1987.

Lowry, Malcolm. *Under the Volcano*. 1947. New York: Harper, 2007.

Luhmann, Niklas. *Risk: A Sociological Theory*. Translated by Rhodes Barret. New York: Aldine de Gruyter, 1993.

Lukas, Scott A. *The Themed Space: Locating Culture, Nation, and Self*. Lexington, MA: Lexington Books, 2007.

Lugo Lovatón, Ramón. *Escombros: Huracán del 1930*. Ciudad Trujillo: Editorial del Caribe, 1955.

Macedo Gomes, Alfredo. *Imaginário social da seca: Suas implicações para a mudança social*. Recife: Fundação Joaquim Nabuco, Massanga, 1998.

MacKinder, Halford. *Democratic Ideals and Reality: A Study in the Politics of Reconstruction*. 1919. Washington, DC: National Defense University Press, 1996.

Magalhães, Josa. "Previsões folclóricas das secas e dos invernos no Nordeste brasileiro." *Revista do Instituto do Ceará* 66 (1952): 253–68.

Magaloni, Beatriz. *Voting for Autocracy: Hegemonic Party Survival and Its Demise in Mexico*. Cambridge: Cambridge University Press, 2006.

Mainardi, Diogo. *O polígono das secas*. São Paulo: Companhia das Letras, 1995.

"O manifesto dos pioneiros da educação nova." 1932. In *Pedagogia em foco*, edited by José Luis de Paiva Bello. Web. Last modified 1 July 2009. Accessed 25 May 2010.

Maloof, Judy. "The Construction of a Collective Voice: New Journalistic Techniques in Elena Poniatowska's Testimonial: *Nada, nadie: Las voces del temblor*." *Hispanófila* 135 (2002): 137–51.

Manzanilla, Linda. "Indicadores arqueológicos de desastres: Mesoamérica, los Andes y otros casos." In García Acosta, *Historia y desastres* 2:33–58.

Martí, José. *Nuestra América*. 1895. Edited by Hugo Achugar. Caracas: Biblioteca Ayacucho, 1977.

Martínez-Vergne, Teresita. *Nation and Citizen in the Dominican Republic, 1880–1916*. Chapel Hill: University of North Carolina Press, 2005.

Martyr d'Anghiera, Peter. *De Orbe Novo: The Eight Decades of Peter Martyr d'Anghiera*. Translated by Francis Augustus MacNutt. New York: Putnam, 1912. *Internet Archive*. Web. Accessed 25 May 2010.

Maskrey, Andrew. *Disaster Mitigation: A Community Based Approach*. Oxford: Oxfam, 1989.

McDowell, Sarah. "Heritage, Memory, and Identity." In Graham and Howard, *Ashgate Research Companion* 37–54.

Melville, Elinor G. K. *A Plague of Sheep: Environmental Consequences of the Conquest of Mexico*. Cambridge: Cambridge University Press, 1994.

Meyer, John M. *Political Nature: Environmentalism and the Interpretation of Western Thought*. Cambridge: MIT Press, 2001.

Milla y Vidaure, José. *La hija del adelantado*. 1866. Guatemala: Editorial José de Pineda Ibarra, 1979.

Miller, Shawn William. *An Environmental History of Latin America*. Cambridge: Cambridge University Press, 2007.

Monsiváis, Carlos. *Entrada libre: Crónicas de una sociedad que se organiza*. Mexico City: Era, 1987.

———. "La autoorganización ciudadana equivalió a una desobediencia civil." Interview in Garza Toledo et al. 6–13.

———. *No sin nosotros: Los días del terremoto, 1985–2005*. Mexico City: Era, 2005.

———. "On the Chronicle in Mexico." Translated by Derek A. Petrey. In Corona and Jörgensen, *Contemporary Mexican Chronicle* 25–36.

Monsreal, Agustín. "Mi ciudad rota." *El Excelsior*, 8 Oct. 1985, 1–2.

Morris, Stephen D. "Political Reformism in Mexico: Salinas at the Brink." *Journal of Interamerican Studies and World Affairs* 34, no. 1 (1992): 27–57.

Moya Pons, Frank. "Modernization and Change in the Dominican Republic." Translated by Christine Ayorinde. In *Dominican Cultures: The Making of a Caribbean Society*, edited by Bernardo Vega, 209–37. Princeton: Markus Wiener, 2007.

Muniz de Albuquerque, Durval, Jr. *A invenção do Nordeste e outras artes*. Recife: Fundação Joaquim Nabuco, Massangana; São Paulo: Cortez, 1999.

Murguía, Alejandro, and Barbara Paschké. Introduction to Murguía and Paschké, *Volcán*.

———, eds. *Volcán: Poems from Central America, a Bilingual Anthology*. San Francisco: City Lights, 1983.

Musacchio, Humberto. *Ciudad quebrada*. Mexico City: Océano, 1985.

Nogueira Galvão, Walnice. *Gatos de outro saco: Ensaios críticos*. São Paulo: Brasiliense, 1981.

———. "*Rebellion in the Backlands*: Landscape with Figures." *Portuguese Literary and Cultural Studies* 4–5 (2000): 149–56.

Nolasco, Margarita, Jorge Legorreta, and María Luisa Acevedo. "Vivienda para los damnificados: Cuatro propuestas de acción." *México en la Cultura* 1235 (20 Nov. 1985): 39–40.

Núñez, Manuel. *El ocaso de la nación dominicana.* Santo Domingo: Letra Gráfica, 2001.

Ochoa, John. *The Uses of Failure in Mexican Literature and Identity.* Austin: University of Texas Press, 2004.

Olímpio, Domingos. *Lúzia-Homem.* 1903. São Paulo: Brasileira, 1949.

Oliveira Paiva, Manoel de. *Dona Guidinha do Poço.* 1891. Edited by Lúcia Miguel-Perreira. São Paulo: Saraiva, 1952.

Oliveira Vianna, Francisco José. *Evolução do povo brasileiro.* Rio de Janeiro: José Olympio, 1956.

Oliver-Smith, Anthony. Introduction to Oliver-Smith, *Natural Disasters and Cultural Responses.*

———, ed. *Natural Disasters and Cultural Responses: Studies in Third World Societies.* Williamsburg, VA: College of William and Mary, Department of Anthropology, 1986.

———. "Peru's Five Hundred Year Earthquake: Vulnerability in Historical Context." In Varley 31–48.

———. "Theorizing Disaster: Nature, Power, and Culture." In Hoffman and Oliver-Smith 23–48.

Oliver-Smith, Anthony, and Susanna M. Hoffman. "Introduction: Why Anthropologists Should Study Disaster." In Hoffman and Oliver-Smith 3–22.

Olwig, Kenneth R. "'Natural' Landscapes and the Representation of National Identities." In Graham and Howard, *Ashgate Research Companion* 73–88.

Oña, Pedro de. *El temblor de Lima de 1609.* Edited by José Toribio Medina. Santiago de Chile: Elzeviriana, 1909.

Osorio Lizarazo, José Antonio. *The Illumined Island.* Translated by James I. Nolan. Mexico City: Offset Continente, 1947.

———. *La isla iluminada.* Santiago: Editorial del Diario, 1947.

Pacheco, Cristina. "Diez años después." In Serna 7–15.

———. *Zona de desastre.* Mexico City: Océano, 1986.

Pacheco, José Emilio. "Las ruinas de México: Elegía del retorno." In *Miro la tierra: Poemas, 1983–1986.* Mexico City: Era, 1986.

Pan-American Health Organization, Programa de Preparativos para Situaciones de Emergencia y Coordinación del Socorro en Casos de Desastre. *Terremoto de México, septiembre 19 y 20, 1985.* Crónicas de Desastres, no. 3. Washington DC: OPS, 1985.

Parentes Fortes, Herbert. *Euclides: O estilizador de nossa história.* Rio de Janeiro: Edições GRD, 1959.

Partido de la Revolución Salvadoreña. *El Salvador: Un volcán social.* [Caracas?]: Ruptura, [1980?].

Patrocínio, José do. *Os retirantes.* 2 vols. 1879. São Paulo: Três, 1972. *Biblioteca Virtual de Literatura.* Web. Accessed 25 May 2010.

Paulos, John Allen. *A Mathematician Plays the Stock Market.* New York: Basic Books, 2003.

Paz, Octavio. "Escombros y semillas." *Vuelta 9,* no. 108 (1985): 8–10.

———. *El laberinto de la soledad.* 1950. Mexico: Fondo de Cultura Económica, 1967.

———. *Posdata.* Mexico City: Siglo Veintiuno, 1970.

Peguero, Valentina. *The Militarization of Culture in the Dominican Republic from the Captains General to General Trujillo.* Lincoln: University of Nebraska Press, 2004.

Perales, Iosú, ed. *El volcán en guerra: El Salvador, 1979–1987.* Madrid: Revolución, 1988.

Pérez Gay, Rafael. "Piedra sobre piedra: Recortes de prensa y crónica del 19 de septiembre de 1985." *México en la Cultura* 1234 (9 Oct. 1985): 41–42, 47.

Pérez-Mallaína, Pablo E. "La fabricación de un mito: El terremoto de 1687 y la ruina de los cultivos de trigo en el Perú." *Anuario de Estudios Americanos* 57, no. 1 (2000): 69–88.

Petit-Breuilh Sepúlveda, María Eugenia. *Naturaleza y desastres en Hispanoamérica: La visión de los indígenas.* Madrid: Sílex, 2006.

Pinoncelly, Salvador. "Expropriación minimosca." *México en la Cultura* 1235 (20 Nov. 1985): 52.

Poniatowska, Elena. *Nada, nadie: Las voces del temblor.* Mexico City: Era, 1988.

———. *La noche de Tlatelolco: Testimonios de historia oral.* Mexico City: Era, 1971.

———. *Nothing, Nobody: The Voices of the Mexico City Earthquake.* Translated by Aurora Camacho de Schmidt and Arthur Schmidt. Philadelphia: Temple University Press, 1995.

Popol vuh. Edited by Agustín Estrada Monroy. Mexico City: Editores Mexicanos Unidos, 1998.

Poy Solano, Laura. "Y la radio salió a la calle." *La Jornada,* 19 Sept. 2005, special edition. Los terremotos de 1985. Web. Accessed 26 May 2010.

Presidencia de la República, Unidad de la Crónica Presidencial. *Terremotos de septiembre: Sobretiro de las razones y las obras, crónica del sexenio 1982–1988, tercer año.* Mexico City: Fondo de Cultura Económica, 1986.

Pym, Anthony. *Negotiating the Frontier: Translators and Interculture in Hispanic History.* Manchester, UK: St. Jerome, 2000.

Queiroz, Rachel de. *O quinze.* 1930. São Paulo: Siciliano, 2001.

Rabello, Sylvio. *Euclides da Cunha.* Rio de Janeiro: Civilização Brasileira, 1966.

Rama, Ángel. *La ciudad letrada.* Hanover, NH: Ediciones del Norte, 1984.

Ramírez, Sergio. *Balcanes y volcanes.* Managua: Nueva Nicaragua, 1983.

———. *Margarita, está linda la mar.* Madrid: Alfaguara, 1998.

Ramírez Saiz, Juan Manuel. "Urban Struggles and Their Political Consequences." In Foweraker and Craig 234–46.

Ramos, Graciliano. *Vidas secas*. 1938. São Paulo: Martins, 1971.

Ramos, Miguel Willie. "The Lukumí Pantheon: Orishas Worshiped by the Lukumí." *Eledá.org*. Web. Last modified 11 Nov. 2008. Accessed 27 May 2010.

Ramos, Samuel. *El perfil del hombre y la cultura en México*. 1934. Buenos Aires: Espasa-Calpe, 1951.

Rangel, Alberto. *Inferno verde: Cenas e cenários do Amazonas*. 1908. Manaus: Valer, 2001.

Reguillo, Rossana. "Border(line) Texts: The Chronicle, Writing in the Open." In Corona and Jörgensen, *Contemporary Mexican Chronicle* 51–59.

Rivera, José Eustasio. *La vorágine*. 1924. Edited by Luis Carlos Herrera. Bogotá: Pontífica Universidad Javeriana, 2005.

Robinson, Scott S., Yolanda Hernández Franco, Rosario Mata Castrejón, and H. Russell Bernard. "It Shook Again: The Mexico City Earthquake of 1985." In Oliver-Smith, *Natural Disasters* 81–122.

Rodríguez Demorizi, Emilio. *Relaciones históricas de Santo Domingo*. Vol. 3. Ciudad Trujillo: Montalvo, 1957.

Rubin, Jeffrey W. "Popular Mobilization and the Myth of State Corporatism." In Foweraker and Craig 247–67.

Rufino Fischer, Izaura, and Lígia Albuquerque. "A mulher e a emergência da Seca no Nordeste do Brasil." *Fundação Joaquim Nabuco: Trabalhos para Discussão* 139 (2002): 1–9. Web. Accessed 18 Jan. 2006.

Saborit, Antonio. "El estruendo que sofoca los gritos." *México en la Cultura* 1234 (9 Oct. 1985): 37–40.

Sahagún, Bernardino de. *Historia general de las cosas de la Nueva España*. Edited by Juan Carlos Temprano. Madrid: Historia 16, 1990.

Salinas Álvarez, Samuel. "La ciudad y su destino." *Universidad de México* 417 (Oct. 1985): 11–18.

San Miguel, Pedro L. *The Imagined Island: History, Identity, and Utopia in Hispaniola*. Translated by Jane Ramírez. Chapel Hill: University of North Carolina Press, 2005.

Schwartzman, Simon. "Brazil's Leading University: Between Intelligentsia, World Standards, and Social Inclusion." In *World Class Worldwide: Transforming Research Universities in Asia and Latin America*, edited by Philip G. Altbach and Jorge Balán, 143–72. Baltimore: Johns Hopkins University Press, 2007.

Sennett, Richard. *The Uses of Disorder: Personal Identity and City Life*. New York: Knopf, 1970.

Serna, Leslíe. *Aquí nos quedaremos: Testimonios de la Coordinadora Única de Damnificados*. Mexico City: Universidad Iberoamericana, Coordinadora Única de Damnificados, 1995.

Serrano, Mónica. "El legado del cambio gradual: Reglas e instituciones bajo

Salinas." In *La reconstrucción del estado: México después de Salinas*, edited by Mónica Serrano and Víctor Bulmer-Thomas, 13–43. Mexico City: Fondo de Cultura Económica, 1998.

Silva Herzog, Jesús. *La revolución mexicana en crisis*. Mexico City: Cuadernos Americanos, 1944.

Slater, Candace. *Stories on a String: The Brazilian Literatura de Cordel*. Berkeley: University of California Press, 1982.

Smith, Anthony. *The Newspaper: An International History*. London: Thames and Hudson, 1979.

Snow, David A., E. Burke Rochford, Jr., Steven K. Worden, and Robert D. Benford. "Frame Alignment Processes, Micromobilization, and Movement Participation." *American Sociological Review* 51, no. 4 (1986): 464–81.

Sommer, Doris. *Foundational Fictions: The National Romances of Latin America*. Berkeley: University of California Press, 1991.

Spivak, Gayatri. "Can the Subaltern Speak? Speculations on Widow Sacrifice." *Wedge* 7–8 (1985): 120–30.

Squier, Ephraim George. *Travels in Central America, Particularly in Nicaragua: With a Description of Its Aboriginal Monuments, People, and Scenery, Their Languages, Institutions, Etc.* New York: Appleton, 1853.

StormCarib: The Caribbean Hurricane Network. "Climatology of Caribbean Hurricanes: Santo Domingo, Dominican Republic (MSDS)." Web. Accessed 25 May 2010.

Strathern, Marilyn. "No Nature, No Culture: The Hagen Case." In *Nature, Culture, and Gender*, edited by Carol MacCormack and Marilyn Strathern, 174–222. Cambridge: Cambridge University Press, 1980.

Suárez R., Gerardo, and Zenón Jiménez J. *Sismos en la ciudad de México y el terremoto del 19 de septiembre de 1985*. Servicio Sismológico Nacional. *Terremoto en México '85*. Web. Accessed 25 May 2010.

Suassuna, Ariano. *Auto da compadecida*. Rio de Janeiro: Agir, 1962.

Superintendência de Desenvolvimento do Nordeste (SUDENE). "Levantamiento histórico de las acciones gubernamentales para minimizar los efectos de las sequías de 1721 a 1995." *Desastres y Sociedad* 5, no. 3 (1995): 64–70. Web. Accessed 25 May 2010.

———. "Relación histórica resumida de las sequías del Nordeste." *Desastres y Sociedad* 5, no. 3 (1995): 59–63. Web. Accessed 25 May 2010.

Taine, Hippolyte Adolphe. *History of English Literature*. 1864. Translated by Henry Van Laun. Vol. 1. New York: P. F. Collier, 1900.

Taliaferro, Charles. "Early Modern Philosophy." In *A Companion to Environmental Philosophy*, edited by Dale James, 130–45. Oxford: Blackwell, 2001.

Tamayo, Jaime. "Neoliberal Encounters: *Neocardenismo*." In Foweraker and Craig 121–36.

Távora, Franklin. *O Cabeleira*. 1876. São Paulo: Martin Claret, 2003.

Teófilo, Rodolfo. *Os Brilhantes*. 1895. Brasília: Instituto Nacional do Livro, 1972.

———. *A fome.* 1890. Fortaleza: Edições Demócrito Rocha, 2002.

———. *O paroara: Romance.* 1899. Fortaleza: Secretaria de Cultura, Desporto e Promoção Social, 1974.

———. *Seccas do Ceará: Segunda metade do século XIX.* Fortaleza: Atheliers Louis, 1901.

Trindade Lima, Nísia. *Um sertão chamado Brasil: Intelectuais e representação geográfica da identidade nacional.* Rio de Janeiro: Revan; Universidade Candido Mendes, Instituto Universitário de Pesquisas do Rio de Janeiro, 1999.

Troncoso Sánchez, Pedro. *Estudios de historia política dominicana.* Santo Domingo: Julio D. Postigo e Hijos, 1968.

Trujillo Molina, Rafael Leonidas. *The Basic Policies of a Regime.* Ciudad Trujillo: Editora del Caribe: 1960.

Turits, Richard Lee. *Foundations of Despotism: Peasants, the Trujillo Regime, and Modernity in Dominican History.* Stanford: Stanford University Press, 2003.

Ubaldo Ribeiro, João. *Sargento Getúlio: Romance.* Rio de Janeiro: Civilização Brasileira, 1971.

Valente, Luiz Fernando. "Brazilian Literature and Citizenship: From Euclides da Cunha to Marcos Dias." *Luso-Brazilian Review* 38, no. 2 (2001): 11–27.

Valle-Castillo, Julio. Introduction to *Cenizas de Izalco,* by Claribel Alegría and Darwin J. Flakoll, 7–12. San Salvador: Consejo Nacional para la Cultura y el Arte, 1997.

Vargas Llosa, Mario. *La fiesta del chivo.* Madrid: Alfaguara, 2000.

———. "'Nos mató la ideología': Una entrevista con Mario Vargas Llosa." Interview with Héctor Aguilar Camín. Zona Abierta 36 Canal 2, El Canal de las Estrellas, Mexico City. Broadcast 27 May 2000. Transcript. Web. Accessed 14 Oct. 2007.

Varley, Ann, ed. *Disasters, Development, and Environment.* Chichester, UK: John Wiley, 1994.

Ventura, Roberto. "Visões do deserto: Selva e sertão em Euclides da Cunha." *História, Ciência, Saúde—Manguinhos* 5 (1998): 133–47.

Veríssimo, José. *Estudos de literatura brasileira: Primera Serie.* Rio de Janeiro: Garnier: 1901.

Vidal e Souza, Candice. *A pátria geográfica: Sertão e litoral no pensamento social brasileiro.* Goiâna: Universidade Federal de Goiâna, 1997.

Villa, Marco Antonio. *Vida e morte no sertão: História das secas no Nordeste nos séculos XIX e XX.* São Paulo: Ática, 2000.

Weiss, Harvey, and Raymond S. Bradley. "What Drives Societal Collapse?" *Science* 291, no. 5504 (2001): 609–10.

Whitmore, Thomas, and B. L. Turner. *Cultivated Landscapes in Middle America on the Eve of the Conquest.* Oxford: Oxford University Press, 2002.

Whitt, Laurie Anne, Mere Roberts, Waerete Norman, and Vicki Grieves. "Indigenous Perspectives." In *A Companion to Environmental Philosophy*, edited by Dale James, 3–20. Oxford: Blackwell, 2001.

Williams, Raymond Leslie. *The Twentieth-Century Spanish American Novel*. Austin: University of Texas Press, 2003.

Wisner, Ben. "Disaster Vulnerability: Scale, Power, and Daily Life." *Geojournal* 30, no. 2 (1993): 127–40.

Wrigley, Richard. "Transformations of a Revolutionary Emblem: The Liberty Cap in the French Revolution." *French History* 11, no. 2 (1997): 131–69.

Záiter-Mejía, Alba Josefina. *La identidad social y nacional en Dominicana: Un análisis psico-social*. Santo Domingo: Editora Taller, 2001.

Zermeño, Sergio. "Crisis, Neoliberalism, and Disorder." In Foweraker and Craig 160–80.

Zimmer, Oliver. "In Search of Natural Identity: Alpine Landscape and the Reconstruction of the Swiss Nation." In *Natures Past: The Environment and Human History*, edited by Paolo Squatriti, 240–69. Ann Arbor: University of Michigan Press, 2007.

Zola, Émile. "The Experimental Novel." 1880. In *The Experimental Novel and Other Essays*. Translated by Belle M. Sherman. New York: Haskell House, 1964.

Index

Vera M. Kutzinski, *Sugar's Secrets: Race and the Erotics of Cuban Nationalism*

Richard D. E. Burton and Fred Reno, editors, *French and West Indian: Martinique, Guadeloupe, and French Guiana Today*

A. James Arnold, editor, *Monsters, Tricksters, and Sacred Cows: Animal Tales and American Identities*

J. Michael Dash, *The Other America: Caribbean Literature in a New World Context*

Isabel Alvarez Borland, *Cuban-American Literature of Exile: From Person to Persona*

Belinda J. Edmondson, editor, *Caribbean Romances: The Politics of Regional Representation*

Steven V. Hunsaker, *Autobiography and National Identity in the Americas*

Celia M. Britton, *Edouard Glissant and Postcolonial Theory: Strategies of Language and Resistance*

Mary Peabody Mann, *Juanita: A Romance of Real Life in Cuba Fifty Years Ago* Edited and with an introduction by Patricia M. Ard

George B. Handley, *Postslavery Literatures in the Americas: Family Portraits in Black and White*

Faith Smith, *Creole Recitations: John Jacob Thomas and Colonial Formation in the Late Nineteenth-Century Caribbean*

Ian Gregory Strachan, *Paradise and Plantation: Tourism and Culture in the Anglophone Caribbean*

Nick Nesbitt, *Voicing Memory: History and Subjectivity in French Caribbean Literature*

Charles W. Pollard, *New World Modernisms: T. S. Eliot, Derek Walcott, and Kamau Brathwaite*

Carine M. Mardorossian, *Reclaiming Difference: Caribbean Women Rewrite Postcolonialism*

Luís Madureira, *Cannibal Modernities: Postcoloniality and the Avant-garde in Caribbean and Brazilian Literature*

Elizabeth M. DeLoughrey, Renée K. Gosson, and George B. Handley, editors, *Caribbean Literature and the Environment: Between Nature and Culture*

Flora González Mandri, *Guarding Cultural Memory: Afro-Cuban Women in Literature and the Arts*

Miguel Arnedo-Gómez, *Writing Rumba: The Afrocubanista Movement in Poetry*

Jessica Adams, Michael P. Bibler, and Cécile Accilien, editors, *Just Below South: Intercultural Performance in the Caribbean and the U.S. South*

Valérie Loichot, *Orphan Narratives: The Postplantation Literature of Faulkner, Glissant, Morrison, and Saint-John Perse*

Sarah Phillips Casteel, *Second Arrivals: Landscape and Belonging in Contemporary Writing of the Americas*

Guillermina De Ferrari, *Vulnerable States: Bodies of Memory in Contemporary Caribbean Fiction*

Claudia Sadowski-Smith, *Border Fictions: Globalization, Empire, and Writing at the Boundaries of the United States*

Doris L. Garraway, editor, *Tree of Liberty: Cultural Legacies of the Haitian Revolution in the Atlantic World*

Dawn Fulton, *Signs of Dissent: Maryse Conde and Postcolonial Criticism*

Nick Nesbitt, *Universal Emancipation: The Haitian Revolution and the Radical Enlightenment*

Michael G. Malouf, *Transatlantic Solidarities: Irish Nationalism and Caribbean Poetics*

Maria Cristina Fumagalli, *Caribbean Perspectives on Modernity: Returning the Gaze*

Vivian Nun Halloran, *Exhibiting Slavery: The Caribbean Postmodern Novel as Museum*

Paul B. Miller, *Elusive Origins: The Enlightenment in the Modern Caribbean Historical Imagination*